Gardening
WITH SHRUBS

UNA VAN DER SPUY

Gardening
WITH SHRUBS

*Shrubs of
the World for Gardens in the
Southern Hemisphere*

DON NELSON
CAPE TOWN

Published by Don Nelson
PO Box 859, Cape Town 8000

ISBN 1 86806 014 4

First edition 1973
Revised edition 1986

Other books by the same author

Gardening in Southern Africa
Ornamental Shrubs and Trees
Garden Planning and Construction
Wild Flowers of South Africa for the Garden
South African Shrubs and Trees for the
Garden
Gardening with Trees
Gardening with Ground Covers
Gardening with Climbers

Designed by Poul-Ejnar Hansen
Photo-typesetting: Diatype Setting,
Cape Town
Lithographic reproduction: Hirt & Carter,
Cape Town
Printed and bound by Interpak,
Pietermaritzburg

Una van der Spuy

Una van der Spuy has lived in all provinces of South Africa and has a sound knowledge of the prevailing climatic conditions in different regions. Her ten books are based on wide practical experience in gardening and in planning gardens for others.

Recently she received a gold medal from the South African Nurserymen's Association for her 'contribution to horticulture'.

The author stresses the importance of creating beauty in one's home surroundings with a minimum of labour and in this book indicates how shrubs can help to do just that.

Frontispiece
The Giant or King Protea *(Protea cynaroides)* produces its large showy flowers from late winter to spring

Contents

Part I

Introduction

Top left
A garden made beautiful by trees, shrubs, roses and lawn. The shrub with white flowers is a Snowball (*Viburnum opulus* 'Sterile')

Top right
A pool surrounded by shrubs and other plants makes a pretty picture

Bottom left
Shrubs, perennials and annuals produce a riot of colour in this rock garden

Bottom right
Grow shrubs to form a background and to protect small plants from wind

Introduction

The purpose of this book is to help gardeners to create a labour-saving garden that costs little to maintain. A garden should be a joy and a delight, but it can be this only if one is not preoccupied or harassed by the number of tasks that need to be done, or is so busy doing them that there is no time to relax.

Whether your garden is a tiny suburban plot or several acres in extent, you can have year-round interest and beauty by growing shrubs. Planted in good soil, they require little or no fertilizer, very little pruning and seldom any spraying against pests or diseases. They will reward you in many different ways . . . by providing colour in the garden each month of the year and sprays of leaves, flowers or berries for indoor arrangements; by sheltering your home from wind; by creating a screen to ensure privacy; by introducing variety in form and foliage texture, and a perpendicular line or mass; and by hiding an ugly view or framing a good one. You do not have to be an enthusiastic plantsman to make a charming shrub garden. You need to know something about the kind of climate they prefer; their height and spread; the season of the year when they are at their best; any special characteristics of their foliage; whether they are deciduous or evergreen; what soil they like; and what situation they prefer – sun or shade. All this information is given in the next section of this book, arranged in tabular form for quick reference, to enable you to select the right shrubs for the right places in the garden.

Planning the shrub garden

If the garden is to be composed mainly of shrubs, it is advisable to plan carefully before planting because, once planted, shrubs should not be moved. Transplanting at a later date may not kill them if it is carefully done, but it entails a good deal of unnecessary work and may slow down the growth of the shrubs for a time.

When making a plan, draw it to scale. On a large sheet of graph paper sketch the size of the plot and the location of the house on the plot, using one or more squares to represent 30 cm. Next, list the special features to be considered, such as – direction and strength of the prevailing winds against which it may be necessary to erect barriers; a fine view to be framed or ugly features you wish to hide in the distant landscape, or on your own or a neighbouring plot (e.g. laundry area, garbage cans). Include on your plan a place for outdoor living, preferably near the kitchen, where it is easy to serve food. This may be a patio, an open terrace or a barbecue.

The plants selected should be drawn in to scale by making a circle indicating their spread. This is the *only* way to know what area the plants will cover, and it is worth doing carefully as it is far easier to use an eraser to make corrections on paper than to transplant shrubs later when they have grown too large. The height to which shrubs grow is indicated in the text. Their spread is usually half to two-thirds their height, unless they are referred to as spreading shrubs, when it may be accepted that the spread is likely to be about the same as the height.

Plan the garden so that most of the shrubs are placed around or near the perimeter of the property, or else in groups – not scattered about singly within the lawn area. If the lawn is very large, one or more groups of shrubs in the lawn will serve to break the monotony of a large expanse of grass. Single shrubs planted here and there in a small lawn make it appear smaller and increase the amount of maintenance required, because the edge of the lawn around each shrub has to be clipped by hand; furthermore, watering shrubs scattered over a wide area is more difficult than watering shrubs planted in groups. The only shrubs to stand alone are those used as accent plants – to create a focal point.

Should a large area of the garden be open to the street, plant groups of shrubs to form a decorative shrubbery and provide privacy for certain points in the garden and home.

Before choosing any shrubs for your own garden, make a note of what is growing on neighbouring properties and use their planting scheme to your advantage. For instance, if your neighbour has tall deciduous shrubs in his garden where it adjoins yours, plant shorter evergreen ones on your side to liven up that area in winter and, if possible, choose those that offer contrast in the colour of flowers or foliage. If he has a hedge of one kind of plant, you can have the fun of growing a wide range of plants in your garden against the background of his hedge.

When planning a border or group of shrubs, aim at having variety in form and colour, unity and balance.

Avoid having a single straight line of different shrubs of more or less the same height. Rather group the shrubs so that they form a curving border to the lawn by placing two or three shrubs of graded height one behind the other, with occasionally a single shrub of unusual shape as a contrast to adjacent plants. Make a point, also, of planting one kind of shrub, or a small group of the same ones, in more than one part of the garden. This occasional repetition of the same shrub or shrubs reduces the possibility of the lay-out looking spotty and restless, and makes the garden appear a unified whole.

Choose shrubs with foliage of different kinds and colours. Remember that good-looking foliage all the year round is more important than beautiful flowers for only three or four weeks. A shrub with dark green leaves makes a pleasant foreground to a taller one with variegated leaves, and a shrub with wine-coloured leaves shows up well next to one with grey foliage. Consider the foliage rather than the flowers when selecting your shrubs. It is not difficult to plan and plant so that it is the colour and texture of the foliage that make the garden attractive.

A collection of shrubs will not necessarily make a pleasing garden, even although each individual shrub is beautiful. It is the way the shrubs are sited or arranged in relationship to one another and to other plants that creates the picture. When making the plan, note the colours of the flowers of the shrubs selected and the season when they bloom. This will enable you to design decorative plant pictures. If, for example, you have chosen a summer-flowering shrub with yellow flowers for a particular situation, plant near to it one which has white, blue or mauve flowers at the same season, rather than a shrub with pink or red flowers. The possible pleasing combinations are endless.

Balance in both mass and colour is an important aspect of the garden.

A garden with a bold group of shrubs on one side, and nothing on the other, will have an unbalanced appearance. Let the planting along the border, or the groups of shrubs, be more or less equal in mass and height. Whether you rely on foliage and flowers or both for colour, plan so as to ensure that all the colour does not appear on one side of the garden only. For example, if all the shrubs in one group or section have foliage that is grey, wine-coloured or different shades of green whilst those in another group, or on the other side, are all dark green, the garden will appear unbalanced. If flowers are to highlight the garden, avoid having all the spring-flowering shrubs in one area and all the autumn-flowering ones in another. Rather group two or three spring-flowering ones together, and two or three autumn, winter or summer-flowering ones near each other in different parts of the garden. The tables on pages 46 to 53 will help you to choose shrubs for seasonal interest.

When sketching the shrubs chosen on the plan, give each one a number, as there is insufficient space on the graph paper to write in the full names. It is as well, also, to write after the number 'Sp' for spring, 'S' for summer, 'A' for autumn, 'W' for winter, and 'F' for foliage. This will enable you to see at a glance how the colour grouping of your plan will appear from season to season. With a pen of a different colour put in figures denoting height to ensure that you do not site low-growing shrubs behind tall ones.

Climate

Choose shrubs to suit your climate. This simplifies gardening. The shrubs described in this book are from all parts of the world. Some are native to tropical regions; some come from temperate climates, some from dry areas, some from very cold countries, and some are indigenous. All of them will grow, and in fact many of them are already growing in gardens in Southern Africa.

Some shrubs grow and flower well only in regions with cold winters that induce a definite period of dormancy, whilst others do best in subtropical areas. The widest range of shrubs can be grown in regions where winters are cool but frost is not severe. In such a region shrubs from cold countries, as well as many of those native to subtropical lands, can be grown.

Climatic conditions in Southern Africa vary considerably from subtropical, through temperate to almost desert-like, with extremes in temperature in some regions. The variation of climate within the individual provinces is also considerable.

In many parts of South Africa and Zimbabwe the climate is temperate enough to allow subtropical plants to flourish side by side with those native to cold regions of the world.

Based on rainfall, Southern Africa can be broadly divided into three zones – the south-western tip near Cape Town, which has regular and good rains in winter and hot, dry summers; the northern Cape, the Karoo and the south of Namibia, which have a meagre and erratic rainfall in summer or winter, and the rest of South Africa, Zimbabwe and the north of Namibia, which have reasonable to good rains in summer and dry winters.

Generally it can be said that the incidence of rain has a marked effect on the growth of plants. It is true that, where the rainfall is low, it may be possible to supply the garden with the water it requires, but there are factors connected with rain that affect the growth of plants, other than the water itself.

During periods of rain the intensity of the sunlight is reduced by clouds and moisture in the atmosphere, with the result that there is far less evaporation from plants and from the soil. Many plants do better under such conditions than when exposed to bright sunlight, which promotes rapid transpiration, even although they may be artificially provided with enough water. Rapid evaporation causes wilting and detracts from the appearance of plants. It should be remembered, too, that the effectiveness of moisture in the soil depends on the rate of evaporation in a particular area. For example, 25 mm of water will maintain vigorous plant growth for two or three times as long in the humid coastal region as it would in arid inland regions.

The Transvaal has good summer rains and severe frost on the Highveld, with mild winters and a lower incidence of rain in the Lowveld and Bushveld, where subtropical plants flourish. Many shrubs native to cold countries of the Northern Hemisphere grow well in Johannesburg and other cold centres, particularly if they have filtered shade for part of the day to reduce the intensity of the sunlight and if they are watered adequately.

The eastern side of the Orange Free State has a good rainfall with very low

drops in temperature at night, which limit the range of shrubs that can be grown. Frost and an erratic rainfall over other parts of this province necessitate careful planning and maintenance to make and keep the garden beautiful.

Natal enjoys widely diverse growing conditions from subtropical near the coast to temperate in the midlands, with sharp frosts in some parts and severe frosts on the highlands. The rainfall on the whole is good, and gardening, whether at the coast or inland, is therefore easier than in most other parts of Southern Africa.

Subtropical shrubs can be grown along the coastal strip of the Eastern Province, but the drops in temperature inland make it difficult to grow plants other than those hardy to frost. The incidence of frost along the south of the Drakensberg is such as to limit the gardener to plants hardy to severe frost.

Temperate conditions and a reliable rainfall along the coast, from west of Port Elizabeth to Cape Town make it possible to grow a very wide range of plants easily. This region is also the natural habitat of a number of very fine shrubs and other plants.

A great deal of the Karoo, the Northern Cape and the southern part of Namibia have a low and erratic rainfall, with sharp to severe frost at night and very high temperatures in summer.

Extremes of temperature are a feature of much of the arid regions where the rate of evaporation is an additional problem for gardeners. Fortunately there are plants that have adapted to these harsh conditions. Some have succulent stems and leaves which help them to survive long hot dry periods, and some remain dormant in winter and grow out only after the period of frost is over.

In regions where a low rainfall and a shortage of water combined with low drops in temperature make gardening

This subtropical garden looks cool and inviting. It depends for its beauty on shrubs, palms and trees surrounding a lawn

Shrubs bring colour to the garden at different seasons of the year

difficult, gardeners should consider making a rock or pebble garden. To be attractive this kind of garden calls for careful planning and planting. Few plants need be used, and if these, together with the rocks, gravel or pebbles are not properly sited in relation to one another, the result may be ugly rather than beautiful. In Japan different types of moss are planted as a ground cover around rocks to add colour and texture to the scene; in South Africa similar use could be made of prostrate succulents with very small leaves and other low-growing plants with small leaves that are resistant to drought and frost.

In Zimbabwe changes in temperatures are not as marked as in wide parts of South Africa. Where the rainfall is low or erratic, but there is sufficient water for artificial irrigation, delightful gardens can be made by growing subtropical plants as well as those which come from cool regions of the world.

Gardeners living in areas that have severe frost, or which are tropical or dry should consult the tables on pages 24 to 28, where the names of shrubs suited to such climates are listed. There are many beautiful shrubs that like frost and equally lovely ones that demand mild winters and humid conditions for their best development.

Frost. In a region where severe frosts are common, it is possible to grow shrubs that are somewhat tender to frost by erecting protective 'tents' or 'wigwams' of hessian or straw around them in autumn and winter, or by placing cardboard cartons over them at night during the first winter after they are transplanted. This form of protection at night is recommended for members of the protea family, which like to have a free circulation of air around them. Many plants may also be raised successfully if planted against a north-

Azaleas highlight a shady part of the garden. The low hedge of Golden Privet adds emphasis to the curve of the path

A broad grass walk bordered by a low trimmed hedge and azaleas leads past a fine piece of topiary to a white bench

facing wall that absorbs heat during the day and gives it off at night. The protection provided by a hedge, or other shrubs or trees is sometimes sufficient to prevent frost-damage to plants which are not quite hardy to severe frost. Mulching the ground will also help to obviate frost-damage.

Frost-damage, particularly to evergreen shrubs, is sometimes due to the fact that the early morning sun striking frosted leaves causes injury to the tissues. Plant shrubs that are not completely hardy to frost in a position where they will be shaded from the early morning winter sun. This allows the air to warm up and dissipate the frost before the sun shines onto the leaves. It is advisable also to water evergreen shrubs regularly in areas where winters are dry and frosty.

Conditions in your neighbourhood and even in your garden can create micro-climates that will differ from the general climate of the area; for example, in a garden on sloping ground, plants at the bottom of the slope are likely to suffer more damage from cold than plants in the same garden at the top of the slope.

Humidity. Many shrubs that occur naturally in tropical and subtropical regions do well only where there is humidity in the air. If your garden is subject to long dry periods and it is impractical or impossible to water sufficiently to create a humid atmosphere, avoid planting shrubs native to warm, humid regions.

Soil
The growth of a shrub depends to a large extent on the soil in which it is planted. Soils differ considerably; they may vary in different parts of the same garden. The best kind of soil, referred to as loam, is friable and rich in humus – neither too porous nor too solid to cultivate. The two extremes that demand thorough initial preparation to ensure good plant growth are sand and heavy clay. Sand is made up of fine or large particles through which water drains quickly. Sandy soils are often deficient in plant nutrients and they need to be watered frequently. Clay soil is made up of particles as fine

as powder. When wet, it is inclined to compact, particularly if worked or walked on. Sandy soil needs less water at a time to percolate to the root-zone than clay, but clay has the advantage of retaining the moisture. Plants growing in clay therefore need to be watered less frequently than those growing in sand. Both sand and clay can be improved by the addition of humus in the form of compost, leaf-mould, rotted straw, composted sawdust, peat or manure.

In regions of high rainfall, where the underlying clay is so impermeable as to prevent the drainage of water from the root-zone, it may be necessary to put in pipes to drain the water away. Generally, however, digging extra large and deep holes and putting rubble or coarse gravel at the bottom will prevent stagnant water lying around the roots. Many plants native to Australia and South Africa, particularly members of the protea and myrtle families, grow well only in soil which has good drainage. This does not signify that such plants will thrive in sand. They require a loose soil with a high humus content.

Where the soil is poor, it is advisable to make holes 45–60 cm wide and deep, and to fill them with a mixture of good compost and loam. A young shrub will grow much quicker in soil improved in this way than in poor, sandy soil or in compacted clay. Compost can be made at home from lawn cuttings combined with household refuse, and an activator that speeds up decomposition of vegetable matter. Such activators are obtainable in powder or liquid form. As the making of compost takes two to four months, many gardeners prefer to purchase it from firms dealing in garden sundries, or from their nurseryman.

Alkaline soil. Many plants grow well in soil which is moderately alkaline, but none will grow in highly alkaline soil. Deep irrigation sometimes helps to wash an excess of harmful salts from the soil in the root-zone but, as alkaline soil is generally to be found in areas of low rainfall, such deep irrigation is not always possible because of a shortage of water. Plants growing in soil which is too alkaline may show stunted growth, or the leaves may turn

brown and look scorched or withered along the margins. Where the alkalinity of the soil is high enough to inhibit growth, gardeners should rely on growing plants in raised beds or containers filled with suitable soil, or make very large holes and fill these with a mixture of good soil, compost and peat. A pebble garden, in which only a few plants need to be grown, is an excellent form of gardening for regions where the soil is strongly alkaline. (See page 32.)

Water used in areas where the soil is alkaline also tends to be alkaline and it may therefore change the nature of the soil used in the containers. The sprinkling of a tablespoonful of iron sulphate, sulphur or alum (aluminium sulphate) on the soil around each plant once a month will help to prevent the water from changing the nature of the soil drastically.

Gardeners who wish to know the nature of their soil should purchase a soil-testing kit or send samples of the soil to a State Department or to a commercial firm which undertakes the testing of soils. The result of such a test is expressed in what is known as the pH value of the soil. A pH of 7 indicates that the soil is neutral – that is, neither alkaline nor acid. A figure above 7 means that the soil is alkaline and one below 7 shows that it is acid. The change in figures is fairly drastic; a pH 5 indicates that the soil is ten times as acid as soil with a pH 6, and pH 4 is one hundred times as acid as pH 6.

Most plants grow well in soil with a reaction of between pH 6 and pH 6,5 – that is, in a slightly acid soil. Many will, however, grow in soil with a higher pH, and lime-loving ones may tolerate a pH up to 8. Plants which like acid conditions need soil with a pH lower than 6. No plants succeed in very acid or in very alkaline soil.

Acid soil. Acid soil generally occurs in areas with a high rainfall. Soil which is slightly acid produces good plant growth, but where the pH is below 6 lime should be applied before planting shrubs, other than those which like acid soil. A rough guide as to the nature of the soil can be ascertained from the colour of the flowers of hydrangeas.

Where these are blue, the soil is likely to be acid; where they are pink the soil is neutral or alkaline. As a general rule, do not apply lime unless the soil is too acid to promote good growth.

When plants which like acid soil show chlorosis − i.e. yellowing of the leaves, particularly the area between the veins, action should be taken to change the pH value of the soil. Chlorosis in such cases usually indicates that the plant is suffering from a deficiency of iron. This may not be due to a lack of iron in the soil but rather to the fact that elements in the soil make the iron unavailable to the plant. Treat the soil, or spray the foliage, with iron chelates according to directions given on the package. This produces a quick reaction. For long-term effect sprinkle a small handful of sulphur, iron sulphate or alum on the ground around the plant and water it in.

Fertilizers

Where the soil is naturally rich in humus or has been improved by the addition of good compost, artificial fertilizer may not be needed to promote the growth of shrubs. However, should shrubs show yellowing of the foliage or fail to grow some months after planting, apply a general garden fertilizer according to directions given on the package. Usually a small handful scattered on the soil from near the main stems to the outer spread of the branches is sufficient. Shrubs that like acid soil should not be treated with a general fertilizer but with one of the special preparations recommended for such plants.

If a shrub is mulched, remove the mulch before applying fertilizer and replace it after soaking the soil. Always soak the soil with water immediately after fertilizing.

Fertilizers may also be applied to the leaves in liquid form. This is known as 'foliar feeding'. The plant reacts more quickly when fertilized in this way but the results do not last as long as when fertilizer is applied to the soil. Particulars as to how to mix and apply such foliar fertilizers will be found on the containers.

The best time to apply fertilizer is early in spring when many plants are starting into vigorous growth, but it may be given during summer too.

Planting

Throughout the year evergreen and deciduous shrubs in leaf are sold established in containers filled with soil or compost, but in winter deciduous ones are obtainable with their roots wrapped in peat, hessian, plastic or waterproof paper. It is advisable to plant deciduous shrubs in winter as they are then dormant and less likely to be adversely affected by transplanting.

Shrubs in containers may be planted out at any time of the year, but the best time to plant is in late winter or early spring after frosts are over, or during the rainy season, as cloudy wet weather makes it unnecessary to shade or water the young shrubs much.

If doubtful about the quality of the soil, dig holes 60 cm wide and deep and prepare a good soil/compost/peat mixture. Put some of this in the bottom of the hole and tread it down firmly. Estimate how much soil to put in the bottom of the hole by standing the plant in its container in the hole. When planted, the soil level about the plant should be more or less the same as it was when in the container. See that there is about 15 cm of good soil around and below the plant to encourage good initial root growth. Remove the plant from the container without disturbing the earth about its roots. It is not difficult to do this if the plant is watered beforehand. Carefully place it in position with its soil around its roots, and then fill in earth firmly around the sides, making sure that the soil around the roots does not crumble away from the roots in the process. Some plants in active growth react badly to the disturbance of soil around their roots.

When planting deciduous shrubs with bare roots in winter, put the roots of the plants in a bucket of water or cover them with wet soil until planting can be done. Ascertain the right size to make the hole by standing the shrub in the hole and allow for 15 cm or more of good soil about the roots. Make a mound of soil in the bottom of the hole and spread out the roots before filling in the soil on top. Should any roots be broken, cut these off with a sharp pair of secateurs before planting. After planting ensure that the soil is firmly pressed down around the plants.

When filling in the soil, leave a saucer-like depression around the shrub at the surface of the ground to hold water, and soak the ground thoroughly immediately after planting. Let the water dribble slowly around the shrub until the water has penetrated deep into the soil.

If planting is done in very hot, dry weather, a shrub in full leaf should be shaded for a few days; although soaking the ground will help it to resist the heat and dryness and prevent wilting, it may not be enough.

Water

In regions where the rainfall is seasonal and erratic, more shrubs die or fail to grow well because of insufficient water than for any other single reason.

How much water a shrub requires, and how often, is a question which cannot be answered in definite terms. It depends on many variable and complex factors.

(1) The nature of the plant. Some plants like an abundance of water to promote good growth; others are by nature adapted to withstand long periods of drought. Deciduous plants require less water in winter than evergreen ones.

(2) The age of a shrub. Shrubs three or more years old will have developed a good root system, which enables them to draw on water present below the surface of the soil, even when the top soil appears to be quite dry. They therefore require less water than newly-planted shrubs.

(3) The root system of the plant. Shrubs such as azaleas, with fibrous roots near the surface, should be watered more often than those with roots that go deep into the soil.

(4) The nature of the soil. Shrubs growing in sandy soil need to be watered more frequently than those growing in clay; but those in clay require more water at a time to penetrate to the roots than those in sandy soil.

(5) Weather. During periods of dry or
    hot windy weather when the rate of
    transpiration is accelerated, shrubs
    naturally require more water than
    during cool, overcast weather.
Watering need not prove an onerous
task. Avoid frequent spraying of the
surface of the soil. Rather soak the soil
thoroughly once a week than sprinkle
it every day. If the shrubs are fairly
near one another, install a perforated
hose to remain in position permanently. This type of hose allows the
water to trickle out slowly. Measure
how much water comes through the
holes in a given time, and estimate
how long the tap should be open to
soak the soil down to the root-zone.

   Where water is in short supply and
droughts are common, plant drought-
resistant shrubs and apply the water to
the root-zone of the plants instead of
on the surface of the soil. This can be
done by installing next to each shrub a
piece of 5–10 cm plastic, iron or clay
pipe so that it penetrates 30 cm beneath the soil surface. The bottom of
the pipe should rest on a thick layer of
coarse gravel. To water, put the hose
into the top of the pipe, and allow the
water to dribble slowly into it.

   A mulch will also ensure that water
is not absorbed quickly from the soil
by the action of sun or wind.

Mulch

In hot dry countries of the world,
mulching to reduce the evaporation of
soil moisture was practised centuries
ago. A mulch may be made of different
materials – straw, chaff, leaves, old
lawn clippings, sawdust, weeds without seedheads, plastic sheets or stones.
Stones have the advantage of being per-
manent and they keep the soil cool
and moist. Plastic sheets are light and
easy to handle but they tend to heat
the soil unless they are put over a layer

Top left
The background of shrubs and perennials
add charm to this water feature

Bottom left
The leaves of Golden Privet (Ligustrum) are
colourful through most of the year

Opposite
A rock and water garden which is enhanced
by its frame of shrubs and perennials

of straw. Organic materials are, however, the best to use as a mulch because they improve the soil. In decomposing, they add to its humus content.

It is better to use composted or partially rotted sawdust, chaff and leaves but, if only fresh material is available, first sprinkle the soil around the plants with a small handful of fertilizer with a high nitrogen content and then put down the mulch. When a mulch is applied the soil bacteria start working on the lower layer of it, decomposing the leaves, straw or whatever you have used. In doing this the bacteria make use of nitrogen in the soil and, if additional nitrogen is not applied with the mulching material, they may use up nitrogen in the soil to the detriment of the plant.

When watering shrubs surrounded by a thick mulch, apply the water direct to the soil under the mulch by removing the nozzle from the hose, or by using a perforated hose which remains permanently in position along the shrub border beneath the mulch. Plants that like acid soil do well if mulched with peat. Saturate the peat before putting it down as otherwise it is likely to absorb moisture from the soil.

Pruning

For most shrubs pruning is unnecessary, unless they are grown to form a hedge. A little trimming or cutting back of shrubs when they become too large for their space in the garden is, however, desirable. When this has to be done, study the growth of the shrub and shape it accordingly. Do not merely cut it straight off across the top and down the sides. Shorten the stems and if the shrub seems to have too many stems coming up from the base, cut some of these at ground level, or dig them up with their roots. With winter and spring-flowering shrubs this cutting or trimming should be done immediately after they have flowered. Shrubs which flower in summer or autumn should be trimmed in late winter or very early spring. Spring-flowering shrubs which have ornamental berries in summer or autumn should not be pruned after flowering, as this is likely to reduce the crop of berries. Rather shorten a few

stems each year, leaving the remaining ones to carry the berries.

There are some shrubs, such as Spanish broom, which need fairly drastic annual pruning to keep them from becoming leggy at the base and gaunt and untidy in appearance. A few shrubs, such as fuchsias, send up long, lanky growth and produce few flowers, on sagging stems, if they are not cut back once or twice a year. Nipping the end of a stem at a leaf junction will promote basal branching and give a better shape, but if these plants are already too tall and straggly, cut them back hard in late winter or early spring. Others, such as melaleuca, callistemon and protea should have the flowering stems shortened after the flowers have faded, to keep the plants tidy.

If shrubs in a garden have been neglected for years and have grown into a jungle, prune them back hard, by cutting or sawing off main stems fairly low down. Any younger stems can be headed back as well.

Cutting or trimming shrubs to form a compact hedge must be done regularly. The first cutting may be done when the shrubs are less than 30 cm high. Shear them off with a pair of hedge clippers and keep the plants low for several months to force dense basal growth. How often a formal hedge should be trimmed depends on the rate of growth of the plants. Some are naturally slow-growers and need trimming only two or three times a year; others, which grow fast, may need grooming once a month during spring and summer, and less often in cold weather.

Trimming shrubs to formal shapes – globes, cones or boxes – should start when the plants are very small. The number of times this trimming is necessary each year will depend on the rate of growth of the plant and the weather.

Standard shrubs are usually grafted onto an understock. Should stems emerge at ground level or along the stem below the head of a standard shrub, cut these out neatly with a knife, slicing into the stem or root-zone. Cutting them off with secateurs will not stop them from growing again, and if they are allowed to grow the

appearance and vitality of the standard will suffer.

With shrubs that produce colourful new growth, trimming may be done two or three times between late spring and autumn, as the beauty of such shrubs lies in the new growth, rather than in the flowers.

Names

Botanical names are long and are often tongue-twisters. It is therefore not surprising that some gardeners feel irritated by writers who use these names in their books. Common names have a more homely sound and, of course, they are far easier to pronounce and remember, but very often common names lead to confusion. The same common name may be used in different parts of a country for different plants. For example, in some regions the word 'japonica' refers to a Japanese flowering quince, whilst in other regions it is used as the common name for a camellia. Then again, in some cases there are many different related plants with the same name, and if you want a particular one, you must know its complete botanical name. Ask a nurseryman for a viburnum or a cotoneaster and he will say: 'I have six or more different species of each; which one do you want?'

Learning botanical names depends to some extent upon one's attitude of mind. Decide that it is interesting and instructive to know them and it will become easy. Nobody quibbles about using names such as rhododendron and magnolia; yet these are both botanical names that have become familiar.

Botanical names often enable one to know something more about the plants and their relationships. Plants, like people, have two names to help one to identify them. The first one is the genus or generic name – equivalent to our surnames, and the second one is the species (or specific name), which may be compared to our first names. Take viburnums again. If you look at the index or the descriptions of viburnums in this book, you will find that there are a number of species. They are similar in a general way, but they have different attributes. Some may be grown for the beauty of their flowers; some for their scent; and some for their berries or foliage. Knowing the species names is essential in this case. Knowing them also often helps one to identify a plant, because the species name may describe the shape or some peculiarity of the leaf, the flower or its general habit of growth. Or the species name may refer to the place of origin of the plant or the person who first discovered it. For instance, *Hydrangea quercifolia* is a hydrangea with leaves rather like those of an oak, from *quercus* (the name for an oak) and *folia* meaning leaves. The species name *odora* indicates that the plant is scented, *prostratum* that it is prostrate in growth, *spinosa* that it is thorny, and *chinensis* that it comes from China.

Until recently gardeners, nurserymen and horticulturists have referred to 'varieties' of plants. For example, we used to refer to varieties of roses, azaleas, pelargoniums and so on. The term 'variety' is now used only for botanical varieties (rarely planted in gardens). In gardening the term 'variety' has been replaced by that of 'cultivar'. A cultivar can loosely be described as a hybrid propagated for general gardening purposes. The name of the cultivar is always written after the botanical name of the plant from which it is derived. It is written with initial capital letters and in single inverted commas. For example, we have the name *Acer palmatum* 'Dissectum Atropurpureum'. The genus name *Acer* and the species name *palmatum* are written in italics, the genus name with an initial capital letter and the species name with a small letter. Then comes 'Dissectum Atropurpureum', which is the cultivar name. If you want this particular plant it is no use asking merely for *Acer palmatum* because there are several hybrids or forms of this. The word 'Dissectum' means finely cut and describes the delightful way in which the leaves are incised, and the word 'Atropurpureum' describes the purple colour of the leaves.

The genus name does not have to be written out in full each time it occurs. The use of the initial capital letter is sufficient. For example, in a description of the genus Abelia, one may simply use the letter 'A' followed by the species names − *A. grandiflora* or *A. schumannii.*

Sometimes the botanical names of plants are changed because of a reclassification of plants or because another name had previously been given. This is unfortunate because a change of names often leads to confusion, and because it is extremely difficult to find out when names have been changed and what the new names are. Where changes have been made fairly recently the previous botanical name is given in brackets beneath the new name.

Plant some indigenous shrubs

South Africa is the home of a large array of splendid shrubs, some of which have become popular in other parts of the world − in California, the south of France, New Zealand and Australia. South African nurserymen are aware of the decorative potential of indigenous plants and many of them stock a wide range, so that it is easy for the gardener to make a selection of these. Many of the spectacular shrubs from the South-Western Cape can be grown successfully in other parts of the country, and many of those native to the summer-rainfall regions can be grown equally well in the winter-rainfall region.

As more and more land is brought under cultivation there will be fewer patches of wild flowers to enjoy, and unless the public becomes more enthusiastic about the protection of its heritage of lovely native plants, it is possible that in the not-too-distant future many species will be found only in national parks and nature reserves. The owners of large estates would be doing their country a great service if they allocated a few acres for the foundation of private nature reserves, and all towns should endeavour to establish a garden of native plants, featuring particularly those of their own area, but growing also some of those that occur naturally in other regions of Southern Africa.

Acknowledgements

The compilation of a book of this kind involves a good deal of research, and, as one cannot grow all of the plants described under different climatic conditions, one must, perforce, draw on the experience of others to fill in the gaps in one's own knowledge.

I am deeply indebted to the enthusiastic and practical gardeners, nurserymen and horticulturists in different parts of this country and in other countries, who have so kindly shared their knowledge and experience with me. I owe a debt of gratitude also to those who were so ready to advise and help when I had difficulty in ascertaining the correct botanical names of some plants, and particularly to Dr John Rourke of the Compton Herbarium, Kirstenbosch, Cape; Mr Peter Hyypio of the Bailey Hortorum, Cornell University, USA, the staff of the Botanical Research Institute, Pretoria and Mr C. Brickell, at the time Director of the Royal Horticultural Society Garden at Wisley.

Una D van der Spuy

Una van der Spuy,
Old Nectar, Stellenbosch, May 1986

Part II

Plant selection guide

The more one knows about the characteristics of shrubs the easier it is to plan and plant a garden so that it will be attractive throughout the year.

The following lists have been compiled to assist gardeners, whatever the climate, to select the right shrub for the right place, to bring colour and interest – whether from flowers, foliage or berries – to different parts of the garden at different seasons of the year.

Japanese style gardens – large and small – furnished with shrubs, trees and climbers

Shrubs for small gardens

The smaller the garden, the more important it is to plan carefully before planting. Shrubs of exuberant growth and those that cannot be restricted to approximately 1 m in spread should not be planted in a small garden. Some of the shrubs listed here are naturally small, and some are large but they do not mind being trimmed or cut back once a year. If, after two or three years, a shrub appears to be outgrowing the space allotted it in the garden, trim back the stems, or remove some of them where they emerge above the ground. Done at the right time of the year, this will not necessarily reduce their flowering and, in some cases, may improve the form of the shrub and the quality of the flowers. Details about the trimming and pruning of shrubs are given on page 16.

In recent years horticulturists have propagated dwarf or miniature forms of some of the large shrubs. These, and shrubs with variegated foliage, which generally grow less vigorously than the species from which they evolved, are eminently suitable for small gardens.

Abelia species and cultivars
Abutilon megapotamicum
Acacia acinacea
Acacia brownii
Acacia pulchella
Acer palmatum cultivars
Adenandra species
Aloe (several species)
Aphelandra species
Ardisia species
Artemisia species and cultivars
Arundo donax cultivars
Aster filifolius
Atriplex species
Aucuba japonica cultivars
Azalea species and cultivars
Azara microphylla 'Variegata'
Baeckea camphorata
Bambusa multiplex 'Fernleaf'
Banksia violacea
Barleria obtusa
Bauera sessiliflora
Beaufortia purpurea
Beloperone guttata
Berberis thunbergii cultivars

Bocconia frutescens
Boronia species
Bouvardia longiflora
Brunfelsia calycina eximia
Buxus microphylla japonica
Callistemon linearis 'Pumila'
Callistemon pinifolius
Callistemon speciosus
Calluna vulgaris
Calocephalus brownii
Calothamnus sanguineus
Cantua bicolor
Caryopteris clandonensis
Ceanothus (some cultivars)
Centaurea species
Centradenia species
Ceratostigma species
Chamaecyparis lawsoniana
    'Erecta Aurea'
    'Lutea Nana'
    'Minima Aurea'
    'Minima Glauca'
    'Nana'
    'Pygmaea Argentea'
Chamaecyparis obtusa
    'Kosteri'
    'Nana'
    'Nana Lutea'
Chamaecyparis pisifera
    'Aurea Nana'
    'Nana'
    'Plumosa Aurea Nana'
    'Squarrosa Aurea Nana'
Chorizema species
Chrysanthemum frutescens
Cineraria maritima
Cistus species
Clerodendrum species
Clianthus puniceus
Codiaeum variegatum
Coleonema species
Convolvulus cneorum
Coprosma repens cultivars
Correa species
Cotoneaster adpressus
Cotoneaster conspicuus
Cotoneaster horizontalis
Cotoneaster microphyllus
Cotoneaster thymifolia
Cryptomeria japonica cultivars
Cuphea ignea
Cyperus haspan
Cyperus papyrus
Cytisus beanii
Cytisus kewensis
Daphne species
Deutzia (some species)
Dichorisandra thyrsiflora

Dicksonia antarctica
Echium fastuosum
Epacris species
Eranthemum nervosum
Erica (most species)
Eriocephalus africanus
Eriostemon species
Escallonia cultivars
Euphorbia species
Euryops (some species)
Eutaxia species
Fabiana imbricata
Felicia amelloides
Fortunella japonica
Fuchsia cultivars
Galphimia glauca
Gardenia jasminoides
Genista hispanica
Genista pilosa
Grevillea (small species)
Halimium lasianthum
Hebe species and cultivars
Heliotropium arborescens
Hovea species
Hydrangea macrophylla
Hydrangea quercifolia
Hypericum species and cultivars
Hypocalymma robustum
Hypoestes aristata
Impatiens species
Iresine herbstii
Isopogon species
Ixora coccinea
Jasminum mesnyi
Jasminum parkeri
Juniperus chinensis cultivars
Juniperus communis 'Compressa'
Juniperus conferta
Juniperus davurica 'Expansa
    Aureospicata'
Justicea carnea
Kunzea parvifolia
Kunzea pulchella
Lantana montevidensis
Lavandula species and cultivars
Lebeckia simsiana
Leonotis leonurus
Leptospermum scoparium (small
    cultivars)
Leschenaultia biloba
Leucadendron floridum
Leucadendron modestum
Leucospermum mundii
Leucospermum prostratum
Leucospermum tottum
Ligustrum (variegated forms)
Ligustrum vulgare 'Nanum'
Lithodora diffusa

Lonicera nitida 'Aurea'
Mackaya bella
Mahonia aquifolium 'Nana'
Micromyrtus ciliata
Mimetes species
Mimulus glutinosus
Murraya paniculata
Mussaenda species
Myoporum parvifolium
Nandina domestica and cultivars
Nymania capensis
Ochna serrulata
Olearia (some species)
Orphium frutescens
Paeonia suffruticosa
Pelargonium species and cultivars
Pentas lanceolata
Pernettya mucronata
Petrophile linearis
Phaenocoma prolifera
Phebalium species
Phlomis fruticosa
Phormium tenax (small cultivars)
Phygelius capensis
Phylica pubescens
Phyllanthus nivosus
Picea glauca 'Conica'
Pimelea species
Plectranthus fruticosus
Plumbago auriculata
Podalyria sericea
Portulacaria afra
Potentilla fruticosa
Prostanthera species
Protea acuminata
Protea aristata
Protea cynaroides
Protea nana
Protea pudens
Protea scolymocephala
Punica granatum 'Nana'
Reinwardtia indica
Rhamnus crocea
Rhododendron (small cultivars)
Ribes species
Romneya coulteri
Rosmarinus officinalis
Russelia equisetiformis
Santolina chamaecyparissus
Sarcococca species
Sasa disticha
Senecio species
Serissa foetida
Serruria species
Skimmia japonica
Spiraea species
Streptosolen jamesonii
Sutherlandia frutescens

Symphoricarpos albus
Syringa persica
Taxus baccata
 'Adpressa Variegata'
 'Repandens'
 'Repens Aurea'
 'Standishii'
Tecoma alata
Tetradenia riparia
Thuja occidentalis cultivars
Thuja orientalis cultivars
Thuja plicata cultivars
Yucca filamentosa
Zenobia pulverulenta

Shrubs with attractive foliage

All too often gardeners choose shrubs because they are charmed by the flowers they bear, forgetting that the beauty of the flowers is transient. Some shrubs flower for a long period, but most of them produce flowers for only three to five weeks. For the remainder of the year their value lies in the beauty of their foliage or form. Before purchasing shrubs assess the value of their foliage and, if the garden is small, let foliage be the final criterion. In a small space one cannot afford to plant shrubs with unattractive foliage even if their flowers are beautiful.

The beauty of foliage may lie in its texture, its form, its arrangement on the plant or its colour. This list should be studied in conjunction with the two following lists that include shrubs with variegated leaves and those with coloured leaves.

Abelia floribunda
Abelia grandiflora
Acacia cardiophylla
Acacia drummondii
Acalypha species
Acer species and cultivars
Acokanthera oppositifolia
Allemanda species
Aphelandra species
Ardisia crispa
Artemisia species
Arundo donax 'Variegata'
Aucuba japonica

Azara microphylla
Bambusa multiplex 'Fernleaf'
Berberis thunbergii and cultivars
Bocconia frutescens
Burchellia bubalina
Buxus sempervirens
Caesalpinia species
Calliandra species
Calothamnus sanguineus
Carissa species
Cassia species
Centaurea species
Chamaecyparis lawsoniana cultivars
Chamaecyparis obtusa cultivars
Chamaecyparis pisifera cultivars
Choisya ternata
Cineraria maritima
Clianthus puniceus
Codiaeum variegatum
Coffea arabica
Convolvulus cneorum
Coprosma repens and cultivars
Cordyline species
Cotoneaster salicifolius 'Floccosus'
Cryptomeria japonica cultivars
Cuphea species
Cyathea species
Cyperus papyrus
Daphne (some species)
Dicksonia species
Embothrium species
Ervatamia divaricata
Escallonia species
Euonymus species and cultivars
Eupatorium sordidum
Euryops acraeus
Euryops pectinatus
Fatsia japonica
Fortunella japonica
Gardenia jasminoides
Gordonia axillaris
Grevillea (some species)
Hakea saligna
Hebe (some species)
Hibiscus rosa-sinensis
Hypericum species
Hypocalymma robustum
Impatiens species
Juniperus cultivars
Justicea carnea
Kalmia latifolia
Lebeckia cytisoides
Leptospermum laevigatum
Leucospermum reflexum
Ligustrum species
Lonicera nitida
Lonicera pileata
Mahonia (some species)

Malvaviscus arboreus
Melianthus major
Murrayà species
Myrtus communis
Nandina domestica
Ochna serrulata
Osmanthus ilicifolius
Paeonia suffruticosa
Pelargonium (some species)
Phormium tenax
Photinia glabra
Photinia serrulata
Phylica pubescens
Phyllanthus nivosus
Phyllostachys castillonis
Picea glauca 'Conica'
Pieris species
Podalyria species
Portulacaria afra
Protea aristata
Pseudopanax lessonii
Punica granatum 'Flore pleno'
Rhododendron (some cultivars)
Ricinus communis
Robinia hispida
Rosmarinus officinalis
Sambucus cultivars
Santolina chamaecyparissus
Sarcococca species
Sasa disticha
Senecio species
Spiraea species and cultivars
Sutherlandia frutescens
Taxus baccata cultivars
Tecoma species
Tecomaria capensis
Tetrapanax papyriferus
Thuja cultivars
Viburnum (some species)
Vitex agnus-castus
Yucca species

Shrubs with variegated leaves

Some of the most attractive garden plants are those with variegated foliage. If they are evergreen plants their leaves highlight the garden throughout the year and, if deciduous, they are decorative for approximately nine months.

The variegated form of a shrub is often less vigorous in growth than the species from which it evolved and therefore more suited to the small garden.

Shrubs with leaves marked with yellow, ivory or white are invaluable for adding light to a dark corner. They should not, however, be planted in complete shade as they need sunlight for some hours of the day to bring out the variation in colour. Many of the small conifers with golden foliage show a tendency to burn if subjected to intense sunlight or much hot, dry wind. If possible plant them where they have shade during the hottest hours of the day and where they are protected from the full strength of the wind.

Sometimes a plant with variegated leaves will send out stems with plain green leaves. These should be cut out as they are more vigorous than those with variegated leaves and, if left to develop, they may take command of the bush.

Abelia cultivars
Abutilon megapotamicum cultivar
Abutilon vitifolium cultivar
Acalypha species
Acer palmatum (some cultivars)
Arundo donax 'Variegata'
Aucuba japonica 'Crotonifolia'
Aucuba japonica 'Gold Dust'
Azara microphylla 'Variegata'
Buxus sempervirens cultivars
Calluna vulgaris 'Aurea'
Chamaecyparis (some cultivars)
Codiaeum variegatum
Coprosma repens 'Argentea'
Coprosma repens 'Picturata'
Coprosma repens 'Variegata'
Cotoneaster horizontalis 'Variegata'
Daphne burkwoodii 'Variegata'
Daphne odora 'Aureo-marginata'
Duranta erecta 'Variegata'
Elaeagnus pungens 'Argenteo-variegata'
Elaeagnus pungens 'Aurea'

Elaeagnus pungens 'Maculata'
Euonymus japonicus cultivars
Fatsia japonica cultivar
Fortunella japonica 'Variegata'
Hebe 'Andersonii Variegata'
Hebe salicifolia 'Variegata'
Hebe speciosa 'Tricolor'
Hibiscus rosa-sinensis cultivar
Hydrangea cultivar
Hypericum moserianum 'Tricolor'
Juniperus chinensis (some cultivars)
Ligustrum japonicum 'Aureum'
Ligustrum lucidum 'Aureo-variegatum'
Ligustrum lucidum 'Tricolor'
Ligustrum ovalifolium 'Aureum'
Ligustrum sinense 'Variegatum'
Lonicera nitida 'Aurea'
Myrtus communis 'Variegata'
Nerium oleander cultivar
Osmanthus ilicifolius
  'Aureomarginatus'
Phormium colensoi 'Tricolor'
Phormium tenax 'Variegatum'
Phyllostachys aurea
Phyllostachys castillonis
Pyracantha cultivar
Sambucus racemosa cultivars
Symphoricarpos orbiculatus
  'Foliis Variegatus'
Taxus baccata (some cultivars)
Thuja orientalis (some cultivars)
Viburnum tinus 'Variegata'
Vitex agnus-castus cultivar
Weigela florida cultivar
Yucca aloifolia 'Variegata'

Shrubs with coloured leaves

A charming and colourful garden can be created by growing shrubs with coloured leaves together with those which have leaves of different shades of green and those with variegated foliage. Many of these shrubs do not produce showy flowers, but they are nevertheless valuable subjects for the garden.

The monotony of a predominantly green garden can be relieved by planting shrubs with blue-green, gold-tinted, grey or wine-coloured leaves. Silver-grey makes a splendid contrast to dark green foliage and it has the merit, too, of adding luminosity to the garden on an overcast day and in the evening. Plants with grey foliage also tone down brilliant colours; they add interest to a shrub or flower border and, in a hot climate, they evoke a feeling of coolness. Some shrubs with coloured foliage do best when planted in a sunny place as their leaves do not colour well in shade, whilst others grow well only in filtered light, but all of them need a certain amount of sun to induce colouring.

Acacia glaucoptera
Acalypha species and cultivars
Acer palmatum 'Atropurpureum'
Acer palmatum 'Aureum'
Acer palmatum 'Dissectum
   Atropurpureum'
Acer palmatum 'Linearilobum
   Rubrum'
Acer palmatum 'Seigai'
Acer palmatum 'Suminagashi'
Artemisia species and cultivars
Atriplex canescens
Berberis thunbergii (some cultivars)
Calluna (some cultivars)
Calocephalus brownii
Centaurea species
Chamaecyparis lawsoniana
   'Erecta Aurea'
   'Lutea Nana'
   'Minima Aurea'
   'Nana Argentea'
   'Pygmaea Argentea'
Chamaecyparis obtusa
   'Fernspray Gold'
   'Nana Lutea'
   'Pygmaea Aurescens'
Chamaecyparis pisifera
   'Aurea Nana'
   'Filifera Aurea'
   'Plumosa Aurea Nana'
   'Squarrosa Aurea Nana'
   'Squarrosa Sulphurea'
Cineraria maritima
Codiaeum variegatum
Convolvulus cneorum
Cordyline australis 'Atropurpurea'
Cotinus coggygria 'Foliis Purpureis'
Dodonaea viscosa 'Purpurea'

A large border composed of shrubs with foliage of different colours

Erica carnea 'Aurea'
Erica cinerea 'Golden Hue'
Euryops acraeus
Euryops pectinatus
Halimium atriplicifolium
Halimium halimifolium
Iresine herbstii
Juniperus chinensis (some cultivars)
Juniperus communis 'Depressa Aurea'
Juniperus x media (some cultivars)
Lavandula spica
Lavandula stoechas
Leptospermum scoparium
  'Red Damask'
Leucospermum reflexum
Phlomis fruticosa
Phormium tenax 'Atropurpureum'
Phormium tenax 'Rubrum'
Phyllanthus nivosus
Physocarpus opulifolius 'Luteus'
Podalyria sericea
Prostanthera induta
Protea (some species)
Ricinus communis
Romneya coulteri
Sambucus cultivars
Santolina chamaecyparissus
Senecio (some species)
Spiraea japonica 'Gold Flame'
Taxus baccata
   'Adpressa Variegata'
   'Aurea'
   'Fastigiata Aurea'
   'Repens Aurea'
   'Standishii'
Thuja occidentalis (some cultivars)
Thuja orientalis (some cultivars)
Thuja plicata (some cultivars)
Viburnum opulus 'Aureum'
Weigela florida 'Foliis Purpureis'

Shrubs with good autumnal foliage

Avoid planting the garden with only ever-green shrubs. Some of the most decorative plants are deciduous ones that are lovely in autumn, when the leaves change colour, and beautiful in spring, too, when the new leaves unfurl.

Only a few deciduous shrubs have colour-ful autumnal foliage, and the degree of the change in colour depends on climatic condi-tions. In areas of mild winters there may be hardly any change at all, whilst in areas where autumn is crisp and frosty the change is pronounced.

The plants listed below are worth grow-ing for their autumnal colour. As few shrubs produce flowers in autumn those which have colourful leaves at this season contribute a great deal to the beauty of the garden. Another good reason for growing some of these shrubs is that their tinted leaves look charming in arrangements.

Acer palmatum 'Chishio'
Acer palmatum 'Linearilobum'
Acer palmatum 'Oshio-Beni'
Acer palmatum 'Seigai'
Acer palmatum 'Suminagashi'
Amelanchier canadensis
Azalea (some deciduous and
  occidentale hybrids)
Berberis aggregata
Berberis julianae
Berberis thunbergii
Berberis wilsoniae
Ceratostigma willmottianum
Chimonanthus praecox
Clethra species
Cornus species
Cotinus coggygria
Cotinus coggygria 'Foliis Purpureis'
Cotoneaster adpressus
Cotoneaster horizontalis
Cryptomeria japonica 'Vilmoriniana'
Disanthus cercidifolius
Enkianthus species
Euonymus alatus
Euonymus europaeus
Hamamelis mollis
Hydrangea quercifolia
Lagerstroemia indica (dwarf cultivar)
Nandina domestica
Photinia serrulata

Photinia villosa
Rhamnus purshiana
Spiraea prunifolia 'Plena'
Spiraea thunbergii
Stachyurus praecox
Stephanandra tanakae
Stranvaesia davidiana
Viburnum burkwoodii
Viburnum carlcephalum
Viburnum opulus
Viburnum opulus 'Sterile'
Viburnum plicatum var. tomentosum

Shrubs hardy to severe frost

Although climatic conditions in gardens in the Southern Hemisphere are for the most part not rigorous, in some areas severe frost limits the range of plants which can be grown. The shrubs given in this list will stand severe cold but not necessarily dry conditions at the same time. Very often shrubs die, not as a result of the degree of frost experienced, but because they have become too dry in winter. Some of the shrubs named in the next list as being suit-able for areas of moderate frost may be grown in areas of sharp frost too, if they are protected during their first two or three years, or if planted in the lee of buildings or of other plants. (See page 11 for information on preventing frost-damage.) Shrubs which flower in winter should be planted so that the early morning winter sun will not strike the flowers as this is likely to damage them.

Abelia species
Acacia (some species)
Acer palmatum and cultivars
Aloe (several species)
Aloysia triphylla
Amelanchier canadensis
Artemisia species
Atriplex species
Aucuba japonica
Azalea species
Azara microphylla
Banksia ericifolia
Bauera sessiliflora
Berberis species

Buddleia species and cultivars
Buxus species and cultivars
Callicarpa species
Callistemon citrinus
Callistemon linearis
Callistemon salignus
Calluna vulgaris and cultivars
Calycanthus floridus
Carpenteria californica
Caryopteris clandonensis
Ceanothus species and cultivars
Centaurea species
Ceratostigma willmottianum
Chaenomeles species and cultivars
Chamaecyparis species and cultivars
Chimonanthus praecox
Choisya ternata
Cistus species and cultivars
Clerodendrum (some species)
Clethra species
Cordyline australis
Cornus species
Cortaderia selloana
Cotinus coggygria
Cotoneaster species and cultivars
Crinodendron hookerianum
Cryptomeria japonica cultivars
Cytisus species and cultivars
Daphne species
Deutzia species and cultivars
Dicksonia antarctica
Dipelta floribunda
Disanthus cercidifolius
Dodonaea viscosa
Edgeworthia chrysantha
Elaeagnus species
Embothrium species
Enkianthus campanulatus
Erica (some species)
Erythrina humeana
Escallonia (some species and cultivars)
Euonymus species and cultivars
Euphorbia venata
Euryops acraeus
Eutaxia species
Exochorda racemosa
Fabiana imbricata
Forsythia species and cultivars
Fuchsia (some cultivars)
Garrya elliptica
Genista species
Gordonia axillaris
Grevillea asplenifolia
Grevillea banksii 'Forsteri'
Grevillea excelsior
Grevillea juniperina
Grevillea 'Porinda' cultivars
Grevillea rosmarinifolia

Hakea saligna
Halimium species
Hamamelis mollis
Hebe species and cultivars
Hibiscus syriacus
Hydrangea species
Hypericum species and cultivars
Jasminum humile
Jasminum mesnyi
Jasminum parkeri
Juniperus species and cultivars
Kalmia latifolia
Kerria japonica
Kolkwitzia amabilis
Lagerstroemia indica (small cultivars)
Lavandula species
Leptospermum (some species)
Leucadendron album
Leucadendron discolor
Leucadendron tinctum
Ligustrum species and cultivars
Lithodora diffusa
Lonicera species
Magnolia liliiflora
Mahonia species
Melaleuca (some species)
Myrtus species
Nandina domestica
Nerium oleander
Notospartium carmichaeliae
Nymania capensis
Olearia species
Osmanthus species
Paeonia suffruticosa
Pelargonium cultivars
Pernettya mucronata
Philadelphus species and cultivars
Phormium species and cultivars
Photinia species
Phyllostachys species
Picea glauca 'Conica'
Pieris species
Potentilla fruticosa
Protea acuminata
Protea aristata
Protea eximia
Protea grandiceps
Protea magnifica
Protea nana
Prunus species
Punica granatum
Pyracantha species
Rhamnus species
Rhaphiolepis species
Rhododendron species and cultivars
Ribes species
Robinia hispida
Romneya coulteri

Rosmarinus officinalis
Sambucus species
Santolina chamaecyparissus
Sarcococca species
Sasa species
Senecio species
Skimmia japonica
Spartium junceum
Spiraea species and cultivars
Stranvaesia davidiana
Symphoricarpos species
Syringa species
Taxus species and cultivars
Thuja species and cultivars
Viburnum species
Vitex agnus-castus
Weigela florida
Xylosma congestum
Yucca species
Zenobia pulverulenta

Shrubs which stand moderate frost

The plants mentioned in the previous list will naturally also grow in regions that have only moderate frost. Very often frost-damage can be obviated by protecting plants when young, or by planting them in a sheltered situation. Often, too, frost-damage is not serious and, in fact, does some good inasmuch as it reduces the size of plants which may otherwise grow too large for their place in the garden. At the end of winter, stems damaged by frost should be cut back to live growth. Some plants not tolerant of frost can be grown in cold regions if planted where they are sheltered from the rays of the early-morning winter sun. (See page 11 for further particulars on the protection of plants against frost.)

Abutilon species
Acacia (some species)
Acokanthera oppositifolia
Adenandra fragrans
Aloe (many species)
Ardisia species
Arundo donax
Aster filifolius
Baeckea species

Bambusa species
Banksia species
Barleria obtusa
Bauhinia galpinii
Beaufortia species
Beloperone guttata
Boronia species
Bouvardia species and cultivars
Brunfelsia species
Burchellia bubalina
Caesalpinia species
Calliandra species
Callistemon (some species)
Calocephalus brownii
Calothamnus species
Cantua buxifolia
Carissa species
Cassia artemisioides
Cassia bicapsularis
Cassia corymbosa
Cassia didymobotrya
Cassia tomentosa
Cestrum species
Chamaelaucium uncinatum
Chorizema species
Chrysanthemum frutescens
Cineraria maritima
Coleonema pulchrum
Convolvulus cneorum
Coprosma repens and cultivars
Corokia species
Correa species
Crotalaria agatiflora
Cuphea ignea
Cyathea species
Cyperus papyrus
Dombeya species
Dovyalis caffra
Dryandra species
Duranta erecta
Echium fastuosum
Epacris species
Erica species
Eriocephalus africanus
Eriostemon species
Erythrina species
Euphorbia species
Euryops species
Fatsia japonica
Felicia amelloides
Fortunella species
Gardenia thunbergia
Grevillea species
Grewia occidentalis
Hakea species
Hamelia chrysantha
Heliotropium arborescens
Hibiscus rosa-sinensis

Holmskioldia sanguinea
Hovea species
Hypocalymma species
Hypoestes aristata
Impatiens species and cultivars
Iochroma cyaneum
Iresine herbstii
Isopogon dubius
Justicea carnea
Kunzea species
Lantana montevidensis
Lavatera assurgentiflora
Lebeckia species
Leonotis leonurus
Leptospermum species and cultivars
Leschenaultia biloba
Leucadendron species
Leucospermum species
Malvaviscus arboreus
Melaleuca species
Melianthus major
Michelia figo
Micromyrtus ciliata
Mimetes species
Mimulus glutinosus
Murraya species
Mussaenda frondosa
Myoporum species
Nylandtia spinosa
Ochna serrulata
Orphium frutescens
Pelargonium species
Pentas lanceolata
Persoonia pinifolia
Petrophile linearis
Phaenocoma prolifera
Phebalium species
Phlomis fruticosa
Phygelius capensis
Phylica pubescens
Pimelea species
Plectranthus species
Plumbago auriculata
Podalyria species
Polygala species
Portulacaria afra
Prostanthera species
Protea species
Pseudopanax species
Punica granatum and cultivars
Reinwardtia indica
Rhapis species
Ricinus communis
Rondeletia amoena
Russelia equisetiformis
Serissa foetida
Serruria species
Stephanandra tanakae

Streptosolen jamesonii
Sutherlandia frutescens
Tecoma species
Tecomaria capensis
Telopea speciosissima
Templetonia retusa
Tetradenia riparia
Tetrapanax papyriferus
Thevetia peruviana
Thryptomene calycina
Tibouchina semidecandra
Wigandia caracasana

Shrubs for tropical and subtropical gardens

Some plants enjoy cold growing conditions and will not thrive in a warm garden; others will grow only in a mild climate. Plants native to warm regions of the world belong to two broad groups. There are those that grow in areas with a dry climate, and others that are native to hot regions with a high rainfall. Many of the most beautiful flowering shrubs native to tropical regions do well only where there is humidity in the air. It is therefore advisable to water them well when they are planted in regions where the rainfall and humidity are low. The natural habitat of some of these shrubs is the jungle. These require some shade when grown in the garden.

Abutilon species
Acalypha species and cultivars
Acokanthera oppositifolia
Allemanda species
Aloe (some species)
Aphelandra species
Ardisia species
Arundo donax
Barleria obtusa
Bauhinia galpinii
Beloperone guttata
Bocconia frutescens
Bouvardia species
Brunfelsia species
Burchellia bubalina
Caesalpinia species
Calliandra species

Callistemon species
Cantua buxifolia
Carissa species
Cassia species
Centradenia species
Cestrum aurantiacum
Cestrum nocturnum
Chrysanthemum frutescens
Clerodendrum (some species)
Codiaeum variegatum
Coffea arabica
Crotalaria species
Cuphea species
Dichorisandra thyrsiflora
Dombeya species
Duranta erecta
Echium fastuosum
Eranthemum pulchellum
Ervatamia divaricata
Erythrina blakeii
Eupatorium sordidum
Euphorbia species
Fatsia japonica
Fortunella species
Fuchsia cultivars
Galphimia glauca
Gardenia species and cultivars
Grevillea (some species)
Grewia occidentalis
Heliotropium arborescens
Hibiscus rosa-sinensis
Hydrangea cultivars
Hypoestes aristata
Impatiens species and cultivars
Iochroma cyaneum
Iresine herbstii
Ixora coccinea
Justicea carnea
Lantana montevidensis
Lavandula species
Leonotis leonurus
Mackaya bella
Malvaviscus arboreus
Megaskepasma erythrochlamys
Melaleuca (some species)
Melianthus major
Michelia figo
Mimulus glutinosus
Murraya species
Mussaenda species
Ochna serrulata
Pelargonium cultivars

Shrubs as a background to a flower border.
Prunus at the back with Brunfelsia in front

Tall and dwarf shrubs and conifers make a
beautiful border to this charming garden

Pentas lanceolata
Phlomis fruticosa
Phygelius capensis
Phyllanthus nivosus
Plectranthus species
Plumbago auriculata
Portulacaria afra
Reinwardtia indica
Rhapis species
Ricinus communis
Russelia equisetiformis
Streptosolen jamesonii
Tecoma species
Tecomaria capensis
Tetradenia riparia
Tetrapanax papyriferus
Thevetia peruviana
Tibouchina species
Westringia rosmariniformis
Wigandia caracasana
Yucca species

Shrubs for dry gardens

In areas where a low rainfall combined with intense sunlight throughout the year leads to the soil and air becoming very dry, many shrubs fail to grow unless they are watered well. In such areas water is, however, often in short supply, but, fortunately, there are some pretty shrubs which will endure dry growing conditions once they are well established.

In dry areas newly-planted shrubs should, if possible, be watered regularly for several months until they have developed a good root system. It is advisable, also, to put down a thick mulch on the ground around the plants to conserve moisture in the soil. Where little water is available for irrigation, gardeners might find it easier to maintain a pebble garden rather than a garden furnished with a large number of plants.

Shrubs marked with an * are more tolerant of dry conditions than the others.

Abelia species
*Acacia acinacea
Acacia decora
Acacia drummondii

*Acacia glaucoptera
*Acacia myrtifolia
Acacia pulchella
*Aloe species
Aloysia triphylla
Artemisia species
Aster filifolius
*Atriplex species
Baeckea virgata
Banksia coccinea
Banksia ericifolia
Bauhinia galpinii
*Berberis species and cultivars
Buddleia alternifolia
Caesalpinia species
Callistemon species
Calocephalus brownii
Calothamnus species
Cantua buxifolia
Cassia artemisioides
Cassia floribunda
Cassia tomentosa
Ceratostigma willmottianum
Chaenomeles speciosa
Chorizema species
Chrysanthemum frutescens
Cineraria maritima
*Cistus species
Coleonema pulchrum
Cordyline australis
Cortaderia selloana
Cotoneaster species and cultivars
Cytisus species and cultivars
*Dodonaea viscosa
*Dovyalis caffra
Dryandra (some species)
Duranta erecta
Elaeagnus species
Erica (some species)
*Eriocephalus africanus
Eriostemon myoporoides
Eriostemon verrucosus
Erythrina acanthocarpa
Erythrina humeana
*Euphorbia leucocephala
*Euphorbia milii
Euryops species
Eutaxia species
Felicia amelloides
Genista species
Grevillea (some species and
  cultivars)
Hakea species
Halimium lasianthum
Hibiscus syriacus
Holmskioldia sanguinea
Hovea species
Jasminum species

Kunzea species
Lantana montevidensis
Lavandula species
*Lebeckia species
Leonotis leonurus
Leptospermum (some species)
Ligustrum species
Melaleuca (many species)
Micromyrtus ciliata
Myoporum species
*Myrtus communis
Nerium oleander
Nylandtia spinosa
*Nymania capensis
Osmanthus species
Pelargonium species
Petrophile linearis
Phebalium bullatum
Phlomis fruticosa
Photinia species
*Plumbago auriculata
Podalyria sericea
Polygala myrtifolia
*Portulacaria afra
Prostanthera species
Punica granatum and cultivars
Pyracantha species
Rhamnus species
Ricinus communis
Romneya coulteri
*Rosmarinus species
Santolina chamaecyparissus
Senecio species
*Spartium junceum
Spiraea cantoniensis
Sutherlandia frutescens
*Tecomaria capensis
Thevetia peruviana
Vitex agnus-castus
*Yucca species
Xylosma congestum

Shrubs for coastal gardens

It is not always easy to establish a garden near the sea because the soil is usually sandy and porous, and because plants may be subjected to strong winds and salt spray. The texture of the soil should be improved by heavy applications of compost, manure and peat, and a windbreak should be made to protect plants. The wind itself may not be as damaging as the salt it carries. Few plants will grow on the seashore itself but a wide range of plants may be planted in coastal gardens away from the beach. Plants which stand salt-laden wind are marked with an *

To prevent sand from piling up over newly-planted shrubs along the seashore, and to prevent wind damage, it may be necessary to erect an artificial barrier or screen before planting. This may be a fence of wood or a strong netting fence laced with reeds, long grass or brushwood.

Abelia species
Acacia acinacea
Acacia spectabilis
Acalypha species
Acokanthera oppositifolia
Adenandra species
Aloe (some species)
Ardisia crispa
Artemisia species
Aster filifolius
*Atriplex species
Banksia ericifolia
Barleria obtusa
Berberis species
Brunfelsia calycina
Burchellia bubalina
Callistemon (some species)
Calocephalus brownii
Calothamnus species
Cantua buxifolia
*Carissa species
Cassia corymbosa
Centaurea species
Cestrum species
Choisya ternata
Chrysanthemum frutescens
*Cineraria maritima
Cistus species
Clianthus puniceus
Codiaeum variegatum

Coffea arabica
Coleonema pulchrum
Convolvulus cneorum
*Coprosma repens and cultivars
*Cordyline australis
*Corokia species
Correa species
Cortaderia selloana
Cotoneaster (some species)
Cuphea ignea
*Cytisus species
Deutzia species
Dodonaea viscosa
Echium fastuosum
*Elaeagnus pungens
Erica (some species)
Eriocephalus africanus
*Escallonia macrantha
*Euonymus japonicus
Eupatorium sordidum
Euphorbia species
Euryops (some species)
Felicia amelloides
Fortunella japonica
Fuchsia cultivars
Gardenia species
Genista species
Grevillea (some species)
Hakea species
Halimum lasianthum
Hamelia chrysantha
*Hebe species
Hibiscus rosa-sinensis
Hydrangea macrophylla
Impatiens species
Iresine herbstii
Lantana montevidensis
Lavandula species
*Lavatera assurgentiflora
Leonotis leonurus
Leptospermum species and cultivars
Leucadendron (some species)
Leucospermum (some species)
Ligustrum species
Lonicera nitida
Lonicera pileata
Mackaya bella
Megaskepasma erythrochlamys
Melaleuca (some species)
*Myoporum species
Myrtus communis
*Nerium oleander
Nylandtia spinosa
Ochna serrulata
Olearia (some species)
Pelargonium species and cultivars
Pentas lanceolata
Phaenocoma prolifera

Phlomis fruticosa
Phormium species and cultivars
Phyllanthus nivosus
Pimelea ferruginea
Plectranthus species
Plumbago auriculata
Podalyria species
Polygala species
Pomaderris elliptica
Protea compacta
Protea cynaroides
Protea eximia
Protea neriifolia
Protea longifolia
*Pseudopanax species
Pyracantha species
Rhamnus species
Rhaphiolepis species
Romneya coulteri
Rondeletia amoena
Rosmarinus species
Santolina chamaecyparissus
Senecio (some species)
*Spartium junceum
Spiraea species
Streptosolen jamesonii
Tecoma species
*Tecomaria capensis
*Templetonia retusa
*Thevetia peruviana
Tibouchina semidecandra
*Westringia rosmariniformis
Wigandia caracasana
Yucca species

Shrubs for shady places

Most gardens have a shady area, but the degree of shade varies considerably. In the Southern Hemisphere the south side of a building has open shade all day. An east-facing wall is shady for only part of the day — in the afternoon, and a west-facing one will have morning shade and afternoon sun. This last position is a difficult one, for no plants grow well if denied morning sun and subjected to the heat of the afternoon sun.

In an established garden there are also

shady places under trees. A large tree with a heavy canopy of foliage produces dense shade whilst a tree with sparse foliage casts light or filtered shade.

Plants marked with an * are shade-loving plants. These grow better in shade than they would in the sun, but most of them prefer dappled shade to dense shade. The others are shade tolerant and do best in part or open shade.

In regions with a low rainfall and continuous intense sunshine, many shrubs that grow naturally in full sunlight in a temperate region, will do better if shaded from the heat of the afternoon sun.

In coastal gardens where there is moisture in the air, some shade-loving plants will thrive exposed to full sunshine.

Abelia species
Abutilon species
*Acer species and cultivars
*Amelanchier canadensis
Aphelandra species
*Ardisia crispa
*Aucuba japonica
*Azalea species and cultivars
Azara microphylla
Barleria obtusa
Bauera sessiliflora
*Beloperone guttata
Berberis darwinii
Berberis julianae
Berberis stenophylla
Boronia (some species)
Brunfelsia calycina and cultivars
*Burchellia bubalina
Buxus species
Calycanthus floridus
Carpenteria californica
Ceratostigma willmottianum
*Chimonanthus praecox
Choisya ternata
Clianthus puniceus
Codiaeum variegatum
*Cornus species
Cotoneaster horizontalis
*Cyathea species
*Daphne species
*Dichorisandra thyrsiflora
*Dicksonia antarctica
Elaeagnus species
*Embothrium species
*Enkianthus campanulatus
Eranthemum pulchellum
Euonymus japonicus
Eupatorium sordidum
*Euphorbia venata

*Fatsia japonica
Forsythia cultivars
*Fuchsia cultivars
Gardenia jasminoides
Garrya elliptica
Grewia occidentalis
Hamamelis mollis
Hebe species and cultivars
Heliotropium arborescens
Hovea elliptica
*Hydrangea species and cultivars
Hypericum species and cultivars
Hypocalymma robustum
Hypoestes aristata
*Impatiens species and hybrids
Iresine herbstii
*Justicea carnea
Juniperus cultivars
*Kalmia latifolia
Ligustrum species
*Mackaya bella
*Magnolia liliiflora
*Mahonia species
Megaskepasma erythrochlamys
Michelia figo
Murraya paniculata
Myrtus communis
Nandina domestica
Ochna serrulata
Osmanthus species and cultivars
Paeonia suffruticosa
Pernettya mucronata
Phebalium dentatum
Philadelphus species
Photinia species and cultivars
*Phygelius capensis
*Pieris species
*Plectranthus species
Potentilla fruticosa
*Reinwardtia indica
Rhamnus species
Rhaphiolepis species
*Rhododendron
*Sarcococca species
*Skimmia japonica
Spartium junceum
Spiraea species
Stephanandra tanakae
Stranvaesia davidiana
*Symphoricarpos species
*Syringa species
Taxus baccata cultivars
Tetradenia riparia
Tetrapanax papyriferus
Viburnum species
*Zenobia speciosa

Shrubs which like acid soil

Most shrubs grow well in soil which is neutral, that is, neither acid nor alkaline, or in soil which is slightly acid or slightly alkaline, but some show a definite preference for acid soil. Such plants will not thrive in soil that is even slightly alkaline. Do not plant them, therefore, unless the soil in your garden is acid or unless you are prepared to make it acid. Particulars as to how to do this are given on page 12.

Some of the most beautiful shrubs are those that like acid soil, and gardeners who wish to grow these in an area where the soil is alkaline should try planting them in large containers or in raised beds filled with an acid-soil mixture. Suitable compost or soil can be obtained from garden supply stores and large nurseries.

Group the plants which like acid soil together, as this makes it easier to ensure that the soil in which they are growing has the right pH value.

The yellowing of the leaves of plants which like acid soil is often an indication that they are not absorbing the iron they need. Spray the foliage or water the soil around the plants with iron chelates, according to directions given on the package, and sprinkle a small handful of sulphur or alum (aluminium sulphate) around the affected plants.

Acer palmatum cultivars
Amelanchier canadensis
Azalea species and cultivars
Baeckea species
Banksia species
Bauera sessiliflora
Beaufortia species
Berberis species and cultivars
Boronia species
Calluna vulgaris
Chamaecyparis cultivars
Clethra species
Coffea arabica
Cornus species
Crinodendron hookerianum
Daphne species
Dichorisandra thyrsiflora
Disanthus cercidifolius
Dryandra species
Edgeworthia chrysantha

Embothrium species
Enkianthus campanulatus
Epacris species
Erica species
Exochorda racemosa
Gardenia species
Cordonia axillaris
Grevillea species
Hamamelis mollis
Hydrangea species and cultivars
Isopogon dubius
Justicea carnea
Kalmia latifolia
Kolkwitzia amabilis
Leptospermum cultivars
Leucadendron species
Leucospermum species
Lithodora diffusa
Magnolia liliiflora
Mahonia species
Mimetes species
Nandina domestica
Pernettya mucronata
Persoonia pinifolia
Petrophile linearis
Phylica pubescens
Pieris species
Pimelea species
Polygala species
Protea species
Rhododendron
Rondeletia amoena
Serruria species
Telopea speciosissima
Xylosma congestum

Group plants to form a harmonious picture. In the foreground is a Japanese Maple (*Acer palmatum* 'Dissectum Atropurpureum') with climbing Petrea behind

Shrubs which grow in alkaline soil

One of the most limiting factors in gardening is alkaline soil. Nothing will grow in highly alkaline soil, but quite a wide range of plants can be grown in soil which is slightly alkaline. Generally the areas where soil is distinctly alkaline are those with a low rainfall, and this is another factor likely to inhibit good growth.

To promote growth in areas where the soil is highly alkaline, prepare large holes for the shrubs and fill these with less alkaline soil and compost. As the water used for irrigation in such regions is likely to be alkaline it will be necessary to treat the soil regularly to prevent the water from changing the character of the soil drastically. A small handful of sulphur or alum (aluminium sulphate) sprinkled on the ground and watered in every two to three months, will help to ensure that the soil does not become affected by the water. More detailed information on soil can be found on pages 12 and 13.

The tolerance of alkalinity of the plants listed varies. Some prefer alkaline to acid soil, whilst others grow well in acid soil but can be grown also where the soil is slightly alkaline. Gardeners living in regions where conditions are alkaline should study the remarks on the culture of the different plants before making a selection.

Acacia (some species)
Acokanthera oppositifolia
Adenandra species
Aloe (most species)
Aloysia triphylla
Artemisia species
Atriplex species
Bauhinia galpinii
Berberis species and cultivars
Buddleia alternifolia
Buxus species
Callicarpa dichotoma
Callistemon (some species)
Carissa species
Cassia species
Ceanothus species and cultivars
Ceratostigma species
Chamaecyparis lawsoniana cultivars

Choisya ternata
Chrysanthemum frutescens
Cineraria maritima
Cistus species
Clerodendrum fargesii
Coleonema species
Convolvulus cneorum
Coprosma repens and cultivars
Corokia cotoneaster
Cotoneaster species
Cytisus (many species)
Daphne mezereum
Deutzia species
Dodonaea viscosa
Dovyalis caffra
Duranta erecta
Elaeagnus species
Erica carnea
Erica irregularis
Erica erigena
Eriocephalus africanus
Escallonia species
Euonymus species and cultivars
Euphorbia leucocephala
Euphorbia milii
Euphorbia pulcherrima
Euphorbia venata
Euryops species
Genista species
Grevillea (some species)
Hakea species
Hibiscus species and cultivars
Hydrangea cultivars
Hypericum species and cultivars
Iresine herbstii
Juniperus species and cultivars
Lantana montevidensis
Lavandula species and cultivars
Lebeckia species
Leucadendron album
Leucospermum conocarpodendron
Leucospermum cuneiforme
Leucospermum patersonii
Ligustrum species and cultivars
Lonicera species
Nerium oleander
Notospartium carmichaeliae
Nylandtia spinosa
Nymania capensis
Olearia species
Osmanthus species
Paeonia suffruticosa
Pelargonium species
Philadelphus species
Photinia serrulata
Plumbago auriculata
Portulacaria afra
Potentilla fruticosa

Protea aristata
Protea cynaroides
Protea eximia
Protea magnifica
Protea neriifolia
Protea obtusifolia
Prunus species
Punica granatum
Pyracantha species
Robinia hispida
Romneya coulteri
Rosmarinus species
Russelia equisetiformis
Santolina chamaecyparissus
Sarcococca species
Senecio leucostachys
Spartium junceum
Spiraea species
Sutherlandia frutescens
Symphoricarpos species
Syringa species
Taxus species and cultivars
Tecomaria capensis
Templetonia retusa
Thevetia peruviana
Thuja species and cultivars
Viburnum betulifolium
Viburnum rhytidophyllum
Vitex agnus-castus
Weigela florida and cultivars
Yucca species

Shrubs which are quick-growing

Most gardeners are in a hurry. They want to see the transformation of a bare plot into a lovely garden in a matter of weeks. This, of course, is impossible, but a great deal can be achieved in a year or two.

Some shrubs are by nature slow in growth whilst others are fast, but even the quick-growing ones may fail to reveal this attribute if conditions are not congenial. For example, a shrub native to a humid tropical region will sulk and fail to respond if planted in a garden that is dry and cool. The shrubs given in the following list are quick-growing under climatic conditions that suit them, and provided they are watered adequately during dry seasons of the year.

It must be remembered, too, that some of

the quick-growing shrubs may eventually
prove too exuberant, taking up more space
than is available in the garden. When the
slow growing plants are established these
quick-growing ones can be drastically
trimmed or removed altogether.

Abelia species
Abutilon species
Acacia (many species)
Acalypha species
Allemanda species
Artemisia species
Barleria obtusa
Bauhinia galpinii
Buddleia species
Caesalpinia species
Calliandra haematocephala
Callicarpa dichotoma
Cantua buxifolia
Cassia species
Ceanothus cultivars
Centaurea species
Ceratostigma species
Cestrum species
Chamaelaucium uncinatum
Choisya ternata
Chorizema species
Chrysanthemum frutescens
Cistus species
Clerodendrum species
Codiaeum variegatum
Coleonema species
Crotalaria species
Cyperus papyrus
Cytisus species
Deutzia species
Dichorisandra thyrsiflora
Dodonaea viscosa
Dombeya species
Duranta erecta
Echium fastuosum
Eranthemum nervosum
Erica (some species)
Ervatamia divaricata
Eupatorium sordidum
Euphorbia pulcherrima
Euphorbia venata
Euryops species
Fuchsia cultivars
Felicia amelloides
Genista species
Hakea species
Hibiscus rosa-sinensis
Hydrangea species
Hypoestes aristata
Impatiens species
Iochroma cyaneum

Iresine herbstii
Ixora coccinea
Jasminum species
Justicea carnea
Kolkwitzia amabilis
Lavandula species
Leonotis leonurus
Leptospermum cultivars
Leucadendron species
Leucospermum species
Lonicera species
Malvaviscus arboreus
Megaskepasma erythrochlamys
Mimulus glutinosus
Murraya species
Mussaenda species
Notospartium carmichaeliae
Pelargonium species
Pentas lanceolata
Phlomis fruticosa
Phormium tenax
Photinia glabra
Phygelius capensis
Plectranthus species
Plumbago auriculata
Podalyria species
Polygala species
Portulacaria afra
Protea (some species)
Ricinus communis
Russelia equisetiformis
Serruria species
Spartium junceum
Spiraea cantoniensis
Streptosolen jamesonii
Sutherlandia frutescens
Tecoma species
Tecomaria capensis
Tetradenia riparia
Tetrapanax papyriferus
Thevetia species
Tibouchina species
Weigela florida and cultivars
Wigandia caracasana

Shrubs for hedges, screens and windbreaks

*For many generations hedges were planted
to define the boundaries of a property, to
ensure privacy, to protect the house and
garden from dust blowing in from the road
or street, and to reduce the force of wind.
These hedges were usually carefully
trimmed to produce a formal effect. Within
the garden itself low-growing hedges were
planted to outline special areas, such as a
rose garden or a formal pool or fountain.
The first break from the traditional clipped
hedge came when gardeners found that untrimmed hedges were more colourful and
less work than trimmed ones. The next
change was made when it was realised that
privacy and shelter could be obtained by
planting a variety of trees and shrubs
instead of a hedge.*

The formal hedge. *The best plants for
formal hedges are those with fairly small
leaves and those which grow slowly. Small
leaves produce a neater appearance when
clipped than large ones, and slow-growing
plants are easier to manage than quick-
growing ones, since they seldom have to be
trimmed. A formal hedge planted to define
a particular area within the garden may be
only 30 cm high and wide, whilst a boundary hedge is usually 2 m or more in height.*

*A trimmed hedge may be flat, rounded or
tapered at the top. It should measure the
same as, or be slightly narrower across the
top than it is across the base, and the den-
sity of growth should be uniform from top
to bottom. To achieve this, set hedge plants
close together and cut them back regularly
when the plants are still small.*

*Most nurseries sell boxes of young plants
for hedges. Plant these small specimens
10–20 cm apart for a low hedge, and up to
60 cm apart for a high one, and trim the
tops when it is necessary, for a year or
more. Cutting back the top growth regularly at an early stage encourages basal
branching.*

The informal hedge. *An informal hedge is
made by close-planting a row of a single
species of plant. In this case the plants need*

not be headed back for a long period, although occasional trimming is desirable during the first year to ensure good basal growth. Informal hedges of flowering shrubs look effective particularly when the shrub comes into flower. Abelia and plumbago, for example, are most decorative in summer, whilst spiraea produces its foaming masses of flowers in late winter or early spring. Informal hedges may require annual trimming to keep them from growing too high and wide. Hedges which flower in winter or spring may be trimmed immediately after they have flowered, whilst those which flower in summer should be trimmed, when necessary, in late winter or early spring.

An informal hedge may consist of more than one species of shrub, but a mixture of shrubs does not look effective unless the hedge is a long one, and one kind of plant is used for a section of not less than 12 m.

Screen. This term is used to denote an arrangement of plants to conceal a part of the garden from view, or to hide an ugly feature on your own, or a neighbouring property. The best plants for this purpose are those that are tall and slender.

Barrier hedge. This type of hedge fulfils a purpose other than that of merely providing privacy and delineating a boundary. It is to prevent people and animals from intruding. The plants to use for this purpose are those with strong spines or thorns, such as Berberis species, Carissa grandiflora, Chaenomeles (flowering quince), Dovyalis caffra and Pyracantha.

Windbreak. Coastal gardens are often subjected to winds of varying intensity at different seasons of the year. Gardening in some inland regions may be difficult for the same reason. Where strong winds prevail the establishment of a windbreak becomes a matter of first priority in the garden. The plants chosen for a windbreak should be suited to local climatic conditions.

Pelargoniums trained along a fence form a decorative hedge very quickly

Abelia with its pretty little honey-scented flowers is a fine plant for a formal or informal hedge

When selecting plants for a hedge, screen or windbreak be guided by the size of the garden. Ascertain not only the height to which the plant is likely to grow in your region, but also its spread. A tall, slender plant can be grown on a small plot, whereas a shrub that spreads itself may become a nuisance and never look attractive, since it has to be cut frequently to keep it from spreading too far and wide. The spread of most shrubs is approximately two-thirds of their height.

The shrubs marked with an * are recommended for low, formal hedges, up to 60 cm, as they don't mind being trimmed back hard.

Abelia species
Acacia decora
Acacia drummondii
Acalypha species
*Atriplex lentiformis
*Atriplex nummularia
Azalea indica
Banksia spinulosa
Bauhinia galpinii
*Berberis buxifolia
Berberis julianae
Berberis stenophylla
*Berberis thunbergii
*Berberis wilsoniae
Buxus sempervirens
*Buxus sempervirens 'Suffruticosa'
Callicarpa dichotoma
Callistemon (some species)
Carissa species
Chaenomeles species
Choisya ternata
*Chrysanthemum frutescens
*Coleonema pulchrum
Coprosma repens and cultivars
Cortaderia selloana
Cotoneaster species
*Cuphea ignea
Cytisus praecox
Deutzia species
Dodonaea viscosa
Dovyalis caffra
Duranta erecta

The colourful Japanese Flowering Quince
(*Chaenomeles*) stands severe frost

In early spring the graceful stems of
Spiraea add charm to the garden

35

Elaeagnus species
Escallonia species
Euonymus japonicus
Grevillea rosmarinifolia
Grewia occidentalis
Hakea species
*Hebe buxifolia
*Hebe cupressoides
Hebe salicifolia
Hibiscus rosa-sinensis
*Hypericum 'Sun Gold'
*Ixora coccinea
Jasminum species
*Lavandula species
*Leptospermum species and
  cultivars
*Ligustrum species and cultivars
*Lonicera nitida
Luculia species
Murraya paniculata
Myoporum insulare
Myrtus (some species)
Nerium oleander
Ochna serrulata
Osmanthus species
Pelargonium (tall cultivars)
Philadelphus species
Photinia species
*Plumbago auriculata
*Portulacaria afra
Prunus laurocerasus
Pyracantha species and cultivars
Rhododendron species and cultivars
*Rosmarinus officinalis
Sambucus species
*Santolina chamaecyparissus
Spiraea cantoniensis
Spiraea prunifolia 'Plena'
Stephanandra tanakae
Taxus baccata (some cultivars)
Tecomaria capensis
Thevetia peruviana
Viburnum rhytidophyllum
Viburnum suspensum
Viburnum tinus
Weigela florida cultivars
Westringia rosmariniformis

Shrubs with fragrant flowers or aromatic leaves

Scent in the air is an essential quality of a pleasing garden. When one sees a beautiful flower, one is tempted to sniff gently, hoping that it will have fragrance; or, one may rub one's fingers against the leaves anticipating that some kind of perfume will escape.

The ideal garden would have plants producing scented flowers or aromatic leaves during different months of the year. It would include, too, plants that give off their scent at night as well as those which scent the air during the daylight hours. The number of shrubs that have scented flowers is not large but, by combining these with climbers, trees and perennials with scented leaves or flowers, one can achieve this ideal garden.

Abelia grandiflora
Acacia species
Acokanthera oppositifolia
Adenandra fragrans
Aloysia triphylla
Azalea (some species and cultivars)
Azara microphylla
Boronia (some species)
Bouvardia species and cultivars
Brunfelsia species
Buddleia (some species)
Calycanthus floridus
Carissa species
Carpenteria californica
Cestrum nocturnum
Chimonanthus praecox
Choisya ternata
Clerodendrum (some species)
Clethra species
Coffea arabica
Daphne species
Erica peziza
Euryops virgineus
Fortunella species
Gardenia species
Genista monosperma
Hamamelis mollis
Heliotropium arborescens
Jasminum humile
Lavandula species
Lebeckia species

Leptospermum citratum
Lonicera fragrantissima
Luculia species
Michelia figo
Murraya species
Osmanthus fragrans
Osmanthus ilicifolius
Pelargonium (some species)
Philadelphus (some species and
  cultivars)
Pimelea physodes
Podalyria calyptrata
Prostanthera species
Rhododendron (some cultivars)
Ribes aureum
Rosmarinus officinalis
Santolina chamaecyparissus
Sarcococca species
Skimmia reevesiana
Spartium junceum
Syringa species and cultivars
Viburnum bitchiuense
Viburnum bodnantense
Viburnum burkwoodii
Viburnum carlcephalum
Viburnum carlesii
Viburnum farreri
Viburnum x 'Juddii'
Viburnum odoratissimum
Zenobia pulverulenta

Shrubs which provide material for arrangements

To be able to create arrangements of plant material gathered from one's own garden makes gardening the more pleasurable.

There are many shrubs with beautiful flowers, foliage or berries, but only those which have the additional merit of being long-lasting in vases are included in this list. Should the stems have woody ends, slit the basal part of the stem, or split a few centimetres of the bottom end with a mallet or hammer, and stand them in a tall jug of water for a few hours before arranging them.

Although this list appears to be fairly short, it must be remembered that some of the names given include many different species of decorative value. For example, there are many boronias, proteas, pyracanthas, leucospermums and heaths. By planting several species of each of these genera one can have flowers for arrangements during different months of the year.

Cutting sprays of flowers, leaves or berries for arrangements is a simple way of pruning shrubs which may be growing too large for their space in the garden.

Abelia species
Acacia (some species)
Acokanthera oppositifolia
Adenandra fragrans
Aloe species
Arundo donax 'Variegata'
Azalea species
Baeckea species
Banksia ericifolia
Beloperone guttata
Boronia heterophylla
Boronia megastigma
Bouvardia species
Callicarpa dichotoma
Centaurea species
Chaenomeles cultivars
Chamaelaucium uncinatum
Chimonanthus praecox
Chrysanthemum frutescens
Coprosma repens
Cortaderia selloana
Cotoneaster species
Cyperus papyrus
Cytisus species and cultivars
Daphne species
Dryandra species
Elaeagnus species
Epacris species
Erica species
Eriocephalus africanus
Euonymus species
Euphorbia leucocephala
Euphorbia pulcherrima
Euphorbia venata
Exochorda racemosa
Fatsia japonica
Forsythia species
Fuchsia cultivars
Gardenia species
Grevillea (some species)
Hamamelis mollis
Hebe armstrongii
Hebe speciosa
Hydrangea species and cultivars
Hypocalymma robustum
Ixora coccinea
Leptospermum cultivars

Leucadendron species
Leucospermum species
Ligustrum species and cultivars
Magnolia liliiflora
Mahonia species
Mimetes species
Nandina domestica
Osmanthus ilicifolius
Paeonia suffruticosa
Pentas lanceolata
Petrophile biloba
Petrophile linearis
Phaenocoma prolifera
Philadelphus species and cultivars
Photinia fraseri
Phygelius capensis
Phylica pubescens
Plumbago auriculata
Polygala virgata
Protea species
Pyracantha species
Rhaphiolepis species
Rhododendron species and cultivars
Senecio species
Serruria species
Skimmia japonica
Spartium junceum
Spiraea species
Stephanandra tanakae
Symphoricarpos species
Syringa species
Telopea speciosissima
Tetradenia riparia
Thryptomene calycina
Viburnum (some species)
Weigela florida cultivars
Zenobia pulverulenta

Shrubs with berries or fruits

When making a selection of shrubs for the garden, consider all the attributes of the plant. The foliage may be the most decorative feature for most of the year, but some shrubs have beautiful flowers and unattractive foliage; others have insignificant flowers but attractive leaves or fruits. Many of the shrubs listed here are worth growing for their pretty berries, but a few have all the attributes — pleasing foliage, attractive flowers and decorative berries. In

some cases berries will form only if plants bearing male and female flowers are near each other.

The majority of plants grown in gardens have perfect flowers — flowers, that is, having both male and female parts (bisexual). There are, however, cases where the male and female parts are on different flowers (unisexual).

In some species the male and female flowers develop on the same plant. These are known as monoecious plants. In others, known as dioecious plants, the male and female flowers appear on different individuals, and to ensure fruiting or berries it is necessary to have plants of both sexes.

There are also polygamous plants, in which bisexual and unisexual flowers may occur on the same or different individuals of the one species. With plants of this nature, it is advisable to plant several specimens to make certain of an abundance of berries or fruits. Examples of this are to be found in Pernettya mucronata and some of the callicarpas and viburnums.

Amelanchier canadensis
Ardisia crispa
Aucuba japonica
Berberis (some species)
Callicarpa species
Carissa species
Chaenomeles japonica and cultivars
Clerodendrum trichotomum
Corokia cotoneaster
Cotoneaster species
Dovyalis caffra
Duranta erecta
Elaeagnus (some species)
Eriocephalus africanus
Euonymus (some species)
Fortunella species
Ligustrum species
Mahonia species
Myrtus communis
Myrtus ugni
Nandina domestica
Nymania capensis
Ochna serrulata
Osmanthus ilicifolius
Pernettya mucronata
Persoonia pinifolia
Photinia serrulata
Photinia villosa
Punica granatum
Pyracantha species
Rhamnus crocea
Rhaphiolepsis species

Ribes species
Sambucus cultivars
Sarcococca species
Skimmia japonica
Skimmia reevesiana
Stranvaesia davidiana
Stranvaesia undulata
Sutherlandia frutescens
Symphoricarpos species
Viburnum (some species)

Shrubs to grow in containers

Plants in containers are frequently used to decorate the home interior, or the patio, pebble garden or terrace. Apart from the fact that well-grown plants in attractive containers make a handsome show indoors and out, there are some good practical reasons for growing them in containers.

In areas where the soil is alkaline it is possible to grow acid-soil plants in containers filled with suitable soil. In a garden devoid of shade, shade-loving plants can be raised in the shade of the house or carport. Where the soil is impermeable clay, shrubs that prefer free drainage can be grown successfully in raised plant-boxes and, where frosts are severe, those which are tender to frost can be raised in pots that can be moved to a sheltered area during winter. One can keep the house, terrace or patio attractive from season to season by removing the containers with plants that have finished flowering, and replacing them with containers of plants coming into flower.

Containers. Containers for plants may be pots, boxes or tubs, of different materials — clay, china, earthenware, asbestos, iron, polystyrene, plastic or wood. The type chosen should be in keeping with its surroundings. A plastic one may be used in or outside a modern home, whereas a wooden or iron one is more suited to an old house. The container in which the plant is growing is often put inside another more attractive container. For example, several plants growing in clay pots may be put into a rectangular window-box, or into a tub on a terrace; and a well-established plant in an unattractive tin-can may be hidden in a good-looking plant-box.

Before planting shrubs in containers make sure that there are drainage holes. In the bottom of a tub have three or more holes 12 mm across, and space them well. Place an angular chip of stone over each hole to prevent the soil from blocking it. Round stones are not suitable as they tend to stop up the hole and prevent free drainage. If a plant is grown in a clay pot inside another container without holes, see that the clay pot is raised slightly so that it does not rest in the water that drains through into the outer container.

Soil for plants in containers. Use a porous soil, not heavy clay. Prepared mixtures are sold by many nurseries and garden supply stores. A suitable mixture for most plants is one combining two parts of good loam with one of peat and one of compost. About a teaspoonful of bonemeal or a balanced plant food can be added to a container measuring approximately 30 cm across at the top. Succulent plants, such as aloes, do better in soil of a gritty or sandy nature, and acid-soil plants should have a special mixture free of lime. Oak-leaf mould and peat suit them best.

Watering plants in containers. No rules can be laid down as to how much to give or how often. First, because different plants require different amounts of water; secondly, because the amount of water required depends on the weather. In hot, dry, windy weather plants in full leaf in containers may need water twice a day, whilst in still, cool or cloudy weather, or when they are semi-dormant, less water will be needed. The general appearance of the plants and feeling the soil will indicate when to apply water. The yellowing of leaves can result from insufficient or too much water, from soil depleted of nutrients, or the wrong kind of soil. Flagging leaves usually indicate that the plants need water and, if the soil is dry below the top 2–3 cm, it is time to water. Pour the water in slowly until it drains through the holes at the bottom. If it drains through rapidly the soil is excessively dry.

As watering naturally leaches out nutrients from the soil, plants growing in containers should be given a little nourishment from time to time. The general appearance of the plant will usually indicate when it is beginning to starve. Apply fertilizer in powder, liquid or tablet form according to directions given on the package, except to plants which like acid soil. These may be given fertilizer made specially for such plants, or they may be re-potted in a fresh mixture of acid soil, peat and compost.

Containers vary in size, and shrubs may be grown in small, medium or large containers. Indoors, small or medium containers are used whilst plants grown outdoors are invariably planted in medium to large containers.

Small container: 20–30 cm across at the top
Medium container: 30–45 cm across at the top
Large container: more than 45 cm across at the top.

Two spring-flowering shrubs which make a pretty picture together. Yellow broom (Spartium) with Eupatorium

Name of plant	Sun or shade	S	M	L	Remarks
Abutilon megapotamicum (Lantern flower)	Part shade		●	●	Needs a support when grown in a pot. Is attractive trailing over edge of tub or hanging basket.
Acalypha cultivars (Copper leaf)	Part shade	●	●	●	Foliage throughout the year. Best in warm regions.
Acer palmatum cultivars (Small maples)	Part shade	●	●	●	Grown for their lovely foliage and form. Acid soil. Good bonsai subjects.
Aloe (small species) (Aloe)	Sun	●	●	●	Unique leaves, colourful flowers. Well-drained soil.
Ardisia crispa (Coral ardisia)	Part shade		●	●	Attractive evergreen foliage and scarlet berries in winter. Good patio plant.
Arundo donax 'Variegata' (Giant reed)	Sun or filtered light			●	Tall plant with elegant leaves to give height to patio.
Artemisia species (Artemisia)	Full sun		●	●	Silver or pale grey foliage. Remains ornamental throughout year.
Aucuba japonica (Japanese laurel)	Part shade		●	●	Foliage is decorative in all seasons. Berries in winter.
Azalea (Azalea)	Dappled shade	●	●	●	Acid soil. Produces beautiful flowers in late winter and early spring.
Beloperone guttata (Lobster or Shrimp plant)	Part shade	●	●	●	Quick-growing with colourful flowering stems for many months of the year.
Bouvardia species (Bouvardia)	Sun Part shade		●	●	Pretty and sweetly-scented flowers in spring to summer.
Buxus microphylla japonica (Japanese box)	Sun Part shade		●	●	Useful plant for training into ornamental shapes or bonsai.
Calluna vulgaris (Scotch heather)	Part shade	●	●	●	Acid, sandy soil. Flowers in spring. Cut back lightly after flowering is over.
Centaurea species (Dusty Miller)	Sun	●	●	●	Silver leaves attractive throughout the year on terrace.
Chamaecyparis cultivars (Cypress)	Sun Part shade		●	●	Decorative foliage. Recommended for patio or terrace.
Chorizema species (Flame pea)	Sun		●	●	Hot regions. Suitable for hanging basket or pot-culture.
Chrysanthemum frutescens (Marguerite, Paris daisy)	Sun	●	●	●	Quick-growing with pretty foliage and ornamental flowers, mostly in spring.
Cineraria maritima (Dusty Miller)	Sun	●	●	●	Silvery-grey foliage a pleasing foil to plants with green leaves. Good terrace plant.
Clerodendrum species (Oxford and Cambridge bush) (Blue butterfly bush)	Part shade		●	●	Graceful shrubs of moderate to quick growth, with pretty flowers.
Clianthus puniceus (Glory pea, Parrot beak)	Part shade	●	●	●	Slender plant which needs support. Beautiful flowers in late winter.

Name of plant	Sun or shade	S	M	L	Remarks
Codiaeum variegatum (Croton)	Part shade	●	●	●	Coloured foliage of decorative value throughout the year.
Coffea arabica (Coffee)	Sun Part shade		●	●	Acid soil, moist air. Good-looking evergreen foliage. Can be trimmed.
Convolvulus cneorum (Bush morning glory)	Sun		●	●	Attractive foliage with a sheen, and pretty flowers in spring. Patio or terrace.
Coprosma repens and cultivars (Mirror plant)	Sun		●	●	Glossy plain green or variegated leaves are ornamental throughout the year.
Cordyline terminalis (Cabbage tree)	Sun		●	●	Plant of exceptional form for large patio or terrace.
Cotoneaster congestus (Dwarf cotoneaster)	Sun	●	●	●	Species with small leaves and crimson berries in autumn.
Cryptomeria japonica cultivars (Japanese cedar)	Sun Part shade	●	●	●	Dwarf forms of cypress for terrace or patio.
Cyperus haspan (Papyrus)	Sun Part shade		●	●	Small papyrus for side of pool or pebble garden.
Cytisus canariensis (Canary Island broom)	Sun		●	●	Robust, quick-growing plant. Cut back hard after flowering is over.
Daphne odora (Daphne)	Part shade		●	●	Slow-growing small plant with neat foliage and pleasing, scented flowers.
Erica (most species) (Erica, Heath)	Sun Part shade	●	●	●	Different species flower different months of the year. Acid soil with free drainage.
Euonymus japonicus cultivars (Japanese laurel)	Sun Part shade		●	●	Beautiful leaves, green or variegated. Trim to formal shape as entrance plant.
Euphorbia leucocephala (Spray Poinsettia)	Sun		●	●	A graceful plant. Trim in spring to keep it compact.
Euphorbia pulcherrima (Poinsettia)	Sun Part shade	●	●	●	Quick-growing under warm conditions. Brilliant flowerheads in winter.
Fatsia japonica (Japanese aralia)	Part shade		●	●	Large and handsome leaves ornamental throughout year.
Fortunella japonica (Kumquat)	Sun Part shade		●	●	Grown as a standard it makes a good plant for entrance or patio.
Fuchsia hybrids (Fuchsia)	Shade Part shade	●	●	●	Quick-growing with long flowering period. Suitable indoors or out, pots or hanging baskets.
Gardenia jasminoides (Double white gardenia)	Sun Part shade			●	Slow-growing with good-looking foliage and sweetly-scented flowers.

Name of plant	Sun or shade	S	M	L	Remarks
Hebe cupressoides (Cypress hebe)	Sun Part shade		●	●	Has neat, small foliage and attractive flowers. Can be trimmed to formal shapes.
Heliotropium arborescens (Heliotrope, Cherry pie)	Part shade		●	●	Quick-growing, dainty shrub with pretty, scented flowers. Needs trimming occasionally.
Hydrangea cultivars (Hydrangea)	Shade Part shade	●	●	●	Handsome heads of flowers all summer long. Fine indoors or on shady patio or terrace.
Impatiens species (Balsam, Busy Lizzie)	Shade	●	●	●	Quick-growing decorative plants for flowers almost throughout the year.
Iresine herbstii (Blood-leaf)	Sun Part shade		●	●	Blood-red or ice-green leaves marked with deeper colours. Shear to maintain neat appearance.
Ixora coccinea (Ixora)	Part shade		●	●	A neat shrub with pretty rose to scarlet flowers in summer.
Juniperus (small cultivars) (Juniper)	Sun Part shade		●	●	Evergreen plants with a fine form and interesting foliage for terrace or patio.
Lantana montevidensis (Trailing lantana)	Sun		●	●	Trailing plant suitable for containers or large hanging basket. Flowers many weeks of year.
Lavandula species (Lavender)	Sun		●	●	May be clipped to shape or left to grow naturally. Aromatic leaves and flowers.
Ligustrum cultivars (Privet)	Sun Part shade		●	●	Grow as standard and trim to formal shape to enhance terrace, patio or entrance.
Lithodora diffusa (Lithospermum)	Sun Part shade		●	●	Needs acid soil and moist growing conditions. Pretty blue flowers.
Lonicera nitida (Box honeysuckle)	Sun Part shade			●	Neat foliage. Looks effective when trimmed to formal shape. Slow.
Mahonia japonica (Leatherleaf mahonia)	Shade			●	Slow plant with good-looking foliage and berries. Needs trimming to keep it neat.
Murraya paniculata (Orange jasmine)	Sun Part shade		●	●	Good soil and moderate winter weather. Dark green leaves and white flowers.
Myoporum parvifolium (Creeping boobialla)	Sun		●	●	Spreading, prostrate plant for spilling over edge of tub or plant-box.
Nandina domestica (Chinese or Japanese sacred bamboo)	Sun Part shade		●	●	Bamboo-like stems and neat leaves for patio, terrace or pebble garden.
Nerium oleander (Oleander)	Sun			●	Trim annually to restrict growth. An abundance of flowers in summer.
Ochna serrulata (Carnival bush, Ochna)	Sun		●	●	Glossy, neat leaves, tinted bronze in spring. Decorative yellow flowers and ornamental seeds.

Top left
The petals of a Snowball *(Viburnum)* pattern the path beside the pool in spring

Above
A Japanese lantern is the central feature to a shrubbery

Right
Dwarf conifers are fine plants for accenting a scene in the garden – large or small

Name of plant	Sun or shade	S	M	L	Remarks
Pelargonium (Geranium, Pelargonium)	Sun	●	●	●	Quick-growing. Many handsome cultivars with glorious flowers, mainly in spring.
Phlomis fruticosa (Jerusalem sage)	Sun		●	●	Grey-green foliage throughout year, and yellow flowers in spring.
Phormium tenax (New Zealand flax)	Sun Part shade			●	Needs space to develop. Interesting leaves. Stands neglect.
Phylica pubescens (Phylica, Flannel bush)	Sun Part shade			●	Most decorative in late winter and early spring. Needs acid soil.
Phyllostachys castillonis (Castillo bamboo)	Sun Part shade			●	Fine plant for perpendicular, year-round interest on terrace or patio.
Picea glauca 'Conica' (Dwarf Alberta spruce)	Part shade			●	Wants cold growing conditions, moisture and good soil. A plant for the connoisseur.
Pieris species (Lily-of-the-Valley bush) (Pearl flower)	Part shade		●	●	Leaves remain decorative throughout the year. Give rich, acid soil and moist conditions.
Plectranthus species (Spur flower)	Shade Part shade			●	Large leaves throughout the year. Handsome heads of flowers in autumn.
Portulacaria afra (Spekboom, Jade plant)	Sun	●	●	●	Needs porous soil and bright light. Succulent leaves and coloured stems.
Protea (small species) (Protea)	Sun Part shade			●	Plant in acid soil with free drainage and water well in winter.
Punica granatum cultivars (Pomegranate)	Sun		●	●	Has neat foliage, colourful flowers and fruits. Trim to maintain appearance.
Reinwardtia indica (Yellow flax)	Part shade		●	●	Quick-growing plant with an abundance of yellow flowers in autumn and winter.
Rhododendron (small species) (Rhododendron)	Shade Part shade		●	●	Handsome leaves and magnificent heads of flowers. Acid soil, moist conditions.
Sasa species (Dwarf bamboo)	Sun Part shade		●	●	Graceful plants for perpendicular effect on terrace or patio.
Spiraea (some cultivars) (Spiraea)	Sun Part shade			●	Need trimming to keep them neat. Flowers in late winter, early spring.
Sutherlandia frutescens (Cape balloon pea, Gansies)	Sun			●	Effective greyish-green foliage and coral-red flowers. Cut back after seedpods have withered.
Taxus (small cultivars) (Taxus)	Sun Part shade		●	●	Attractive conifers to enhance patio, terrace or entrance.
Thuja (small cultivars) (Thuya, Arborvitae)	Sun Part shade		●	●	Slow-growing conifers of perennial value on patio or terrace, or in pebble garden.

Shrubs for the rock or pebble garden

Rock gardening has been popular for generations, but pebble gardens are fairly new to the Western world. To be attractive both should be carefully designed and planted. The placing of rocks in a rock garden is not easy, for the final result should resemble a rocky outcrop as it would appear in nature. Far too often the so-called rock garden is merely an ugly conglomeration of stones and unsuitable plants. The plants for a rock garden should not be of invasive or spreading growth, as such plants will hide the rocks altogether within two or three years.

Pebble gardens have been made in China and Japan for centuries. The most beautiful of these are those composed of coarse sand or gravel, or small stones of natural shades. The patterns evolved by the raking of the gravel or sand is an art inherited by the Japanese and appreciated by them to the full. The combination of curving and straight lines certainly evokes a feeling of peace and repose. In many of their gardens the coarse gravel is made up of round and angular pieces of stone 1 cm in diameter.

In some Japanese gardens, however, small angular pieces predominate, with round ones being used to create a special effect. The style of pebble gardens which has evolved in Western countries is different from the Oriental to a degree. Here small river stones measuring 2–8 cm are often used. Stones of this size cannot be raked to form a pattern. Small chips of grey granite and coloured scoria or gravel are also used in occidental pebble gardens.

The plants in a pebble garden must be of limited growth. Plants that tend to root themselves and spread (e.g. Pampas grass and some bamboos) should be planted in strong containers sunk into the ground. In a pebble garden it is the pebbles that are important rather than the plants, and only a few plants are needed to create a picture. In a small pebble garden two may be enough — a miniature bamboo and a dwarf conifer, or an aloe and three or four other succulents. Because few plants are needed, this form of gardening is recommended for dry regions where water is not available for irrigation, and for areas where the high degree of alkalinity of the soil restricts the number of plants which can be grown. A pebble garden can be made in part shade or full sunshine.

When making a pebble garden, lay down a piece of thick plastic sheeting to prevent the growth of weeds through the pebbles. After the pebbles, gravel or coarse sand have been placed in position over the plastic, procure one or two (or more) large rocks or boulders and site them somewhere in the area of pebbles — preferably towards the side rather than in the centre. If two boulders are to be used, let one represent height and the other spread. The plants to be grown in the pebble garden can be planted in the ground by making a hole through the plastic, or they can be grown in pots sunk between the pebbles. Embellishing the pebble garden with plants in containers has the advantage that one can change the plants from season to season.

Acer palmatum cultivars
Adenandra fragrans
Aloe (some species)
Ardisia species
Artemisia cultivars
Arundo donax 'Variegata'
Aster filifolius
Azalea (small forms)
Azara microphylla 'Variegata'
Bambusa multiplex 'Fernleaf'
Barleria obtusa
Beloperone guttata
Berberis buxifolia and cultivars
Berberis thunbergii (some cultivars)
Bocconia frutescens
Buxus microphylla japonica
Callistemon phoeniceus 'Prostrata'
Calocephalus brownii
Calothamnus sanguineus
Calothamnus villosus
Cantua bicolor
Centaurea species
Ceratostigma species
Chamaecyparis (small cultivars)
Chorizema species
Chrysanthemum frutescens
Cineraria maritima
Cistus cultivars
Convolvulus cneorum
Cordyline australis
Correa pulchella
Cotoneaster adpressus
Cotoneaster congestus
Cotoneaster horizontalis
Cotoneaster microphyllus

Cotoneaster thymifolius
Cryptomeria japonica (small cultivars)
Cuphea ignea
Cyperus papyrus
Cytisus beanii
Cytisus kewensis
Daphne species
Dichorisandra thyrsiflora
Dicksonia antarctica
Eranthemum nervosum
Erica (small species)
Eriocephalus africanus
Euphorbia leucocephala
Euphorbia milii
Eutaxia microphylla
Fatsia japonica
Felicia amelloides
Forsythia cultivars
Fuchsia cultivars
Gardenia jasminoides 'Radicans'
Halimium lasianthum
Hebe armstrongii
Hebe cupressoides
Hebe pinguifolia
Hypericum 'Sun Gold'
Hypocalymma robustum
Impatiens holstii
Impatiens sultanii
Iresine herbstii
Jasminum parkeri
Juniperus (small cultivars)
Lantana montevidensis
Lavandula species
Lebeckia simsiana
Leschenaultia biloba
Leucadendron floridum
Leucospermum prostratum
Leucospermum tottum
Lithodora diffusa
Lonicera nitida 'Aurea'
Micromyrtus ciliatus
Mimulus glutinosus
Nandina domestica
Ochna serrulata
Orphium frutescens
Pelargonium cultivars
Phaenocoma prolifera
Phlomis fruticosa
Phormium tenax (small cultivars)
Phygelius capensis
Phyllostachys aurea
Portulacaria afra
Protea acuminata
Protea grandiceps
Protea minor
Protea nana
Punica granatum 'Nana'
Reinwardtia indica

45

Romneya coulteri
Rosmarinus species
Russelia equisetiformis
Santolina chamaecyparissus 'Nana'
Santolina chamaecyparissus 'Weston'
Sasa disticha
Senecio species
Serruria species
Spiraea cultivars
Streptosolen jamesonii
Taxus (small cultivars)
Thuja (small cultivars)
Yucca species

Colour through the seasons

Colour plays a significant part in the garden. Yellow is both gay and stimulating; red is a hot colour and should be used with discretion; blues are cheerful, and shades of mauve are cool and restful. Orange and purple are colours that do not mix happily with others; they are strong colours, effective in the right place. Pink is one of the in-between shades that blends well with many others. White adds light and brightness to the garden by day and by night. Like the pastel shades, it is useful for toning down the more vivid colours, and it provides an effective contrast to them.

When choosing shrubs it is usual to consider the colours of the flowers, but one should also know when they produce their flowers or, if the flowers are insignificant, when the shrubs are at their most ornamental because of their foliage or berries. Knowing this makes it easier to design the garden so that it is colourful throughout the year.

The tables that follow have been compiled to help gardeners choose plants to bring colour to the garden from season to season. The colours and flowering seasons given are approximate.

The plants are shown under eight basic colours, but there are infinite gradations of shades in these colours. Pink, for example, includes many shades from the palest blush pink, through shrimp pink, apricot pink, dusty pink to rose and cyclamen. A flower that is flame may be listed under orange or red, depending on which of these two colours appears to predominate. Where a plant is listed under three or more colours it does not necessarily indicate that it has flowers of these different colours. The flowers may be shaded with the colours mentioned.

By consulting these charts together with those on pages 21, 22, 23 and 24, which list plants with ornamental leaves, it should not be difficult to design a beautiful and colourful garden of shrubs. When selecting shrubs, try to visualize the result, and arrange groups to enhance the garden from season to season. Here is an example of an autumn group: Pyracantha angustifolia, *which has orange-red berries;* Cassia tomentosa *and* Reinwardtia indica, *with golden-yellow flowers; and* Viburnum opulus 'Sterile', *which has richly coloured autumn foliage.*

The time when a plant flowers varies according to climatic conditions. A shrub that flowers in a warm garden in late winter may not flower in a cool garden until a month later, in spring. The following are the dates used in this book to cover the seasons:
Spring: September to November
Summer: December to February
Autumn: March to May
Winter: June to August
E = evergreen; D = deciduous.

An easy-to-keep garden composed of a pool, lawn, shrubs and trees

An attractive cosy corner sheltered by trees and shrubs and ornamented by white furnishings

Spring

Abelia species (E) Pink, white

Abutilon species (D, E) Yellow, orange, red, pink, mauve, purple

Acacia (some species) (E) Yellow

Acokanthera oppositifolia (E) Pink, white

Aloe (several species) (E) Yellow, orange, red

Amelanchier canadensis (D) White

Ardisia crispa (E) Pink, white

Aster filifolius (E) Mauve

Azalea species and cultivars (D, E) Yellow, orange, red, pink, mauve, purple, white

Baeckea behrii (E) White

Baeckea virgata (E) White

Banksia (many species) (E) Yellow, orange, red

Bauera sessiliflora (E) Pink, mauve

Beloperone guttata (E) Yellow, brick

Berberis buxifolia (E) Yellow, orange

Berberis darwinii (E) Yellow

Berberis stenophylla (E) Yellow

Boronia caerulescens (E) Blue

Boronia denticulata (E) Purple

Boronia heterophylla (E) Red

Boronia serrulata (E) Pink

Bouvardia longiflora cultivars (E) Pink, white

Brunfelsia calycina (E) Mauve, purple, white

Buddleia alternifolia (D) Mauve, purple

Burchellia bubalina (E) Red

Calliandra tweedii (E) Red

Callistemon brachyandrus (E) Red

Callistemon citrinus (E) Red

Callistemon phoeniceus (E) Red

Callistemon rigidus (E) Red

Callistemon salignus (E) Yellow

Callistemon viminalis (E) Red

Calluna vulgaris (E) Pink, mauve, purple, white

Calothamnus (some species) (E) Red

Cantua buxifolia (E) Yellow, red

Cassia (some species) (E) Yellow

Ceanothus cultivars (D, E) Blue, mauve, purple, white

Ceratostigma willmottianum (D) Blue

Chamaelaucium uncinatum (E) Pink, white

Choisya ternata (E) White

Chorizema species (E) Orange, red

Chrysanthemum frutescens (E) Yellow, pink, mauve, white

Cistus species (E) Pink, mauve, white

Clianthus puniceus (E) Red

Coleonema pulchrum (E) Pink, white

Convolvulus cneorum (E) White

Cornus species (D) Yellow, pink, white

Corokia cotoneaster (E) Yellow

Correa alba (E) White

Crinodendron hookerianum (E) Red

Crotalaria agatiflora (E) Chartreuse

Cuphea species (E) Red

Cytisus species and cultivars (D, E) Yellow, purple, white

Daphne burkwoodii (D, E) Pink, white

Daphne genkwa (D) Mauve

Deutzia species and cultivars (D) Pink, white

Dipelta floribunda (D) Pink

Dryandra (some species) (E) Yellow, orange, tan

Echium fastuosum (D, E) Blue, mauve, purple

Edgeworthia chrysantha (D) Yellow, white

Embothrium species (E) Red

Enkianthus campanulatus (D) White

Epacris longiflora (E) Red, pink

Erica (many species) (E) Yellow, red, pink, mauve, purple, white

Eriostemon species (E) Pink, white

Erythrina acanthocarpa (D) Red

Erythrina blakeii (D) Red

Escallonia cultivars (E) Red, pink, white

Eupatorium sordidum (E) Mauve

Euryops species (E) Yellow

Eutaxia obovata (E) Yellow, orange

Exochorda racemosa (D) White

Felicia amelloides (E) Blue

Forsythia species (D) Yellow

Fortunella species (E) White

Galphimia glauca (E) Yellow

Genista species (E) Yellow, white

Grevillea (many species) (E) Yellow, orange, red, pink

Grewia occidentalis (E) Pink, mauve

Hebe speciosa (E) Mauve, purple, white

Heliotropium arborescens (E) Mauve, purple

Hibiscus rosa-sinensis (E) Yellow, orange, red, pink, white

Hovea species (E) Mauve, purple

Hypocalymma robustum (E) Pink

Impatiens cultivars (D, E) Orange, red, pink, white

Isopogon dubius (E) Pink

Kalmia latifolia (E) Pink

Kerria japonica (D) Yellow

Kolkwitzia amabilis (D) Pink, white

Kunzea species (E) Red, mauve, white

Lantana montevidensis (D, E) Mauve

Lebeckia species (E) Yellow

Leptospermum cultivars (E) Red, pink, white

Leschenaultia biloba (E) Blue

Leucadendron species (E) Yellow, green

Leucospermum (many species) (E) Yellow, orange, red, pink

Ligustrum cultivars (D, E) White

Lithodora diffusa (E) Blue

Lonicera species (D, E) Yellow, pink, white

Mackaya bella (E) Mauve

Mahonia lomariifolia (E) Yellow

Melaleuca (many species) (E) Yellow, red, pink, mauve

Michelia figo (E) Burgundy

Micromyrtus ciliata (E) Pink, white

Mimetes species (E) Yellow, red

Mimulus glutinosus (E) Yellow, orange

Myoporum species (E) White

Nylandtia diffusa (E) Mauve

Nymania capensis (D, E) Russet seedheads
Ochna serrulata (D, E) Yellow
Olearia species (E) Mauve, white
Osmanthus species (E) White
Paeonia suffruticosa (D) Yellow, red, pink, mauve, purple, white
Pelargonium cultivars (E) Red, pink, mauve, purple, white
Pernettya mucronata (E) Pink, white
Petrophile linearis (E) Pink
Phaenocoma prolifera (E) Pink
Phebalium glandulosum (E) Yellow
Philadelphus cultivars (D) White
Phlomis fruticosa (E) Yellow
Photinia species (D, E) White
Phygelius capensis (D, E) Red, pink
Phylica pubescens (E) Lime-green growth
Pieris species (E) White
Pimelea (some species) (E) Pink, white
Podalyria species (E) Pink, mauve
Polygala species (E) Mauve, purple
Pomaderris kumeraho (E) Yellow
Potentilla fruticosa (D) Yellow
Prostanthera species (E) Pink, mauve, purple, white
Protea (many species) (E) Yellow, red, pink, rust, tan, green
Prunus (small species) (D) Pink, white
Punica granatum cultivars (D) Yellow, orange, red
Pyracantha species (E) White
Rhaphiolepis species (E) Pink
Rhododendron cultivars (D, E) Yellow, red, pink, mauve, purple, white
Ribes species (D, E) Red, pink
Robinia hispida (D) Pink
Serruria species (E) Pink
Spartium junceum (E) Yellow
Spiraea cultivars (D) Pink, white
Stephanandra tanakae (D) White
Streptosolen jamesonii (E) Yellow, orange
Syringa species (D) Pink, mauve, purple, white
Tecoma species (D, E) Yellow
Telopea speciosissima (E) Red
Templetonia retusa (E) Red
Thryptomene calycina (E) Pink, white
Viburnum species (D, E) Pink, white
Weigela florida (D) Red, pink
Wigandia caracasana (E) Mauve, purple
Zenobia pulverulenta (D) White

Summer

Abelia species (E) Pink, white
Aloe (some species) (E) Yellow, orange, red
Ardisia crispa (E) Pink, white
Baeckea species (E) Pink, white
Banksia caleyi (E) Orange
Banksia occidentalis (E) Red
Bauhinia galpinii (D, E) Brick
Beaufortia purpurea (E) Purple
Beaufortia sparsa (E) Red
Berberis wilsoniae (D, E) Yellow
Boronia serrulata (E) Pink
Bouvardia longiflora (E) Pink, white
Buddleia colvilei (D, E) Pink, mauve
Buddleia davidii cultivars (D, E) Pink, mauve, purple, white
Caesalpinia species (D) Yellow, red
Calliandra brevipes (E) Pink
Calliandra tweedii (E) Red
Callicarpa dichotoma (D) Pink
Callistemon citrinus (E) Red
Callistemon linearis (E) Red
Callistemon phoeniceus (E) Red
Callistemon pinifolius (E) Lime-green
Callistemon rigidus (E) Red
Callistemon salignus (E) Yellow
Callistemon speciosus (E) Red
Carissa species (E) White
Carpenteria californica (E) White
Centaurea species (E) Yellow, purple
Ceratostigma willmottianum (D) Blue
Cestrum species (E) Yellow, red, pink, purple
Chrysanthemum frutescens (E) Yellow, pink, mauve, white
Cineraria maritima (E) Yellow
Clerodendrum (some species) (D, E) Red, pink, blue, white
Cortaderia selloana (E) Pink, white
Cotinus coggygria (D) Green, purple
Cotoneaster species (E) Pink, white
Crotalaria agatiflora (E) Chartreuse
Dichorisandra thyrsiflora (D, E) Purple
Duranta erecta (E) Blue, white
Erica (some species) (E) Yellow, orange, red, pink, mauve, purple, white
Ervatamia divaricata (E) White
Fabiana imbricata (E) White
Fuchsia cultivars (D) Red, pink, mauve, purple, white
Galphimia glauca (E) Yellow
Gardenia cultivars (E) White
Grevillea (some species) (E) Yellow, red
Hebe species and cultivars (E) Pink, mauve, purple, white
Hibiscus rosa-sinensis (E) Yellow, orange, red, pink, white
Holmskioldia sanguinea (E) Brick
Hydrangea macrophylla (D) Pink, blue, white
Hydrangea quercifolia (D) White
Hypericum species and cultivars (E) Yellow

Opposite top
Snowball (*Viburnum opulus* 'Sterile')
highlights the garden in spring when it
flowers and in autumn when the leaves
turn lovely colours

Opposite bottom
A charming combination of pool, statue
and choice shrubs for the small garden

Top
Note how the shrubs invite one to walk
towards the curving steps

Above
A trimmed shrub is a pleasing contrast to
the exuberant plants on either side

Right
Plant Hydrangeas to gladden a shady area

Impatiens cultivars (D, E) Orange, red, pink, white
Iochroma cyaneum (D, E) Purple
Ixora coccinea (E) Red
Justicea carnea (D, E) Pink
Lavandula species (E) Mauve, purple
Leucospermum cordifolium (E) Pink
Ligustrum species (D, E) White
Malvaviscus arboreus (E) Red
Melaleuca (some spesies) (E) Green, red, mauve, purple
Mimulus glutinosus (E) Yellow, orange
Murraya paniculata (E) White
Mussaenda species (E) Yellow, orange
Myrtus communis (E) White
Nandina domestica (E) White
Nerium oleander (E) Red, pink, white
Ochna serrulata (D, E) Seedheads
Olearia species (E) Mauve, white
Orphium frutescens (E) Pink
Pentas lanceolata (D, E) Red, pink, white
Persoonia pinifolia (E) Yellow
Phygelius capensis (E) Red, pink
Plumbago auriculata (E) Blue, white
Protea aristata (E) Red, pink
Protea cynaroides (E) Pink
Protea longiflora (E) Yellow, pink
Punica granatum and cultivars (E) Yellow, orange, red
Romneya coulteri (D) White
Russelia equisetiformis (E) Red
Santolina chamaecyparissus (E) Yellow
Stranvaesia davidiana (E) White
Streptosolen jamesonii (E) Yellow, orange
Symphoricarpos species (D) Berries
Tecomaria capensis (E) Yellow, orange
Thevetia peruviana (E) Yellow
Thevetia thevetioides (E) Yellow
Vitex agnus-castus (D) Mauve, purple

Autumn

Aloe (some species) (E) Yellow, orange, red
Amelanchier canadensis (D) Red berries
Ardisia crispa (E) Red berries
Barleria obtusa (E) Mauve
Beloperone guttata (E) Yellow, brick
Calliandra haematocephala (E) Pink
Callicarpa dichotoma (D) Mauve berries
Caryopteris clandonensis (D) Blue, mauve
Cassia species (E) Yellow
Cotoneaster species (E) Red berries
Crotalaria agatiflora (E) Chartreuse
Dichorisandra thyrsiflora (D, E) Purple
Dombeya cayeuxii (E) Pink
Duranta erecta (E) Orange berries

Erica fascicularis (E) Pink
Erica glandulosa (E) Pink
Erica oatesii (E) Red, pink
Erica sessiliflora (E) Green
Erica vagans (E) Pink, mauve, purple, white
Erica versicolor (E) Red, pink
Ervatamia divaricata (E) White
Fortunella species (E) White
Gordonia axillaris (E) White
Grevillea fasciculata (E) Orange, red
Grevillea rosmarinifolia (E) Red
Hibiscus rosa-sinensis (E) Yellow, orange, red, pink, white
Hibiscus syriacus (D) Red, pink, mauve, purple, white
Holmskioldia sanguinea (E) Brick
Hydrangea species and cultivars (D) Pink, blue, white
Hypoestes aristata (E) Purple, white
Lavandula species (E) Mauve, purple
Leonotis leonurus (D, E) Orange, white
Luculia gratissima (E) Pink
Megaskepasma erythrochlamys (E) Red bracts
Mussaenda species (D, E) Red, white
Nandina domestica (E) Red berries
Photinia villosa (D) Red berries
Plectranthus species (E) Pink, mauve
Protea burchellii (E) Green, pink
Protea longifolia (E) Yellow, pink
Protea minor (E) Tan
Protea neriifolia (E) Green, pink
Protea nitida (E) Yellow
Protea repens (E) Yellow, pink
Pyracantha species (E) Orange or red berries
Reinwardtia indica (E) Yellow
Ribes sanguineum (D) Berries
Rosmarinus officinalis (E) Mauve
Symphoricarpos species (D) White berries
Tecomaria capensis (E) Yellow, orange
Tetradenia riparia (D) Mauve
Tibouchina semidecandra (E) Purple
Viburnum betulifolium (D) Red berries
Viburnum dilatatum (D) Red berries
Viburnum farreri (D) White
Viburnum opulus (D) Red berries
Viburnum rhytidophyllum (E) Red berries

Winter

Acacia (some species) (E) Yellow
Adenandra fragrans (E) Pink, white
Aloe (some species) (E) Yellow, orange, red
Ardisia crispa (E) Red berries
Aster filifolius (E) Mauve
Aucuba japonica (E) Red berries
Azalea species and cultivars (D, E) Yellow, orange, red, pink, mauve, purple, white
Azara microphylla (E) Yellow
Banksia ashbyi (E) Orange
Banksia brownii (E) Orange, red
Banksia ericifolia (E) Amber, red
Banksia spinulosa (E) Amber
Bauera sessiliflora (E) Pink, mauve
Beloperone guttata (E) Yellow, brick bracts
Berberis aggregata (D) Red or pink berries
Boronia heterophylla (E) Red, purple
Burchellia bubalina (E) Red
Calliandra haematocephala (E) Pink
Calothamnus quadrifidus (E) Red
Cassia artemisioides (E) Yellow
Chaenomeles cultivars (D) Red, pink, white
Chamaelaucium uncinatum (E) Red, pink, white
Chimonanthus praecox (D) Yellow
Chorizema species (E) Orange, red
Coleonema species (E) Pink, white
Correa pulchella (E) Pink
Correa reflexa (E) Red
Cotoneaster (some species) (E) Red berries
Cytisus praecox (E) Yellow, white
Daphne (some species) (E) Pink, white
Dombeya cayeuxii (E) Pink
Dryandra nobilis (E) Yellow
Dryandra polycephala (E) Yellow
Dryandra praemorsa (E) Yellow
Dryandra speciosa (E) Yellow, tan
Echium fastuosum (D, E) Blue, mauve, purple
Epacris impressa (E) Pink, white
Eranthemum nervosum (E) Blue
Erica (many species) (E) Yellow, orange, red, pink, mauve, purple, white
Eriocephalus africanus (E) White
Euphorbia species (D, E) Yellow, red, pink, white
Euryops species (E) Yellow
Forsythia species (D) Yellow
Garrya elliptica (E) Chartreuse
Gordonia axillaris (E) White
Grevillea lavandulacea (E) Red
Grevillea petrophiloides (E) Red, pink
Grevillea rosmarinifolia (E) Red
Grevillea wilsonii (E) Red
Hamamelis mollis (D) Yellow
Heliotropium arborescens (E) Mauve, purple

Hypocalymma robustum (E) Pink
Jasminum (some species) (D, E) Yellow
Kerria japonica (D) Yellow
Lebeckia species (E) Yellow
Leonotis leonurus (D, E) Orange, white
Leptospermum cultivars (E) Red, pink, white
Leucadendron species (E) Yellow, green
Leucospermum (some species) (E) Yellow, orange, red, pink
Magnolia liliiflora (D) Mauve, purple, white
Mahonia lomariifolia (E) Yellow
Nylandtia spinosa (E) Mauve
Nymania capensis (D, E) Russet seedheads
Osmanthus species (E) White
Paeonia suffruticosa (D) Yellow, red, pink, mauve, purple, white
Photinia species (E) White
Phylica pubescens (E) Lime-green growth
Podalyria species (E) Pink, mauve
Polygala species (E) Mauve, purple
Protea burchellii (E) Green, pink
Protea compacta (E) Pink
Protea eximia (E) Pink
Protea grandiceps (E) Pink
Protea magnifica (E) Yellow, pink
Protea nana (E) Rust
Protea neriifolia (E) Green, pink
Protea obtusifolia (E) Green, pink
Protea pudens (E) Tan
Protea repens (E) Yellow, pink
Protea scolymocephala (E) Green
Pyracantha species (E) Orange or red berries
Reinwardtia indica (E) Yellow
Rhaphiolepis species (E) Pink
Rosmarinus officinalis (E) Mauve
Sarcococca ruscifolia (E) White
Serruria species (E) Pink
Skimmia japonica (E) Red berries
Spiraea cantoniensis (D) White
Stranvaesia davidiana (E) Red berries
Sutherlandia frutescens (E) Red
Templetonia retusa (E) Red
Tetradenia riparia (D) Mauve
Tetrapanax papyriferus (D, E) White
Thryptomene calycina (E) Pink, white
Tibouchina semidecandra (E) Purple
Viburnum bodnantense (D) Pink, white
Viburnum burkwoodii (E) White
Viburnum carlcephalum (D) White
Viburnum carlesii (D) White
Viburnum farreri (D) White
Viburnum rhytidophyllum (E) Red berries
Viburnum tinus (E) White

Part III

Descriptions and culture

Hydrangeas and Golden Privet make a colourful contrast

Abelia ABELIA

DESCRIPTION. These ornamental shrubs are usually evergreen but may lose some of their leaves where winters are very cold. They have gracefully arching stems of attractive little leaves, some of which are bronze in spring. The clusters of scented, funnel-shaped flowers are decorative for a long period in summer. When the flowers drop the sepals turn pink and remain colourful for several weeks. Abelia can be effectively trimmed to form a piece of topiary or a neat hedge. Untrimmed, it makes a pleasing informal hedge.

CULTURE. They are fine shrubs, especially for gardens where winters are severe. They are tolerant of dry growing conditions as well as frost. To keep the plants from becoming too large for their position in the garden, thin out some of the stems of mature plants or trim them all over in late winter. They grow in full sun or part shade.

A. floribunda MEXICAN ABELIA
Has a height and spread of 1–2 m. The oval leaves are smooth and glossy, bronze when young, turning a rich deep green later. The pendulous, rosy pink, funnel-shaped flowers are carried in small clusters. Each flower is only 2–3 cm in length but they make a delightful show. This species is not as hardy to cold as the others but it stands 10 degrees of frost.

A. grandiflora GLOSSY ABELIA
Is the most widely grown of the abelias. It stands cold winters and dry winds. The plant is evergreen, reaching a height of 2 m or more, with a spread of as much. It can, however, be trimmed to keep it to half this size. This species makes a good specimen shrub and is popular in many regions as a hedge plant. The neat, glossy, dark green leaves are tinged with bronze when young. In summer it becomes festooned with clusters of small flowers. They are white tinged with pink, and have a pleasant honey-like scent. When the flowers fade the sepals turn pink and bronze. 'Edward Goucher' is a pretty cultivar with pink flowers. *Abelia grandiflora* 'Prostrata' is a low-growing cultivar that makes a good ground cover. It is a useful one for small gardens as it grows to only 45 cm

in height and spread. 'Francis Mason' is a handsome cultivar with leaves edged with gold.

A. schumannii *(A. longituba)*
Is evergreen as a rule but where winters are very cold it sheds most of its leaves. Its height and spread are 1 m. The flowers which appear in late spring and early summer are white flushed with pale pink. The leaves are small and not as glossy as in the other species.

Abutilon

LANTERN FLOWER, CHINESE BELLFLOWER
DESCRIPTION. The species described differ widely in appearance. Where conditions suit them they look attractive in the garden and in containers.

CULTURE. Although many abutilons are native to warm or temperate regions of the world, the two mentioned here tolerate moderate frost. They grow far more quickly, however, in gardens where winters are mild. To promote good flowering and to keep the plants neat, trim them back once a year after they have flowered. Plant them in good soil in full sun near the coast and in partial shade in hot inland areas. Where winters are very cold, plant them against a wall which radiates heat at night.

A. megapotamicum
BRAZILIAN LANTERN FLOWER
Grows in a semi-prostrate fashion and should be trained to a trellis, or planted so that it spills over a wall or bank. The leaves are heart-shaped at the base, 5–10 cm in length and have serrated margins. The calyx is a rich ruby-red, and from it emerges a flower of clear canary-yellow, making an unusual combination of colour. The flowers hang down gracefully from the main branches, attached by their own long slender stems. There are several pretty cultivars, one of which has foliage mottled with gold. The plant may be cut down by frost but it usually comes up again quickly and flowers from spring to autumn.

A. vitifolium FLOWERING MAPLE
Reaches a height of 2–4 m and has large maple-like leaves 10–15 cm long, with three to five lobes. They are

downy and coarsely toothed. In spring it bears clusters of lavender, saucer or bowl-shaped flowers. Does best in gardens that are not subject to hot drying winds. In addition to this species cultivars with flowers of different colours and with variegated leaves are available. They are smaller and more attractive than the species.

Acacia ACACIA, WATTLE, MIMOSA

DESCRIPTION. Most of the decorative acacias are native to Australia which is the home of more than 600 species fairly widely distributed throughout the continent. Many of them are tree-like in form. Only some of those of shrubby form are described here. They are all evergreen except in cold gardens, where some may lose their leaves for a short time.

CULTURE. Many species will grow under difficult conditions. Some stand fairly severe frost and, once established, they will also tolerate long periods of dry weather. They grow in clay or sandy soil and some do well in seaside gardens.

A. acinacea GOLD DUST WATTLE
A shrub reaching 2 m with tiny leaves, which give the plant a rather graceful appearance. In late winter and spring it bears sprays of bright yellow balls of flowers. It grows fairly well in areas that have long dry summers, in frosty regions, and in coastal gardens.

A. brownii BROWN'S WATTLE
A good-looking little wattle growing to about 1 m in height and spread. It does best in a warm, moist climate. It has thorn-like leaves and produces golden-yellow flowers in late winter.

A. buxifolia BOX-LEAF WATTLE
A neat, shrubby plant 2 m or more in height that has spreading stems of small leaves rather like those of the box plant. In spring it becomes wreathed in bright yellow flowers. It is hardy to sharp frost.

A. cardiophylla WYALONG WATTLE
A fine species which grows to 3 m. It has arching stems of small fern-like leaflets and showy yellow flowers in spring.

A. cultriformis KNIFE-LEAF ACACIA
This tall species reaches 2–3 m and is slender and graceful in form. The neat leaves are shaped like a small knife blade, which accounts for the common name. In late winter and early spring it becomes festooned with gay balls of golden-yellow flowers. It stands both frost and drought.

A. decora SHOWY WATTLE
A decorative small species growing to 2 m with slender leaves 2–5 cm long and pretty sprays of yellow flowers in spring. It makes a good informal hedge. Does well in dry areas.

A. drummondii DRUMMOND WATTLE
This is one of the most ornamental of the shrubby acacias and a good one for a trimmed or untrimmed hedge. It reaches a height of 2–3 m or more, and has small feathery leaves and cylinders of lemon-yellow flowers in spring. Does well in coastal gardens and is hardy to frost.

A. glaucoptera CLAYBUSH WATTLE
In late winter and spring it bears canary-yellow flowers, but its pearl-grey foliage makes it attractive throughout the year. It grows to 2 m and stands drought and cold.

A. myrtifolia MYRTLE WATTLE
A useful shrub which is 2 m tall and has narrow oval leaves. The balls of sulphur flowers that appear in late winter are very showy. It stands frost and drought.

A. notabilis FLINDERS WATTLE
This is a good-looking plant worth trying in dry areas. It reaches a height of 2–3 m and bears globular flowers of bright yellow in late winter. It stands moderate frost.

A. polybotrya WESTERN SILVER WATTLE
A large shrub or small tree growing to 3 m or more, with drooping stems of soft, fern-like foliage and sprays of golden flowers in late winter.

A. pulchella PRICKLY MOSES
This species stands long dry periods and moderate frost. It grows to 2 m and has fern-like foliage and attractive golden balls of flowers in spring.

A. spectabilis MUDGEE WATTLE
Is a well-proportioned shrub with a height and spread of 3 m. It has fern-like, sage-green leaves and sprays of golden balls of flowers in late winter. Is hardy to sharp frost.

Acalypha wilkesiana
COPPER LEAF
DESCRIPTION. A pretty evergreen plant, native to the islands of the South Pacific, which deserves a place in the garden because of its decorative foliage. It grows quickly to a height of 2 m or more, and has handsome ovate leaves richly coloured with splashes of rose, pink and crimson against a background of olive-green or bronze. This is a delightful plant for gardens where winters are mild. Where winters are cold it can be grown in a pot in a protected place. It is a good patio or terrace plant and it makes a pleasing informal hedge. Other species worth growing are *A. godseffiana* and *A. hispida*. Many lovely colourful cultivars are available.
CULTURE. Plant in good soil and water well until established. Does well near the coast but will not tolerate drying winds inland, nor much frost. Grows in full sun or part shade.

Acer palmatum MAPLE
DESCRIPTION. Maples are amongst the most decorative of all shrubs, not because of their flowers, but because of their lovely foliage. This species has beautifully shaped leaves with five lobes, 6–12 cm long and almost as broad. Most maples are trees but there are some ornamental shrubby ones well worth a place in gardens large and small. Here only these small types are described under their different names.
CULTURE. These plants require much the same kind of growing conditions as azaleas (see page 63). They grow well in gardens where winters are cold but they cannot tolerate hot drying winds or alkaline soil. Plant them in acid soil, rich in humus, in partial shade, and water them abundantly during dry periods of the year. Regions with a cool misty summer and a cold winter suit them best.

The following cultivars of *Acer palmatum* are recommended:

'Atropurpureum' RED JAPANESE MAPLE
Grows to 2–3 m and is almost tree-like in form, with leaves which are beautifully coloured bronze or purple-red. The leaf colour is particularly rich in spring when the new leaves emerge.
'Aureum'
A charming plant which grows to 3 m and has lime-green to lemon-yellow foliage.
'Chishio'
Reaches a height of 1 m and has leaves that are flame in spring, green in summer and red in autumn.
'Crippsii'
A graceful shrub with finely-cut green foliage on plants 1–2 m tall.
'Dissectum'
This lovely cultivar grows to 2 m and has very deeply and delicately cut leaves. A well-grown specimen is a delightful sight.
'Dissectum Atropurpureum'
A highly ornamental plant with lacy foliage that is a rich purple colour in spring. It seldom grows to more than 1 m in height and spread, although under optimum conditions in cool gardens it may reach twice this size.
'Dissectum Ornatum Variegatum'
Has delicately cut foliage edged with pink and cream on plants 1 m or more tall. A plant to be cherished.
'Linearilobum'
Reaches a height of 2 m and has five long leaflets spread like fingers, with almost smooth margins. They are a delicate green in summer and brightly coloured in autumn. The form known as 'Linearilobum Rubrum' has purple foliage.
'Oshio-beni'
A colourful and interesting cultivar that grows to 2 m and has leaves of soft green which turn brilliant colours in autumn.
'Roseo-marginatum'
This pretty one reaches a height of 2 m and has new spring leaves of green edged with coral pink.
'Seigai'
Is known as the red-stemmed maple. It has young stems of a coral colour and pretty orange foliage in autumn.
'Suminagashi'
A striking small plant with new leaves of deep crimson and bright autumn colouring. It grows to 1–2 m.

Glossy Abelia (*Abelia grandiflora*) has flowers with the scent of honey

Brazilian Lantern Flower (*Abutilon megapotamicum*) can be trained against a wall, draped over a bank or grown in a hanging basket

The golden flowers of wattle (*Acacia cultriformis*) bring sparkle to the garden in late winter and early spring

Acokanthera oppositifolia

BUSHMAN POISON BUSH

DESCRIPTION. A slow-growing evergreen shrub to 3 m with neat oval pointed leaves with a slight gloss. In spring it bears clusters of highly-scented, funnel-shaped flowers of ivory tinged with pink. When picked for an arrangement, the flowers close up but their strong scent remains for many days. The flowers are followed by oval fruits that turn purple when ripe and look like small plums. The fruit and other parts of the bush are poisonous and children should therefore be taught to recognize the plant. It is advisable to remove the fruit as it forms.

CULTURE. This pretty shrub is native to South Africa where, it is said, the Bushmen used the fruit to prepare poison for the tips of their arrows. It does well in warm, coastal gardens. Is tender to frost.

Adenandra fragrans

ADENANDRA, CHINA FLOWER

DESCRIPTION. A charming evergreen South African flowering shrub, neat in habit of growth and well suited to small gardens and rock or pebble gardens. It grows to 60 cm in height and spread and has very small leaves that give off an aromatic scent when crushed. The tiny flowers, which look as though they have been fashioned from the most delicate porcelain, make a delightful show towards the end of

winter. They are carried in clusters, each dainty flower being about 2 cm across with five rounded petals of a delicate shade of ivory or blush pink. The petals are flushed with deeper pink on the reverse side and embellished with a rose line down the middle. The flowers last well in arrangements. *A. uniflora* and *A. villosa* are other pretty species worth growing. These are very similar to *A. fragrans* in appearance.

CULTURE. Adenandras grow best in soil that has a crumbly sandy texture and drains readily. They will endure long periods of dry weather in summer but should be watered in winter when they start to form their flowers. The plants are hardy to 5 degrees of frost.

Allemanda ALLEMANDA

DESCRIPTION. This genus includes quick-growing plants native to tropical America. Some of them are rounded in form and some are scandent in growth. The prettiest of the shrubby types are *A. neriifolia* and *A. schottii*. They grow to 2 m or more in height and spread. *A. cathartica* is a taller plant with spreading stems which can be trained against a wall or trellis. They all have good-looking foliage and tubular or bell-shaped flowers opening to a face made up of five rounded segments. They are buttercup to golden-yellow in colour and make a charming show in the garden between spring and autumn.

CULTURE. Plant in good soil and water well during dry periods of the year. They are tender to frost and do well only in subtropical and tropical gardens.

Aloe ALOE

DESCRIPTION. Although aloes are not shrubs, they are included in this book as, in very dry areas, they are planted with or instead of shrubs. Southern Africa is the home of about 140 species, many of which are handsome when well grown. The leaves are unusual and the plants are sometimes dramatic in form. The leaves are thick and fleshy and generally curved from the base. In the dry, almost desert-like areas where some of them grow naturally, the succulent leaves relieve the monotony of the dry landscape. The tubular flowers are carried in long slender cylindrical spikes or in rounded or conical heads. The predominating colours of the flowers are red, orange and yellow. Many of them flower in autumn and winter and make a fine show when there is little else flowering in the garden. The small species are fine plants for the rock or pebble garden and the tall ones are useful in providing a perpendicular line in gardens where a dry climate makes it difficult to establish trees.

CULTURE. Aloes like well-drained soil. Some of them must have very dry conditions to promote growth, whilst others need water during prolonged

Copper Leaf (*Acalypha wilkesiana*). A quick-growing shrub for warm, humid gardens

This little maple with plum-coloured leaves (*Acer palmatum* 'Dissectum Atropur-pureum') is a charming plant for a cool shady garden

China Flower (*Adenandra uniflora*) is an attractive shrublet for the small garden

periods of drought. Some stand severe frost whilst others do best where winters are mild. Most of those described here will grow equally well in slightly alkaline or acid soil.

A. arborescens TREE ALOE
A robust species which may grow to 2–3 m. The plant gives rise to numerous rosettes of leaves, each of which bears showy pyramidal cones of coral-red flowers in autumn and winter. Once established it stands fairly severe frost and drought.

A. aristata GUINEA-FOWL ALOE
A small neat plant for the rock or pebble garden or for pot-culture. Its rosettes of leaves measure only about 15 cm across and less in height. The little leaves are dark, dull green with light spots or blotches, reminiscent of the markings on a guinea-fowl, which accounts for its common name. The flower spike grows to 45 cm in height and bears dainty, coral flowers in late spring and early summer. It stands severe frost and drought.

A. brevifolia MINIATURE ALOE
A delightful species for the small garden or the rock or pebble garden. The neat rosettes of glaucous-green leaves only 7 cm long are attractive throughout the year and, in spring, it sends up spikes of tomato-red flowers. The plant stands fairly severe frost.

A. candelabrum CANDELABRA ALOE
This decorative aloe will grow in areas of moderate frost but does best in warm regions. The grey-green leaves arch up and are a fine foil to the candelabra-like heads of flowers, which are cadmium-yellow, orange or brick-red.

A. capitata MADAGASCAR ALOE
A charming small aloe which likes warm growing conditions. It has sharply-pointed, grey-green leaves that are of ornamental value throughout the year. In late winter and early spring it produces delightful heads of sulphur-yellow flowers.

A. ciliaris
Is a species with slender stems which sprawl unless given some support. They may grow to 3 m in length. The leaves are sparsely carried on the lower part of the stem but clustered together towards the ends of stems. The pretty tomato to coral-red flowers make a fine show in spring and during other seasons, too. It needs warmth and some shade for its best development. Not recommended for areas of severe frost.

A. comptonii
Has grey-green leaves which turn inwards at the top, forming a neat compact rosette. In spring and summer it has dainty candelabra of rounded heads of coral-red flowers on stems about 1 m tall.

A. cryptopoda SPIRE ALOE
This aloe has green or grey-green leaves which turn up sharply from the base. In summer and autumn its flower stem grows to 1–2 m and bears conical flowerheads of brick-red shaded to yellow. There is also a form with pure yellow flowers. It stands intense heat, dryness and fairly severe frost.

A. ferox BITTER ALOE
Grows to 2 m or more. When young this is an attractive plant but as it gets older and taller the basal part tends to look untidy because the old leaves persist on the plant after they have dried. Plant it behind shrubs that will hide the bottom part of the stem. It has handsome spikes of crimson flowers that make a splendid show in winter. Does best in regions where frosts are not severe.

A. krapohliana MINIATURE ALOE
This little aloe is not easy to grow as it needs almost desert-like conditions. Too little sunlight and too much water may cause it to die off. Its leaves, banded with green or brown, form a neat rosette. Dainty flowers of brick, coral or crimson appear in winter on stems 45 cm tall.

A. longistyla   KAROO ALOE

A small aloe that is ideal for a rock or pebble garden. The leaves covered with white spines turn up from the base forming a neat rosette. The rounded flowerheads carried on short stalks make a fine show in winter, when the coral to rose-red flowers open. It stands considerable frost and needs good drainage.

A. melanacantha   BLACKTHORN ALOE

Is a species for very dry areas. It has pointed cylinders of flowers which are red in the bud turning yellow as they age. The word *melanacantha* means 'black thorns' and refers to the thorns covering the leaves.

A. petricola

Makes a splendid show in winter, when it bears long spikes of handsome flowers shaded from ivory-yellow to brick-red. The leaves form a compact rosette and the inflorescence rises to 1 m from the ground. Stands moderate frost.

A. plicatilis   FAN ALOE

The leaves of this aloe differ from those of the others. They are strap-shaped and arranged like a fan, not in whorls or rosettes. The plant grows to 2–3 m and has a gaunt but attractive appearance as it ages. In late winter clusters of bright tomato-red flowers appear above each fan of leaves. It prefers acid to alkaline soil and does best when watered well in autumn and winter.

A. reitzii

A summer-flowering species that stands heat and frost. The flower stem grows to 1 m or more in height and has a branched top bearing slender cylinders of flowers of yellow to apricot and brick-red.

A. striata   CORAL ALOE

An attractive species for large or small gardens. It has a whorl of grey or blue-green leaves with smooth margins. In late winter and early spring the flower stem rises to 1 m and bears heads of coral-red flowers. It stands fairly severe frost.

A. thraskii   COAST ALOE

A tall-growing species which reaches a height of 2 m. The bright green leaves arch and curve down. The flower stem forms a candelabra bearing ornamental yellow to orange flowers in winter. A fine species for the coastal garden. It is tender to sharp frost.

Aloysia triphylla   *(Lippia citriodora)*

LEMON VERBENA

DESCRIPTION. Is a leggy plant to 1–2 m. This deciduous or partly evergreen shrub is not decorative. Neither the leaves nor the flowers are attractive, but it is nevertheless worth a place somewhere in the large garden because of the delightful lemon scent of its leaves. They are useful for potpourri and for flavouring food and iced drinks.

CULTURE. It stands considerable frost and does well in poor soil. Once established it will also grow well in dry regions.

Amelanchier canadensis

SHAD BUSH

DESCRIPTION. Under optimum conditions this deciduous plant will grow to the size and form of a tree. Generally, however, it reaches no more than shrub size – 2 m. It is a fine sight in early spring when it becomes covered with arching stems of small white flowers before the new leaves appear. The new spring foliage of bronze is even more attractive than the flowers. In autumn the leaves become brightly coloured. It carries maroon berries at this season too.

CULTURE. Shad Bush is a cool-climate plant. It needs cold, frosty winters and moisture for its best development. Plant in partial shade, in acid soil rich in leaf mould.

Aphelandra squarrosa

APHELANDRA

DESCRIPTION. A robust shrub from Brazil which can be kept trimmed to 1 m in height and spread. Its large and unusual leaves are clearly veined with white. The waxy, yellow flowers are carried in colourful spikes towards the ends of stems. *A. tetragona* is a smaller species with decorative leaves and scarlet flowers.

CULTURE. They need a mild climate and in hot inland gardens they should be planted in filtered shade rather than in full sun. Water plants well during dry periods of the year, and cut them back hard after their flowering is over to keep them neat and compact.

Ardisia crispa   *(A. crenata)*

CORAL ARDISIA

DESCRIPTION. This is a good-looking plant for the patio or terrace, or for growing indoors, as well as being suitable for the garden. It is an evergreen growing to 1 m with good, glossy deep-green leaves tapering to both ends, 3–6 cm in length, with scalloped margins. In spring to summer it bears clusters of insignificant flowers. These are followed by showy clusters of bright scarlet berries that continue into winter. *A. japonica* is another pretty species suitable for the small garden or for a rock or pebble garden.

CULTURE. Ardisia will stand mild frost but does best in gardens where winters are warm. Near the coast it will thrive in the open but in hot, inland gardens it should be planted where it is shaded from the sun and sheltered from drying winds. Plant in acid soil rich in humus.

Artemisia   ARTEMISIA

DESCRIPTION. Artemisias are grown not because of the flowers they bear but because of their ornamental silver or pearl-grey leaves. These evergreen shrubs, which grow to 1 m or a little more in height and spread, are valuable plants in the garden. Their light-coloured foliage acts as a foil to shades of green and the more vivid colours of flowers near by. Some species have rather fine, lacy foliage which gives the garden a cool, misty appearance in hot weather. They add attraction to the flower border, they look effective at the front of a group of shrubs with dark leaves, as a foreground to roses, and in the rock garden.

Some decorative species are *A. arborescens*, *A. absinthium*, *A. ludoviciana*, *A. maritima*, *A. palmeri*, *A. stelleriana* and *A. umbelliformis*. 'Silver Queen' is a splendid cultivar.

CULTURE. Artemisias do best in full sun and in well-drained soil. Most of them will grow in part shade but they tend to become straggly in deep shade. They stand frost and hot conditions and are also useful plants for seaside gardens.

Arundo donax GIANT REED

DESCRIPTION. A reed-like plant which is effective in a tub on a patio, or in the ground near a pool or stream. It sends up strong, woody stems to 3 m. The leaves are blade-like, about 60 cm in length and 8 cm wide. The flowers are insignificant, the plant being grown for foliage effect. *Arundo donax* 'Variegata', which has leaves striped with white or yellow, is an elegant cultivar providing interesting stems for arrangements.
CULTURE. Set the plant in rich, moist soil or water abundantly if planted in a dry place. In warm gardens it is apt to spread rapidly. In cold gardens it may be damaged by frost unless the roots are covered by a mulch. The stems should be cut down to ground level in early spring to encourage the development of new spring growth and to keep the plant tidy. In the small garden, or rock or pebble garden, it is advisable to restrict the spread of the roots by planting it in a container sunk into the ground.

Aster filifolius

(Diplopappus filifolius)
SOUTH AFRICAN ROCK DAISY, WILD ASTER
DESCRIPTION. Is a fine plant for the rock garden or for growing on dry walls or banks. The shrub grows to 45 cm in height and spreads across twice this, hugging the soil. It has minute leaves, and in late winter and early spring it becomes wreathed in masses of pretty mauve daisies with bright-yellow centres.
CULTURE. Like many other South African plants this is a splendid one for gardens where growing conditions are not good. It does well in coastal gardens and stands long periods with little water and hot dry winds. It will tolerate fairly severe cold too.

Atriplex SALTBUSH

DESCRIPTION. This genus of plants includes shrubs and ground covers that stand harsh conditions. They are not showy plants but, where the soil is poor, they relieve the bare landscape and help to stop soil erosion. Some species will also serve to halt the drift of sand in coastal areas.
CULTURE. The species described include plants that are tolerant of alkaline soil, moderate to severe frost, seaside and almost desert conditions. They generally do best in sandy or gravelly soil.

A. canescens FOUR-WING SALTBUSH
A species from the western United States which is hardy to severe frost. It grows to 2 m and has slender greyish-white leaves 2–5 cm long, and insignificant flowers.

A. halimus
This species from the Mediterranean seaboard is a spreading plant which reaches a height of 1–2 m. It has silvery-grey stems and leaves, and makes a good cover in seaside gardens. The stems of grey leaves are charming in arrangements.

A. hymenelytra
Grows naturally in dry parts of the United States from Southern California to Arizona. It grows to 30–60 cm high and has grey-green leaves with deeply toothed margins.

A. lentiformis QUAIL BUSH
Occurs in semi-desert regions of the southern United States where the soil is alkaline. It makes a mound of growth 2 m high and as much across. The grey-green leaves are 2–5 cm long. This is a useful screen or hedge plant in regions with alkaline soil.

A. nummularia OLD MAN SALTBUSH
An Australian species growing to a height of 2 m. It is a good screen or hedge plant in dry areas and in seaside gardens. It stands 10 degrees of frost.

Aucuba japonica

JAPANESE LAUREL
DESCRIPTION. An ornamental evergreen shrub growing to 2 m or more, and almost as wide. It has handsome, glossy dark green leaves, oval in form, 7 to 20 cm in length, and toothed at the apex. The small maroon flowers are not showy and the plant is grown for the beauty of its foliage and for the clusters of scarlet berries that appear in winter. In order to ensure fruiting, male and female plants must be planted together. Several hybrids with variegated leaves or leaves of different shapes have been originated. Two cultivars suitable for the garden or for pot culture are 'Crotonifolia', which has leaves marked with gold – (male plant) and 'Gold Dust', which has foliage speckled with gold – (female plant). The names of others will be found in nursery catalogues.
CULTURE. Plant in rich soil in a shady place, protected from sun, and desiccating winds. It can stand sharp cold but not dry conditions. Japanese laurel is a decorative plant for a shady corner of the garden or for a shady patio or terrace. It looks handsome when grown in a container indoors, too. Will grow in slightly alkaline or acid soil.

Azalea AZALEA

DESCRIPTION. Azaleas are now known botanically as rhododendrons but since gardeners are likely to continue to call them by the more familiar name of azalea, they are described under this heading here. A large number of different species of azalea were introduced into Europe from the East, and numerous very lovely cultivars have been developed from these. For the sake of simplicity it is convenient to divide azaleas into two main groups: Evergreen types, which include the Indicas, Kaempferi, Kurumes and Macrantha; and the deciduous ones, which include Knap Hill-Exbury, Mollis and Occidentale hybrids. All azaleas are beautiful in the garden, in containers on a shady terrace or patio, and in arrangements. They flower from late winter to mid-spring.

Evergreen Azaleas

Azalea indica. Most of the evergreen azaleas popular in gardens in different countries of the world belong to this group. They include many single and double-flowered cultivars. The plants vary considerably in size, from shrubs 1 m tall and wide, to those which are 2 m or more in height and spread. The leaves are usually soft and pointed, and the flowers are funnel-shaped. Where soil and climatic conditions suit them these are amongst the loveliest of all flowering shrubs, producing an abundance of flowers for a long period. There are now hundreds of named cultivars. The colours include white, pastel shades and brilliant tones of colour. This class of azalea will stand

Giant Reed (*Arundo donax* 'Variegata'). An ornamental pool-side plant

10 degrees of frost but the flowers are apt to be spoiled where frosts are more severe.

Kaempferi hybrids. These beautiful azaleas are hardy in freezing conditions. Where the cold is severe they may lose most of their leaves. The funnel-shaped flowers are shades of salmon to red, mauve and pink, and the plants are often large. They tend to flower later than other species.

Kurume azaleas. These Japanese azaleas are hardier than the Indicas. They are also smaller in growth with smaller flowers, but what they lack in size they make up for in the great profusion of flowers they carry. Very often the leaves are completely hidden by the abundance of flowers. Some of the flowers bear one flower inside the other. These are referred to as 'hose in hose' varieties. The small-growing varieties are excellent for small gardens and rockeries. They are also fine plants for growing in containers in the house or on a shady terrace or patio. There are many named cultivars available in all countries of the world. The colours include shades of pink, mauve, cyclamen, vermilion and crimson.

Madagascar Aloe (*Aloe capitata*) is a dainty species for the small garden

Plant *Aloe ferox* (Bitter Aloe) for a striking display in winter

Plant the South African Rock Daisy or Wild Aster *(Aster filifolius)* on a dry bank

Azalea indica makes a fine show in spring

Azalea indica 'Elizabeth' has exceptionally pretty flowers

Macrantha azaleas. These are pretty plants for small gardens and rockeries. They are generally compact and low-growing. The flowers may be small or large. These are also sometimes referred to as Gumpo azaleas.

Deciduous Azaleas

These are most rewarding plants with flowers of glowing shades of yellow, apricot, orange, flame, red, pink and white. The three main groups are Knap Hill-Exbury, Mollis and Occidentale hybrids.

Knap Hill-Exbury hybrids. Include spreading and upright plants to 2 m in height. The flowers are large and carried in clusters. They may have a scent and some have ruffled margins to the petals. These are also referred to as 'Rothschild' azaleas because many of the hybrids were created on the Rothschild estate in England. There are many named cultivars of these. The colours include charming shades of yellow, salmon, orange and red.

Mollis hybrids. Are upright in growth to 2 m with large flowers in clusters of seven or more. These azaleas are spectacular plants when in flower. The colours vary from yellow through orange to tangerine-red. The brightest of them is known as 'Koster's Brilliant'. Some of them have leaves that turn pleasing shades in autumn.

Occidentale hybrids. These often have scented flowers of the same size as the Mollis hybrids, but the plants are generally taller — often to 2,5 m in height, and tend to open later in spring than the Mollis azaleas. The colours are white and shades of pink and rose. The foliage of many of them assumes pretty tints in autumn.

CULTURE. Azaleas are not adaptable as to soil and situation as is the case with many other shrubs. They will not grow unless they have the kind of soil they like. They require a loose acid soil with a pH rating of 4,5 to 5,5 (see page 12). There must be no lime in the soil and it should not dry out quickly.

If acid compost is not available work peat into the soil in which they are to be planted. In areas where the soil is alkaline, plant them in containers above the ground or sunk into the ground, filling the containers with acid soil and compost, or with this mixed with peat.

Should the leaves of azaleas show signs of yellowing (chlorosis) it is an indication that soil conditions are not acid enough, and the plants may succumb quickly if action is not taken to change the nature of the soil. This can be done by sprinkling a tablespoonful of aluminium sulphate, sulphate of iron, or sulphur over the soil and watering it in, and by applying iron chelates to the plants or the soil, according to the directions given on the package. These commodities can

Azaleas are decorative plants for gardens large and small

The yellow azalea is a pleasing foreground to Purple Prunus

63

be obtained from shops dealing in garden supplies.

Plant azaleas in dappled shade. They will grow in the open in gardens near the coast, but inland the intensity of the sunlight is too much for them. They make a charming picture if planted under tall trees that shade them but, at the same time, allow light to filter through onto them.

The roots of azaleas are fibrous and remain near the surface of the soil. To prevent them from drying out, put a mulch of compost or of old oak leaves or decomposed pine needles over them. If these are not available, use a mulch of straw or peat. They should never be given ordinary fertilizer. Fertilizers specially prepared for plants that require acid soil may be applied from time to time. Most beautiful azaleas are grown without any artificial fertilizer or manure. Water the plants liberally and regularly, particularly in areas where hot dry winds prevail.

Most azaleas are resistant to sharp frost and do better in a cool climate than a subtropical region. The deciduous azaleas and the Kaempferi and Kurume azaleas are particularly hardy. The Indicas may suffer some frost damage in a very cold garden. These also generally tolerate more warmth and will do better therefore in gardens where winters are mild than the others will.

Azaleas seldom suffer from insect pests. In some areas leaf-eating grubs, thrips, leaf miner or red spider may cause damage in spring. If such insects appear to be damaging the plants, apply a systemic insecticide according to directions given on the package.

Azara microphylla

BOXLEAF AZARA
DESCRIPTION. An evergreen shrub introduced from Chile, suitable for large gardens and parks. The plant grows to 4–5 m in height and has arching spreading stems. The leaves are very small and neat, shiny and dark-green. In late winter it bears clusters of small yellow flowers that give off a faint vanilla-like scent. A cultivar with variegated leaves, known as *A. microphylla* 'Variegata', seldom grows taller

than 1 m and is therefore more suited to the small garden or the large rock garden.

CULTURE. Azara is slow-growing for the first year or two but, once established, it grows fairly fast. Trim it occasionally to keep it from becoming leggy and cut out some of the old stems at the base every other year allowing the newer ones to develop. It stands severe frost but little dryness, and does best in acid soil and partial shade.

Baeckea   HEATH MYRTLE

DESCRIPTION. Evergreen Australian shrubs, of which there are more than sixty species. They grow to 1–2 m in height and spread and have small leaves carried on twiggy stems. The flowers are white, pink or mauve. They are effective in the garden and provide flowers for arrangements in spring and summer.

CULTURE. They do best in loose soil that drains readily and is free of lime. Once established, they will tolerate dryness in summer but should be watered in winter to encourage flowering. In hot inland gardens grow them in part shade. They stand moderate frost.

B. behrii   BROOM HEATH MYRTLE
Grows to 2 m and has slender stems of small white flowers, rather like those of the tea tree. The flowering time is spring to summer.

B. camphorata
CAMPHOR HEATH MYRTLE
A pretty, small shrub from Western Australia which grows to about 60 cm and becomes covered with small pink flowers in summer.

B. virgata   TWIGGY HEATH MYRTLE
Reaches a height of 2 m and carries a profusion of small, starry, white flowers in late spring and early summer. They last well in arrangements.

Bambusa   BAMBOO

DESCRIPTION. Bamboos are really giant grasses with woody stems bearing long leaves. These are generally green but there are some charming ones with variegated leaves. They are graceful plants worth a place in gardens large and small. Grow them in groups, or singly, at the edge of a stream,

amongst other shrubs or in front of trees; or plant them in a container (which restricts the spread of their roots) and use them on the patio or terrace and in the rock or pebble garden.

Centuries ago a Chinese philosopher, discussing the design of a garden for contemplation, made the following suggestion. Those with only a square metre should plant a tree paeony, but if there were 1,5 square metres a bamboo should be planted too. He was allowing little space for the spread of the bamboo but he recognized its worth to his fellow-men. He pointed out that they could eat the young bamboo shoots; build a house and make a conduit for water from the stems; make armaments to defend themselves, and household utensils and furniture from it. He concluded by pointing out that they could also hide from scolding wives and concubines in a bamboo grove! Chinese paintings and porcelain feature the bamboo that plays such an important part in their lives.

CULTURE. Once established, bamboos grow with cheerful abandon. They develop from underground stems called rhizomes that increase in size each year. Some of them tend to send out runners all over the garden and care should be taken to dig these up before they become too deeply rooted. In small gardens it is advisable to plant them in containers sunk into the ground. Tall-growing types should be trimmed off to keep them from becoming too tall. Many of them tolerate cold winters. They like soil rich in humus and an abundance of moisture. Under dry conditions they will not develop rapidly.

B. beecheyana   BEECHEY BAMBOO
Will grow to 9 m unless trimmed. It forms clumps, with individual stems which grow to almost 7 cm in diameter. A plant for the large garden or park.

B. multiplex   HEDGE BAMBOO
This species makes a dense mass of growth to about 5 m. The stems are 2–3 cm in diameter. It is a good plant for a screen.

B. multiplex 'Fernleaf' (*B. nana*)
FERNLEAF BAMBOO

A species for the small garden and for growing in a large container. It reaches 2–3 m in height and has stems only 1 cm across, and dainty fern-like leaves.

Other plants known generally as bamboos are referred to botanically under different names. See under *Phyllostachys* and *Sasa*.

Banksia

AUSTRALIAN HONEYSUCKLE, BANKSIA

DESCRIPTION. This genus includes about fifty species of evergreen shrubs and small trees, most of which are native to Western Australia. Many of them are ornamental plants well worth a place in the garden. The leaves vary quite considerably in the species described. The flowers appear from late winter to summer, generally in showy cylinders or spikes of different colours. The individual flowers are small but closely crowded in dense heads. As the flowers mature, the colourful and gleaming styles emerge making an impressive sight.

CULTURE. Banksias belong to the same family as the proteas and require the same kind of growing conditions. Most species like a well-drained, acid soil. Heavy clay which holds the water does not suit them. They do best in regions where the summer and autumn are rather dry but should be watered well in winter. Transplant them when small, as plants that are large often fail to take. Occasional light pruning may be necessary. Cutting off flowers with a good length of stem will help to keep the plants trim. Most species are hardy to sharp frost. Nearly all of them attract birds that feed on the nectar carried in the decorative flowers.

B. ashbyi
Grows naturally on sandy plains of Western Australia. This is a large shrub reaching 2–3 m in height and spread. The long narrow leaves are deeply cut into triangular segments. In late winter it carries tapering cylinders of showy cadmium to orange-yellow flowers. Is tender to frost.

B. brownii
Is a robust species which grows to 3 m in height and has pleasing foliage. In winter it carries scarlet and gold flowers arranged in a bottlebrush head. Likes mild growing conditions.

B. coccinea   SCARLET BANKSIA
Grows to 2–3 m and has broadly oval, leathery leaves with small spines, and squat cylinders of bright scarlet flowers. This species needs water in winter for its best development. It tolerates long periods with little water from summer to late autumn. The flowering time is spring to summer.

B. ericifolia   HEATH BANKSIA
This one, as its name implies, has leaves like a heath or erica. It is one of the easiest to grow, is hardy to sharp frost and probably the most popular species. The plant reaches a height of 3 m or more and has handsome cylinders of flowers up to 30 cm in length. They are amber to tan in colour and appear during winter, and on and off during other seasons, too. They last well in arrangements.

B. lemanniana
This banksia has a height and spread of 2–3 m. It stands mild frost and is impressive in spring and early summer when it bears its yellow flowers.

B. occidentalis
Is an attractive species growing to 3 m or more, with slender leaves. Spectacular cylindrical spikes of crimson flowers appear in summer and highlight the plant for a long time. This species likes moist growing conditions.

B. prionotes   ORANGE BANKSIA
This is a handsome and robust species which grows to 3–6 m or more. Its leaves are slender and up to 30 cm long with saw edges. The fine cones of orange-yellow flowers appear in winter. It does well in heavy soils, and can be used as a tree.

B. repens   CREEPING BANKSIA
This species is a fine one for a steep, well-drained bank. It grows to only about 45 cm in height, and spreads its long leaves across the ground. Yellow to amber flowers ornament the plant in spring. It stands fairly sharp frost.

B. speciosa
Is 2 m or more in height and spread, and has slender sage-green leaves up to 30 cm long and only 1 cm wide, with triangular teeth. The cone-shaped flowerheads are suffused with silver-grey in the bud and turn yellow on opening. It is a fine sight in spring and early summer when it flowers.

B. spinulosa   (*B. collina*)
A species from the eastern side of Australia. It is a robust plant growing to 3 m in height and spread, with cones or cylinders of yellow to tan flowers in late winter and spring. It stands fairly severe frost and grows in semi-shade or full sun. The flowers with their abundance of nectar attract birds.

Barleria obtusa   BARLERIA
DESCRIPTION. A quick-growing evergreen South African shrub with soft sage-green foliage carried on pliable stems. It reaches a height of 2 m but looks best and flowers well if cut back occasionally. This is a useful shrub for the small garden. In autumn it becomes covered with dainty mauve flowers measuring 2–3 cm across. It looks most attractive when planted next to a shrub that bears yellow flowers at the same time of the year.

CULTURE. Grows readily in sand, gravel or clay. Once established will stand moderate frost, but it is not suited to gardens that are cold for long periods. It does well in subtropical regions and in coastal gardens. In hot dry gardens, plant it in partial shade.

Bauera sessiliflora
SHOWY BAUERA

DESCRIPTION. An evergreen Australian plant of heath-like appearance, seldom growing taller than 2 m. It has small leaves, divided into three small leaflets, arranged in clusters up the slender stems. In late winter and spring it bears clouds of starry pink to cyclamen flowers closely attached to the branches. In full flower it is a delightful sight.

CULTURE. This plant will stand considerable cold, but not dryness. Near the coast it can be grown in the open but in hot inland gardens it should be planted in partial shade. It needs an

Orange Banksia *(Banksia prionotes)* is a handsome plant for the large garden

This shrubby Bauhinia *(Bauhinia galpinii)* grows well in warm gardens

Shrimp Plant *(Beloperone guttata)* looks effective in a container and in the garden

Banksia spinulosa bears pretty cylinders of flowers

In autumn Barleria brightens the garden with its dainty flowers of palest mauve

abundance of moisture and acid soil. Prepare holes with peat and compost. Transplant it when very small.

Bauhinia galpinii
ORCHID BUSH, PRIDE OF DE KAAP
DESCRIPTION. A shrubby South African bauhinia of exuberant growth. It is an evergreen which will grow to 3 m in height and spread, if it is not trimmed back from time to time. The plant has soft stems that bear unusual leaves divided in the middle into two rounded sections. It has handsome brick-red flowers from mid-summer to late autumn. This bauhinia makes a good informal hedge or screen.
CULTURE. Grows well in warm, dry areas and also in areas where the rainfall is high, but will not tolerate much frost. Is recommended for large gardens where winters are not severe.

Beaufortia BRUSH MYRTLE
DESCRIPTION. Evergreen shrubs from Western Australia, closely related to melaleuca and callistemon. They have numerous long stamens that project, giving the flowerhead the appearance of a bottlebrush or fluffy round head.
CULTURE. They do best in loose soil that drains readily, but this does not mean that they thrive only in arid places. They should be watered in winter and spring. These plants require acid soil. Once established, they tolerate fairly sharp frost. Transplant when very small as large plants resent being moved.

B. purpurea
A neat shrub for the small garden or patio. It grows to 1 m and produces a mass of dainty maroon flowers in rounded heads. Flowers in spring and summer.

B. sparsa SWAMP BRUSH MYRTLE
This plant, which grows to 2 m, has tiny dark green leaves and showy terminal flowers with long bright orange to red stamens. The flowerhead resembles a bottlebrush in form. It needs an abundance of water but free drainage. Grow it in full sun or partial shade and behind other shrubs, as it tends to become leggy at the base. The flowering time is summer.

Beloperone guttata
LOBSTER OR SHRIMP PLANT
DESCRIPTION. This plant is effective in the garden and when grown in containers on a patio. It is an evergreen Mexican shrub with soft arching stems growing to 1 m in height and a little more across. It has ovate leaves and flowers carried in drooping spikes. The flowers, which are white marked with purple, are very small and not particularly showy. The attraction of the plant lies in the large copper-coloured bracts which enclose the flowers for many months of

The plum-coloured Barberry *(Berberis thunbergii* 'Atropurpurea') is decorative standing alone or when planted with other shrubs.

the year, particularly in winter and spring. The formation of the spikes resembles a shrimp which accounts for the common name. A cultivar named 'Chartreuse' has lime-yellow bracts.
CULTURE. Grow in shade or partial shade, and protect from drying winds. Once established, it stands moderate frost. In regions with severe frost plant it in a container which can be stored in a sheltered place over winter. Trim plants back lightly after the flowers fade, to keep them neat and compact.

Berberis BARBERRY

DESCRIPTION. Evergreen and deciduous shrubs native to Asia, India, Japan and America. Some species are grown for the beauty of the foliage, some for their showy berries, and some because they have both. Those with purple foliage should be grown in full sun as the leaves become pale in shade. The flowers are generally yellow and appear in spring. Most species have sharp spines on their stems. These are useful plants for large and small gardens. They do not mind being cut back and grow very readily. Some species trim well to make a neat hedge and some look best when grown as an informal hedge. They can be used effectively, too, as single trimmed or untrimmed shrubs. Grow them on large banks or along roadsides for quick cover.
CULTURE. All species enjoy considerable cold and, once established, they will also endure fairly long periods with little water. They grow in alkaline or acid soil. Not recommended for subtropical gardens.

B. aggregata
Reaches a height of 2 m with a spread of as much, and has oval leaves 2–3 cm long that change to yellow and orange in autumn. Bears pink or rose berries in winter. Some fine cultivars have been developed from this species.

B. buxifolia MAGELLAN BARBERRY
An evergreen of upright growth to 2 m. Has small leaves, orange-yellow flowers and dark purple berries. The cultivars 'Nana' and 'Pygmaea' are much smaller in growth and more suited to small gardens or to cover a large bank. They are good plants for a low hedge.

B. darwinii DARWIN BARBERRY
A Chilean species of spreading growth to 2 m or more, with leathery, shiny, prickly leaves and a mass of bright-yellow flowers which show up beautifully against the dark foliage in spring. This highly ornamental species was discovered in 1835 by Charles Darwin on his voyage in the *Beagle*.

B. gagnepainii
Reaches 1–2 m in height and spread but can be trimmed to smaller size. Has spear-shaped dark-green leaves and yellow flowers. This evergreen does well in alkaline soil.

B. julianae WINTER BARBERRY
A good evergreen for cold gardens. Grows to 2 m and has leathery, dark-green leaves that are copper coloured when young. It has strong spines and makes a good barrier hedge.

B. stenophylla ROSEMARY BARBERRY
An evergreen growing to 3 m if not trimmed, with arching stems of slender leaves. It bears a mass of yellow flowers in spring. Trimmed, it makes a decorative hedge. Cultivars developed from this are smaller and more compact in growth, and therefore better suited to gardens of average size. 'Corallina' and 'Gracilis' are two recommended.

B. thunbergii
A deciduous species that was once very popular as a hedge plant. It has leaves which turn autumn colours. Improved forms of this are the following: 'Atropurpurea' with purple leaves and 'Rose Glow', with leaves that are pink at first later changing to purple. 'Crimson Pygmy' is a small form, and 'Atropurpurea Nana' is another pretty, small cultivar with wine-coloured foliage. 'Aurea' is a charming small cultivar with foliage of lime-green, and 'Silver Beauty' has light green leaves splashed with silvery white and pink. They provide interesting material for arrangements. Cultivars with coloured foliage are most ornamental as specimen shrubs near plants with grey or light green foliage and when grown as a hedge.

B. wilsoniae WILSON BARBERRY
Deciduous in cold climates and evergreen where winters are mild. Grows to 2 m and makes a good hedge. The small green leaves take on brilliant colours in autumn. It has bright-yellow flowers in summer followed by salmon to red berries. It produces more berries when grown in rather poor soil, or when closely crowded as in a hedge.

Bocconia frutescens
TREE CELANDINE
DESCRIPTION. This is a fine-looking shrub from the West Indies and Mexico which does well in subtropical gardens. It is an evergreen growing to about 2 m with large and handsome, deeply-lobed leaves 15–30 cm long and 10–20 cm wide. They are a delightful shade of silver-green and ornamental for most of the year. It bears large panicles of creamy-white flowers. Plant it at the back of a flower border or in a group of shrubs. It is effective, too, when standing alone or planted in a container on a patio or terrace.
CULTURE. Near the coast it will grow in full sun. In dry gardens inland it does better if planted in filtered shade. It is tender to frost.

Boronia BORONIA
DESCRIPTION. An Australian genus of which there are more than eighty species. Some are worth growing for their scent and others for their attractiveness in form and flower. They are evergreens with small leaves that give off an aromatic scent when crushed. The flowers have four petals and are bell or star-shaped. Boronia flowers may be different shades of pink, bronze, purple, chartreuse, brown or crimson. Some species have flowers that are charming in arrangements as well as decorative in the garden. The main flowering time is winter and spring.
CULTURE. Boronias prefer acid to alkaline soil and do best in sandy soil which drains readily. Where drainage is poor they may die in a few years. Most of them stand quite considerable frost, but a few enjoy subtropical conditions. Transplant when very small. They grow in full sunshine and in partial shade. In hot inland areas mulch the ground around the plants and

water them regularly during dry periods of the year. They should be cut back lightly after flowering to keep them neat and compact.

B. caerulescens BLUE BORONIA
A pretty little shrub for the small garden. It has a height and spread of about 60 cm. Flowers of pink to lavender-blue highlight the plant in late winter and early spring.

B. denticulata MAUVE BORONIA
A good-looking species growing to 2 m. It has bright-green leaves and starry flowers of cyclamen to mauve in late winter and early spring.

B. filifolia
A dainty species for the small garden. It grows to about 60 cm in height, and has foliage which varies in colour from olive-green to russet-red. Although the starry pink flowers appear mostly in spring it bears some flowers almost throughout the year.

B. heterophylla RED BORONIA
Is the most striking of the boronias. It grows to 2 m and is slender in habit. In spring it bears a profusion of cyclamen bell-shaped flowers with a sweet scent. Water it regularly and trim it lightly once or twice after flowering is over.

B. megastigma BROWN BORONIA
This is not a particularly showy plant, but it is well worth growing for its rich fragrance. The bell-shaped flowers, which are brownish-purple on the outside and creamy-yellow inside, last well in arrangements. The flowering time is late winter and early spring but it bears some flowers during other seasons, too. The cultivar 'Lutea' (Yellow Boronia) has chartreuse flowers. Water it well during dry periods of the year.

B. pinnata PINNATE BORONIA
Grows to 1 m or a little more in height and spread and has sweetly-scented pink flowers in spring. The fern-like foliage is scented too. Water this species regularly throughout the year.

B. serrulata SYDNEY ROCK ROSE
An attractive little shrub growing to 1 m. In spring and early summer it bears compact clusters of fragrant, rose-pink flowers. It does well in warm areas provided it is watered regularly. Plant it in partial shade inland.

Bouvardia longiflora BOUVARDIA
DESCRIPTION. A fine evergreen shrub growing to 1 m or more. It becomes rather straggly in growth if it is not cut back hard after flowering. It is also advisable to nip off the tops of the new shoots in spring to encourage bushiness at the base of the plant. The tubular or funnel-shaped flowers are carried in clusters. They are attractive in the garden and in arrangements. The cultivar 'Albatross' has large white, sweetly-scented flowers from late spring to autumn. Other cultivars are available with flowers varying in colour from palest pink to crimson.
CULTURE. Once established, it will stand mild frost, but it does best in subtropical gardens where winters are warm and the rainfall is high. If they are to be grown where winters are cool plant them where they have protection against cold. In areas with dry winds, plant in semi-shade in a sheltered corner.

Brunfelsia calycina
YESTERDAY-TODAY-AND-TOMORROW
DESCRIPTION. An evergreen or deciduous shrub growing to 2 m with oval leaves, dark green on the upper surface and paler below. The funnel-shaped, sweetly-scented flowers open to a rounded, five-lobed face about 5 cm across. They are dark purple and carried in clusters in spring. The hybrids described are more attractive and better known plants.
CULTURE. Brunfelsia is native to Brazil and likes warm, humid growing conditions. It will stand moderate frost when two or three years old, but it is not recommended for gardens where winters are cold. Plant in soil rich in humus and water well, particularly during dry periods of the year. Can be grown in a container and stored under cover during winter. Does well in coastal gardens.

B. calycina eximia
YESTERDAY-TODAY-AND-TOMORROW
Grows to 1–2 m and bears delightful, fragrant flowers which open purple, then fade to lavender and finally become white. The common name originated from the fact that the colour of the flowers changes from day to day.

The flowers are pretty at all stages. The main flowering time is mid-spring but it bears some flowers at other seasons too.

B. calycina floribunda
YESTERDAY-TODAY-AND-TOMORROW
In warm gardens this plant may reach a height of 3 m but it can be kept to smaller size by regular cutting back after the flowering period, which is mainly spring and summer. It grows well in the open near the coast but does best in partial shade inland. The flowers are larger than those of *B. calycina eximia*.

Buddleia BUTTERFLY BUSH
DESCRIPTION. Deciduous and evergreen shrubs and small trees, many of which come from China and India. They are graceful, quick-growing plants with leaves that vary according to species. They carry spikes, balls or cones of tubular or funnel-shaped flowers in pretty shades of mauve, purple, pink and white. The flowering time is late spring and summer.
CULTURE. These are hardy plants in every sense of the word. They stand cold and frost, and once established they will endure long periods with little water. They grow quickly if planted in good soil but they also perform well in poor soil. They are not recommended for subtropical regions. They look neater if the flowering stems are cut off after the flowers have faded. This will also help to keep them from growing too large.

B. alternifolia BUTTERFLY BUSH
A deciduous or evergreen shrub to 3 m or more with arching stems sparsely covered with oval leaves. In spring it bears clusters of lilac flowers with a sweet fragrance. It does well in poor, dry and alkaline soil. Prune after flowering by cutting out some of the older stems at ground-level. It can be trained to form a small tree by cutting out the basal growth to allow one main stem to develop.

B. colvilei
This is a vigorous plant that may grow to tree size. It reaches a height of 6 m and is therefore suitable only for large gardens or parks. The flowers, which

Butterfly Bush or Summer Lilac *(Buddleia davidii cultivar)* produces its lovely flowers in late spring and early summer

appear in summer, are a rosy-crimson colour. 'Kewensis' is an attractive cultivar.

B. davidii   *(B. variabilis)*
BUTTERFLY BUSH, SUMMER LILAC
A lovely deciduous shrub to 4 m. The leaves have serrated edges and are felted grey on the underside. Long clusters or spikes of scented, lilac to purple flowers appear in summer. The flowering stems, very like those of the lilac, are decorative in the garden and in arrangements. The following are the names of a few of the cultivars developed from this species: 'Charming' (lavender-pink); 'Dubonnet' (rich purple); 'Empire Blue' (mauve-blue); 'Fascination' (pink); 'Fortune' (lilac, with particularly long flowering spikes); 'Royal Red' and 'White Bouquet'.

B. globosa   BUDDLEIA
A semi-evergreen shrub which does well under difficult conditions. It grows to 3 m in height and spread and has pendant balls of honey-scented, orange-yellow flowers in spring and summer.

The pale, silver grey-green leaves of Bocconia lend elegance to the garden

Bottlebrush *(Callistemon linearis)* has attractive cylinders of flowers

Bird of Paradise Flower (*Caesalpinia gilliesii*) grows quickly in gardens where winters are not cold

Calliandra is a graceful plant which bears its powder-puff flowers in mid-spring

Calothamnus: An Australian shrub which does well in gravelly soils and stands dry conditions

Burchellia bubalina

WILD POMEGRANATE

DESCRIPTION. A shapely evergreen shrub or small tree which grows slowly to 2–3 m. It is worth growing for its attractive lustrous, dark green leaves that remain of value throughout the year. In late winter and early spring it bears rounded heads of pretty tubular flowers of bright coral-red. It is a fine shrub for subtropical regions.

CULTURE. This South African plant is tender to sharp frost and does best in warm gardens. Once established it will endure moderate frost. At the coast it grows in full sunshine but it should be planted in filtered shade when grown inland. Plant in soil rich in humus and water well during dry periods of the year.

Buxus BOX

DESCRIPTION. The genus includes about thirty species of evergreen shrubs and small trees, some of which have been used extensively in gardens in Europe because of their resistance to cold. They are grown mainly for their neat foliage and because they can be trimmed to many different shapes, and transplanted when quite large and old, to form ornamental hedges or topiary specimens.

CULTURE. The species used for low hedges and topiary are slow-growing. This characteristic minimizes the amount of trimming necessary. Most species will grow in shade as well as sun, but they are not suited to subtropical gardens. They grow in alkaline or acid soil.

B. microphylla japonica JAPANESE BOX
A shrub to 1–2 m which grows in dry regions with fairly warm winters. The leaves are dark green in summer and brown in winter. It trims well to form a low hedge or individual topiary specimen, either in the ground or in containers.

B. sempervirens ENGLISH BOX
Will not stand dryness. Likes cold winters and an abundance of moisture. Has small lustrous, dark green, ovate leaves which make a neat hedge. The plant may grow to 5 m if not trimmed. There are numerous cultivars of garden merit. 'Arborescens' makes a pretty tree with glossy leaves; 'Argentea' has leaves marked with yellow or white. 'Suffruticosa' is the best one to use for a low hedge. There is a variegated form of this one, too, with leaves edged with white. They are all very slow-growing.

Caesalpinia

DESCRIPTION. Evergreen and deciduous shrubs of the legume family, quick-growing and elegant. They have graceful foliage and flowers of unusual form.

CULTURE. Both species described thrive in tropical and subtropical gardens. They can be grown where winters are fairly cool but do not flower so well. They are tender to severe frost. These plants enjoy hot sun and an abundance of moisture, but once established will tolerate fairly long periods with little water.

C. gilliesii (*Poinciana gilliesii*)
BIRD OF PARADISE FLOWER
A delightful shrub growing to 3 m and a little more in warm, humid regions. It has graceful stems of finely cut foliage which it may lose where winters are cool. In late spring and summer it bears elegant flowers composed of five yellow segments, from which emerge long curving, glistening, scarlet stamens.

C. pulcherrima (*Poinciana pulcherrima*)
PRIDE OF BARBADOS
A quick-growing plant to 2 m with acacia-like foliage and orange or crimson flowers with crinkled edges to the petals and long, drooping scarlet stamens. The flowering time is summer.

Calliandra SHUTTLECOCK FLOWER

DESCRIPTION. Ornamental evergreen shrubs that need sunshine for their best development. They reach a height of 3 m or more. Most species have attractive foliage rather like that of the acacias with feathery leaves. The elegant flowers have long and beautifully coloured stamens which make a sparkling show.

CULTURE. They grow well in regions with dry summers and wet winters. Will stand moderate frost when established but continued sharp frosts may cut them down to the ground.

71

C. brevipes (C. sellvi)
SHUTTLECOCK FLOWER

A Brazilian species growing to 2 m with pompons of pink flowers in summer. It stands fairly severe frost.

C. haematocephala PINK POWDER PUFF

A fast-growing Bolivian shrub to 3 m or more, with pretty leaves which are copper-coloured when new, turning dark green as they mature. It bears big powder puffs of flowers with showy pink stamens in autumn and winter. Needs light soil and plenty of water.

C. tweedii
BRAZILIAN FLAME BUSH, RED CALLIANDRA

Grows to 2 m and has lacy, fern-like leaves divided into tiny leaflets. Bright red flowers appear in spring and summer. Prune to keep it shapely. If cut back by frost it usually grows up again quickly. Does best, however, in regions where winters are mild.

Callicarpa dichotoma
BEAUTY BERRY

DESCRIPTION. A deciduous plant from China growing to 2 m with gracefully arching branches. The leaves are oval and about 10 cm long. It bears small clusters of pink flowers in summer. These are not as showy as the bunches of glossy, bead-like, lilac berries that appear in autumn. These are pretty in arrangements. It is quick-growing and useful for making a hedge or screen whilst plants of slower growth are developing. Other species worth growing are *C. giraldiana*, *C. japonica* and *C. rubella*.

CULTURE. All except *C. rubella* will tolerate frost. If damaged by frost they recover quickly. These plants do not mind poor soil. Where space is limited, prune them in winter to keep the plants small. They grow in alkaline or acid soil.

Callistemon BOTTLEBRUSH

DESCRIPTION. These evergreen shrubs and small trees, native to Australia, have become popular in many parts of the world. The height and spread of the plants are given under the species described. They have rather narrow leathery leaves with a well-defined midrib. In some species the new growth is tinged with bronze. The common name of bottlebrush describes the cylindrical inflorescence of many of them. The flowers are made up of prominent stamens that project, giving the flowerhead the appearance of a bottlebrush. In most species the flowerheads are a cheerful shade of scarlet or crimson, but they may be yellow. The seeds remain on the plants for a long time. Callistemons look effective in any part of the garden – close together to form a screen or informal hedge; in groups in a shrubbery; against a wall, or as individual specimens next to a pool. The main flowering time is spring and summer. It is advisable to cut off the flowers with a length of stem as they fade, to keep the plants tidy and compact.

CULTURE. These are quick-growing plants tolerant of a wide diversity of climatic conditions. They will grow in areas which experience long periods of hot dry weather, and frosts of 5–10 degrees. Some species do not mind alkaline soil. They thrive in coastal gardens and inland, too, preferring full sunshine to partial shade.

C. brachyandrus
PRICKLY OR MALLEE BOTTLEBRUSH

Grows to 2–3 m and is slender in form with pine-like leaves only about 2 cm long. The lovely crimson flowers show up well against the leaves. The flowering time is spring to summer. It is very resistant to hot dry conditions and poor soil.

C. citrinusm (C. lanceolatus)
LEMON OR SCARLET BOTTLEBRUSH

A handsome species which grows to 5 m and can be trained to form a tree by trimming out the basal growth. The new leaves are coppery and then turn bright green. They give off a lemon-like scent when crushed which accounts for its common name. The scarlet or crimson flowers that appear from late spring to autumn make a fine show. 'Splendens' and 'Compacta' are two decorative cultivars. They stand severe frost.

C. linearis
NARROW-LEAFED BOTTLEBRUSH

Bears ornamental crimson brushes 10 cm long in summer. The plant reaches a height of 3 m but can be kept trimmed back to smaller size. 'Pumila' is smaller, with shiny new growth and longer flowerheads. These stand sharp frost.

C. phoeniceus FIERY BOTTLEBRUSH

This species from Western Australia grows to 3 m and is similar in appearance to *C. citrinus*. It is very attractive, with brilliant heads of ruby-red flowers. 'Prostrata' is a low-growing cultivar useful for the rock garden or for small gardens. The flowering time is from late spring to mid-summer.

C. pinifolius
PINE-LEAFED BOTTLEBRUSH

Has very narrow leaves like pine needles and slender lime-yellow flowerheads in summer. The plant grows to 2 m. A cultivar 'Viridis' has green flowers.

C. rigidus STIFF BOTTLEBRUSH

In summer it bears an abundance of red flowers in showy spikes. The plants, 2–3 m high, are erect in growth and have slender pointed leaves. It does well in coastal gardens.

C. salignus YELLOW BOTTLEBRUSH

A large shrub or small tree reaching a height of 6 m or more. The new growth is copper-coloured. The leaves are willow-like in form, and the yellow flowers are carried in small cylinders. This species makes a useful windbreak. It tolerates severe frost when established.

C. speciosus UPRIGHT BOTTLEBRUSH

This tall species from Western Australia is a very decorative one growing to 2–4 m. It has long slender leaves and ruby-red bottlebrush flowers. The main flowering time is spring to summer.

C. viminalis WEEPING BOTTLEBRUSH

A species that assumes a tree-like form with weeping branches clothed with slender mid-green leaves and cascading bottlebrush flowers in spring and summer. An elegant shrub for the back of a large border or as a specimen alone on a lawn. Height 3–4 m.

Calluna vulgaris SCOTCH HEATHER

DESCRIPTION. A fine plant for a rock garden and for growing in pots as well as in the garden. It grows to 1 m in height and spread. The leaves are very

small and closely attached to the stems. The flowers stud the stems making long and colourful sprays in spring. There are several cultivars with flowers varying in colour from pink to rose, mauve, purple and white. 'Aurea', 'Cuprea' and 'Gold Haze' have colourful foliage as well as decorative flowers. Prune plants hard after their flowering is over.
CULTURE. Scotch heather will stand intense cold and does well in poor, sandy or gravelly soil provided that it is acid. It will not grow in alkaline soil nor in subtropical regions.

Calocephalus brownii

CUSHION BUSH
DESCRIPTION. An evergreen Australian shrub grown for its unusual form and foliage. The plant reaches 60 cm in height and spreads across as much or more. It has white stems of twiggy, angular growth and very small, silver-white leaves that make a charming contrast when planted near shrubs with dark-green leaves. It bears clusters of tiny white flowers. This plant is worth growing in a large rock garden or as ground cover on a bank, together with other shrubs. The foliage is attractive in arrangements as well as in the garden.
CULTURE. Cushion bush is not suited to cold damp gardens. It likes full sunshine and sandy soil which allows for good drainage. Grows well near the coast and inland where winters are not very severe.

Calothamnus   NET BUSH

DESCRIPTION. Decorative evergreen shrubs from Western Australia which are related to callistemon and thrive under the same conditions. The leaves are variable in shape. The fringed flowers are carried in heads which, in some species, resemble a one-sided bottlebrush in form. Plant them in groups on a large dry bank, or make an informal hedge of one species. They will grow in coastal gardens.
CULTURE. Most species stand harsh growing conditions such as long dry periods, very hot days followed by cold nights, and poor soil. They are not suitable for damp shady gardens. To keep them neat cut the plants back after their flowering period.

C. quadrifidus   CRIMSON NET BUSH
Grows to 2 m and more and has almost pine-like leaves 1–3 cm long on slender stems. The flowers, with prominent ruby-red stamens, look attractive against the dark foliage. The flowering time is winter and early spring.

C. sanguineus   RED NET BUSH
This ornamental hardy evergreen shrub reaches 2 m in height. In spring it produces a lovely profusion of crimson flowers.

C. villosus   WOOLLY NET BUSH
Is 1 m tall and has soft hairy leaves only 1 cm long, and clusters of crimson flowers. This is a good plant for a large rockery.

Calycanthus floridus

CAROLINA ALLSPICE
DESCRIPTION. A deciduous shrub growing to 2 m with a spread of almost as much. The oval leaves are 10 cm long, green on the upper surface and greyish-green beneath. Flowers made up of narrow, strap-shaped segments of a dusty maroon colour appear in late spring and early summer. They are not showy but the plant is worth growing for the scent of the flowers and twigs.
CULTURE. It enjoys frost and does well in sun or partial shade. It thrives also in poor soil but needs frequent watering.

Cantua buxifolia

SACRED FLOWER OF THE INCAS
DESCRIPTION. A quick-growing evergreen shrub of rather straggly habit reaching 2 m. It has tiny leaves, sparsely carried on drooping stems. Because the plant tends to be unattractive when not in flower, it should be planted at the back of a shrub border. In spring it produces lovely flowers of a luminous coral-red, which look as though they have fluorescent lights behind them. The flowers are carried in bunches and hang down prettily from the drooping stems. *C. bicolor* has smaller flowers of yellow and red.
CULTURE. It stands moderate frost and does well in full sunlight near the coast. In hot inland gardens plant it where it gets some shade during the hottest hours of the day. It is not particular as to soil, growing well in clay or

sandy soil. Trim plants after their flowering period is over.

Carissa

NATAL PLUM, AMATUNGULU, HEDGE THORN
DESCRIPTION. Evergreen shrubs native to Southern Africa, with attractive leaves and pretty scented flowers. They grow to 2–3 m in height. The oval leaves are deep green and lustrous, and the flowers, composed of five, waxy-white rounded petals, have a scent rather like that of jasmine. They appear in summer, and when they fade the plant carries scarlet fruits the size of small plums. A plant often bears flowers and fruits at the same time. They show up beautifully against the dark green of the foliage. The fruit makes a pleasant acid jelly when cooked.

Planted close together carissa will form a good impenetrable screen or hedge, as the stems are armed with strong thorns. It can be grown as a windbreak, too. Prune hard annually for a hedge of normal size. Both species and cultivars are splendid plants for seaside gardens as they do not mind coastal sand and salt spray.

C. edulis and *C. grandiflora* are the names of the two species worth growing. Several cultivars of *C. grandiflora* more suited to gardens of average size have been introduced. Some of these grow to only 60 cm in height and spread.
CULTURE. Will tolerate occasional mild frost, but they are happiest in warm gardens near the coast. They will grow in hot inland areas where frosts are not severe, in full sun or part shade.

Carpenteria californica

CALIFORNIAN MOCK ORANGE
DESCRIPTION. A slow-growing evergreen plant reaching 2 m or more. It has narrow leaves, pointed at both ends, up to 10 cm in length, dark green on the upper surface and pale grey beneath. In summer it carries white flowers with a faint perfume. These are about 5–7 cm across, with a pretty central boss of stamens. They look somewhat like a single dogrose in form.
CULTURE. Is not suited to hot dry areas nor to subtropical regions. Does best where winters are cool to cold and when grown in light shade. Plant in rich soil for best results.

The fluorescent flowers of Cantua appear in spring

Autumn Cassia (*Cassia corymbosa*) makes the garden glow with colour

Peanut Butter Cassia (*Cassia didymobotrya*) is a quick grower

Caryopteris clandonensis

BLUE SPIREA, BLUEBEARD

DESCRIPTION. A deciduous shrub which grows to 2 m. The plant is rounded with narrow, sage-green leaves and clusters of tiny blue or mauve flowers carried along the ends of the stems. The flowering time is summer and early autumn. 'Heavenly Blue' and 'Blue Mist' are two charming cultivars developed from this species. Another decorative species worth trying is *C. incana*, with flowers of misty blue to lavender.

CULTURE. Blue Spirea stands sharp frosts and it will also grow well in fairly warm districts, but it is not happy in subtropical areas. Cut back fairly hard in late winter or early spring to encourage good flowering and to keep it shapely.

Cassia   CASSIA, SENNA

DESCRIPTION. The name includes a wide variety of trees and shrubs with good-looking foliage and flowers. Some of them are evergreen, some partly so, and some are deciduous. Those described are ornamental plants adaptable to a wide range of growing conditions. The leaves are often fern-like, being cut into small leaflets; the flowers are shades of yellow. The flowering time differs according to species.

CULTURE. Cassias grow readily in almost any soil, but prefer one which drains readily to a heavy clay which tends to hold water for long periods. Some species will stand moderate to severe frosts for short periods, but most of them do best where winters are not severe and in subtropical regions.

C. artemisioides   SILVER CASSIA

A pretty Australian evergreen shrub growing to 2 m with a spread of as much. Its silvery leaflets are only 2–3 cm in length and very slender, giving the shrub a pleasant appearance even when it is not in flower. In late winter and early spring the sulphur-yellow flowers show up well against the foliage. It stands harsh growing conditions, such as intensely hot days followed by frosty nights. Needs well-drained soil.

C. bicapsularis   AUTUMN CASSIA

A quick-growing evergreen shrub reaching a height of 3 m, with attractively divided leaves and bright yellow flowers. This shrub well deserves its popularity as it produces a charming show of colour in autumn. It is tender to severe frost, but when cut to the ground it often grows up quickly to flower again the following autumn. In warm areas, prune it each year or the plant will grow too large and become woody about the base.

C. corymbosa   (*C. floribunda*)

AUTUMN CASSIA

This is very like the species described above. It grows to 2 m in height and spread and is therefore more suited to large gardens than small, but it does not mind an annual pruning. The colour of the flowers is a clear, deep golden-yellow that shows up well against the soft green hue of the leaves. The flowering time is autumn.

C. didymobotrya

PEANUT BUTTER CASSIA

An evergreen plant from East Africa which, if left unpruned, will grow into a small tree 3 m in height. It has pretty leaves divided into many pairs of oval leaflets 5 cm in length. It bears decorative heads of flowers in spring, and on and off during other seasons too. They are carried in upright spikes and are sulphur-yellow tipped with brown in the bud. Suited to areas where frosts are never more than moderate.

C. tomentosa   WOOLLY SENNA

A quick-growing robust plant to 4 m which can be pruned back but generally is recommended only for large gardens. From late autumn to early spring the rich yellow flowers are carried in upright spikes at the ends of stems. They show up very well against the pale-green foliage. It will stand mild frost.

Here shrubs in the background emphasize the beauty of the foreground planting

Ceanothus

WILD OR CALIFORNIAN LILAC

DESCRIPTION. Most of the species are quick-growing evergreen plants reaching a height of 2 m. They bear tiny flowers arranged in rounded or oval clusters. The colours include blue, violet, purple or white. *C. caeruleus, C. cyaneus, C. papillosus* and *C. thyrsiflorus* are the names of popular species. Many beautiful cultivars have been evolved and these are now more widely grown than the species. Ceanothus is valuable in the garden because of the blue colour of its flowers. This varies from pale and misty blue to vivid azure blue.

CULTURE. Plant them in soil which drains readily. They like cold and, once established, will tolerate long periods with little water. To produce good flowering they should be watered in winter and spring. They grow in alkaline or acid soil. Trim plants back immediately after flowering to keep them neat and compact.

Centaurea   DUSTY MILLER

DESCRIPTION. Three decorative plants for the garden and for pot-culture belong to this genus. They are grown for their silver or white foliage which remains ornamental throughout the year. Plant them near shrubs with dark green or purple foliage. The leaves are useful for flower arrangements.

CULTURE. They grow well in sandy or gravelly soil to which a little humus has been added. Once established they tolerate fairly long periods with little water and generally survive severe frost.

C. cineraria

This species which is also referred to as *C. candidissima,* is an ornamental Italian species which grows into a mound of lacy, silvery-grey leaves. It bears mauve flowers in summer. The plant looks attractive anywhere in the garden and the leaves are charming in small arrangements.

C. gymnocarpa

Is native to an island in the Mediterranean. It grows to 30–60 cm and has indented, velvety white leaves. The purple flowerheads appear in summer but are usually almost hidden by the leaves.

C. ragusina

A neat little plant from Crete growing to 60 cm, with beautifully indented pearl-grey leaves and yellow flowers in summer. It is a delightful plant for the flower border or to plant in front of a shrub border, or in a rock garden. The leaves are decorative in small arrangements or posies.

Centradenia inaequilateris

CENTRADENIA

DESCRIPTION. This is a quick-growing little evergreen shrub with a height and spread of less than 1 m. Its leaves are lanceolate and hairy. In summer it bears clusters of small pink flowers with rounded petals. It is a useful shrub for quick cover and looks effective towards the front of a shrubbery or at the back of a flower border. *C. grandifolia* is not as pretty but its flowers last well in arrangements.

CULTURE. Plant in full sun or part shade and water in spring and summer. It does best in regions where winters are mild. Tender to frost.

Ceratostigma willmottianum

CHINESE PLUMBAGO

DESCRIPTION. This is a gay little plant for the small garden or for a rock or pebble garden. It grows to about 1 m in height and spread, sending out a mass of wiry, twiggy growth from the ground. The leaves turn colour in autumn before falling. Throughout summer it is covered with rounded heads of small phlox-like flowers of bright cornflower blue. *C. plumbaginoides* (Dwarf Plumbago) is very similar but more prostrate in growth.

CULTURE. Stands severe frost and considerable drought too. Will grow in full sunshine or semi-shade. If cut back by frost it grows up again quickly to flower by summer. If not cut down by frost, prune it in late winter by cutting back the stems fairly hard.

Cestrum   CESTRUM

DESCRIPTION. Ornamental, quick-growing, evergreen shrubs native to the warm regions of central America. They tend to be tall and slender in growth and look best if trimmed lightly each year after flowering. If planted close together they make a pleasing screen or informal hedge.

CULTURE. Cestrums do best in regions with mild winters but they stand moderate frost. They often rise again after being frosted to the ground. Water them during dry periods of the year.

C. aurantiacum   YELLOW CESTRUM

A well-proportioned plant that is evergreen in warm climates and semi-deciduous in cold areas. In summer it bears showy bunches of orange-yellow tubular flowers. It grows to 2 m and looks effective at the back of a shrub border.

C. elegans   CESTRUM

A tall plant to 3 m which can be kept trimmed back to smaller size. It carries wine-coloured, tubular flowers in pendant clusters at the ends of pliable stems.

C. newellii   RED CESTRUM

Grows gracefully to 2 m and has pretty soft leaves and pendant clusters of glossy tubular flowers of sealing-wax red or rose-pink in summer.

C. nocturnum   NIGHT-SCENTED JASMINE

This robust evergreen is valued for the scent of its flowers. Too large for the average garden, it makes a good background shrub in a large garden or park. It grows to 4 m and has narrow leaves 12 cm in length, and clusters of creamy-yellow, highly-scented flowers in summer. This plant from the West Indies is best suited to subtropical gardens.

Chaenomeles

JAPONICA, JAPANESE FLOWERING QUINCE

DESCRIPTION. Fine flowering shrubs highly prized in most countries of the world because of the colourful flowers they produce during winter. They make a gay show in the garden and charming arrangements of a Japanese character. The species *C. japonica* is a spiny shrub that grows to 1–2 m and has crimson to scarlet flowers followed by yellow fruits like small apples. *C. speciosa* (*C. lagenaria*), the true Japanese quince, is a robust plant growing to 2–3 m with large red flowers. Both species have given rise to numerous lovely cultivars with red, white, pink or rose flowers. Planted close together they make a good impenetrable hedge.

CULTURE. Japanese flowering quince stands very severe frost. Once established it will also tolerate fairly long periods with little water. Plants should be watered from late autumn to winter to promote good flowering. Plant in soil rich in humus. Where the soil is alkaline plants may show chlorosis (yellowing of the leaves). Should this happen apply a sprinkling of sulphur, aluminium sulphate or iron chelates to the soil according to directions given on the package. Prune plants, if necessary, by cutting stems for arrangements or, if they are too big, cut them back hard immediately after flowering.

Chamaecyparis CYPRESS
(Pronounced **Kammi-siperis**)
DESCRIPTION. The genus includes evergreen shrubs as well as trees. Cultivars of great merit with leaves of different colours − green, metallic blue, silver, grey and gold are decorative plants for large or small gardens. These small cypresses can be planted alone on a lawn, together with other shrubs in a border, in a rock or pebble garden, in a Japanese-style garden, as a hedge, or in large containers on a terrace or patio. Most of the shrub-like cultivars have been developed from trees named: *Chamaecyparis lawsoniana, C. obtusa* and *C. pisifera.*
CULTURE. Neither the species nor the cultivars are suitable for subtropical gardens. They do well where winters are cool to cold and where the rainfall is good. They do better in acid than in alkaline soil.

The following are some of the named cultivars of *Chamaecyparis lawsoniana:*
'Ellwoodii'
Grows slowly to a height of 6 m and forms an oval, pointed column 1–2 m across at its widest. It makes a good specimen tree or large shrub but can be grown as a container plant, too. The foliage is soft and has a blue-grey tinge in winter. Cultivars with more distinctive colouring, derived from this one, have been propagated. 'Chilworth Silver', 'Ellwood Gold' and 'Ellwood Pillar' are three likely to prove popular.
'Erecta Aurea'
A slow-growing cultivar which reaches a height of 1−2 m, with attractive sprays of golden foliage. Not recommended for regions where hot dry

winds blow as the foliage tends to scorch.
'Fletcheri'
Is columnar in habit with a broad base. It is very slow but may eventually grow to 6 m. In foliage and form it is very like 'Ellwoodii'.
'Forsteckensis'
Has a globular form, growing very slowly to 1 m, with a broader spread. It has decorative fern-like sprays of greyish-blue foliage.
'Lutea Nana'
This slow-growing bush may eventually reach a height of 2 m. It is a fine little plant with flat sprays of golden-yellow arranged in a dense fashion.
'Minima Aurea'
Is one of the best dwarf conifers for the small garden. It is conical in form with upright sprays of golden foliage. The ultimate height, after twenty years, may be only about 1 m.
'Minima Glauca'
A slow cultivar, globular in form, that grows to 1 m in height and spread in a generation. It is a neat plant with compact sprays of sea-green foliage.
'Nana'
Grows slowly to a height of 2 m and is of bushy habit. Its foliage is dark green and arranged in short, almost horizontal sprays.
'Nana Argentea'
Similar in form to 'Nana', but the foliage is prettily coloured with cream and grey.
'Pygmaea Argentea'
A splendid little plant for the small garden in a cool climate. When mature it has a height and spread of only 1 m, and forms a rounded bush with graceful sprays of green foliage tipped with silvery cream.
'Rogersii'
A globe-shaped plant with glaucous blue-green, thread-like foliage. It grows slowly to 2 m in height and spread.
'Tamariscifolia'
This is a cultivar for the large garden or park. It grows slowly to a height of 3 m with a spread of as much or more, forming a rounded mound. The fans of sea-green foliage overlap each other in a graceful fashion.

The following are cultivars of *Chamaecyparis obtusa.*
'Fernspray Gold'
Grows very slowly to a height of 2 m and has a spread of 1,5 m. The rich golden-yellow foliage is carried in fern-like sprays.
'Kosteri'
A dwarf conifer reaching 1 m in height and spread. It is a good plant for the rock garden. The bright green leaves turn bronze in winter.
'Nana'
This one is suitable for the small garden. After a generation it will be somewhat less than 1 m in height and spread. It forms dense, rounded branchlets of dark-green foliage arranged in tiers.
'Nana Gracilis'
A cultivar for the large rock garden or to plant as a specimen shrub or tree. It grows to a height of 5 m and has dense, rounded sprays of dark-green foliage.
'Nana Lutea'
Grows very slowly to 1 m and is somewhat conical in form with neat open fans of foliage coloured from cream to gold. One of the prettiest of the dwarf conifers, suitable for growing in a container or the garden.
'Pygmaea'
A loosely branched form which reaches a height of 1 m and spreads across more than this. The foliage is dark green, turning to bronze-green in winter. 'Pygmaea Aurescens' is similar but has foliage tinged with yellow.

The following are some cultivars of *Chamaecyparis pisifera:*
'Aurea Nana'
This very slow dwarf conifer is globular in form. It has sprays of yellow foliage and is a fine plant for the cool rock garden.
'Boulevard'
May grow to 4 m in height and is conical in form, with attractive soft steel-blue foliage that turns bronzy-purple in winter. Is listed in some books as 'Cyanoviridis'.
'Filifera Aurea'
Grows slowly into a mounded plant about 2 m in height and spread, but it can be trimmed to keep it smaller. The cord-like stems of yellow foliage arch out and down gracefully.

Ceanothus has dainty heads of tiny flowers

Dusty Miller (*Centaurea cineraria*) is a fascinating plant for the terrace, garden or patio

Another form of Dusty Miller with attractive foliage

'Nana'
One of the smallest of these dwarf cultivars – seldom more than 60 cm in height and somewhat more in spread. It is globular in form with densely arranged sprays of dark-green foliage. 'Nana Aureovariegata' has foliage tipped with gold.

'Plumosa Aurea Nana'
A very slow-growing cultivar that reaches about 1 m in height and spread. Its foliage is held erect and prettily coloured yellow to gold.

'Squarrosa Aurea Nana'
This dwarf conifer is very slow in growth. It is compact in form with dense foliage tinged with yellow. Suitable for a rock or pebble garden.

'Squarrosa Dumosa'
A rounded dwarf type that grows to 1 m in height and spread. In summer the foliage is grey-green; in winter it becomes bronze in hue.

'Squarrosa Sulphurea'
This cultivar has foliage of sulphur-yellow in spring, green in summer and green tinged with bronze in winter. It forms a conical plant to a height of 2–3 m.

Chamaelaucium uncinatum
GERALDTON WAXFLOWER
DESCRIPTION. This evergreen shrub, native to Western Australia, has a graceful habit of growth. It is quick-growing with small leaves on slender arching stems. It reaches a height of 2 m or more and bears sprays of dainty flowers, rather like those of the tea tree (leptospermum). They appear in late winter and spring, and are decorative in the garden and long-lasting in arrangements. There are several lovely named cultivars with flowers of white, pink, rose and crimson.
CULTURE. Plant in soil which drains easily. It stands fairly severe frost and long periods with little water. Groom the plants each year to keep them from becoming too large and leggy. It likes an abundance of sunshine.

Chimonanthus praecox
ALLSPICE, WINTERSWEET
DESCRIPTION. A deciduous shrub growing to 3 m with numerous stems from the base. It has fairly large tapering leaves which colour prettily where early frosts are experienced in autumn. The pale yellow flowers appear in winter when the plant is bare of leaves. They are only 2–3 cm across and not particularly showy but they give off a sweet scent for which the plant is grown. The flowers are useful also for winter arrangements. Cultivars known as 'Grandiflorus' and 'Luteus' have larger flowers of deeper colour. This is a plant for large gardens or parks.
CULTURE. Likes cool to cold winters and will not flourish in subtropical regions. Prune it back after flowering to keep the plant within bounds. In areas where the sunlight is intense throughout the year, plant it in shade.

Choisya ternata
MEXICAN ORANGE BLOSSOM
DESCRIPTION. A pleasing, quick-growing evergreen 2 m in height and spread. It has an abundance of pretty, dark green, lustrous leaves divided into leaflets arranged in threes. These keep the plant attractive throughout the year. In spring it carries white, five-petalled flowers of rounded form arranged in clusters. They give off a faint scent of orange blossom which accounts for the common name. It makes a good informal hedge or screen but can be kept trimmed to formal shape also.
CULTURE. This plant will stand quite considerable frost. It grows in soil which is acid or slightly alkaline. Add compost or soil rich in humus to the holes before planting. In hot inland gardens plant it in partial shade. Near the coast it does well in full sun.

Chorizema FLAME PEA
DESCRIPTION. The name of this Western Australian plant is derived from the Greek *khoros*, a dance, and *zema*, a drink. It is said to have been given as an expression of joy at the finding of a spring of clear, sweet water, by a party which had endured many thirsty days of travel under desert conditions. These are low-growing plants suited to small gardens and for growing in a rock garden or container. They are sparse in growth, sending out stems close to the ground. They seldom grow to more than 1 m in height and spread,

Chinese Plumbago (*Ceratostigma willmottianum*) is a fine plant for small gardens and large containers. It bears a gay profusion of deep blue flowers all summer long

Red Cestrum. A quick-growing shrub for gardens large and small

Japanese Flowering Quince (Chaenomeles) provides colour in the garden and charming flowers for winter arrangements

and carry pea-shaped flowers made up of orange and crimson segments. The flowering time is late winter and early spring.

CULTURE. They endure several degrees of frost and grow well in hot inland regions. They grow quickly even in poor soil. In regions of high rainfall, plant them in soil which drains readily.

C. cordatum HEART-LEAF FLAME PEA
A gay little shrub with heart-shaped leaves with prickles along the margins, and small sprays of red and yellow flowers.

C. ilicifolium HOLLY FLAME PEA
Grows to 1 m and has slender stems of small leaves which look somewhat like those of holly. Red and yellow flowers festoon the plant in late winter.

C. varium BUSH FLAME PEA
A shrub for the front of a border. It has ovate leaves with spiny edges and gaily coloured little flowers of red, yellow and purple.

Chrysanthemum frutescens

MARGUERITE, PARIS DAISY
DESCRIPTION. These quick-growing daisies have been popular since Great-grandmother's day, and well they deserve this popularity, for few plants are easier to grow and few yield such an abundance of flowers for so long. The main flowering season is spring to summer, but if the plants are trimmed back at the end of spring, they will

come on and bloom again and again before the cold of autumn inhibits further flowering. The bushes, which grow to 1 m in height and spread, tend to become leggy. Grooming the plants once or twice a year will help to keep them tidy. The colours of the flowers vary from plain white, to white with a pink centre, pink, rose, lavender and many shades of yellow. They are decorative interplanted with flowers in a flower border, and they make an effective show also when planted at the front of a shrub border, or in pots or tubs on a terrace. Planted close together, they will make a charming low and colourful border or hedge. Such a border should be made of one strain or colour. The flowers are delightful in arrangements as well as being ornamental in the garden. Some strains have single flowers and others have double ones. Many named cultivars are available.

CULTURE. When buying plants select small ones rather than those which have already developed a woody main stem. A plant only 20 cm tall will develop into a bushy shrub laden with flowers in two or three months, whereas a tall plant may become leggy and untidy. It is advisable to renew the plants every two to three years. They root very easily from cuttings made during the warm months of the year. They grow in any soil but like an abundance of sunshine. They do remarkably well in sandy soil and near the

Plant Flame Pea (*Chorizema cordatum*) in the rock garden

Single and double forms of Marguerites produce masses of flowers, which are charming in the garden and in arrangements

79

coast. In cold gardens frost may cut back the top growth but, if the roots are covered with a thick mulch, they are unlikely to be damaged and the plants shoot up rapidly once more in spring.

Cineraria maritima

(Senecio cineraria) DUSTY MILLER
DESCRIPTION. This is a decorative small foliage plant from the Mediterranean region with deeply cut, pearl-white leaves and heads of yellow flowers in late spring and early summer. The flowers are pretty, but the plant is grown for its leaves rather than the flowers. Plant it towards the back of a flower border or in front of a shrub border. It looks particularly effective in front of shrubs or trees with wine-coloured leaves. The cultivar 'Candicans' is an improvement on the species.
CULTURE. Grows readily from seed or cuttings and stands severe frost and dry weather, but not long periods of drought.

Cistus   ROCK ROSE, SUN ROSE

DESCRIPTION. The genus includes some pretty quick-growing evergreen shrubs native to the Mediterranean littoral. They can be found in dry areas of North Africa and the western parts of Syria and Israel. They grow to 1–2 m and have very slender leaves, dark green or greyish-green in colour. The stems and leaves are often sticky. In early spring they bear lovely, five-petalled flowers which look like single roses. The petals, as they open, have a papery appearance. In addition to the species there are several named cultivars. 'Silver Pink' (pale pink flowers with golden stamens) and 'Sunset' (wine-rose flowers) are two very attractive small ones growing to only 60 cm in height.
CULTURE. These are splendid plants for hot, dry gardens, and for covering large dry banks. They tolerate falls in temperature to 10 degrees below freezing and they do well in poor gravelly or sandy soil. They do not thrive in damp, subtropical gardens but do well in coastal gardens. Plant them in full sunshine.

C. crispus   ROCK ROSE
A charming plant for a rock-garden. It grows to 1 m and has exceptionally pretty pink to cyclamen flowers in mid-spring.

C. ladanifer
Reaches a height of 2 m and has very sticky stems, long leaves and large decorative pure white flowers with crimson blotches at the base of each petal.

C. laurifolius
A quick-growing plant to 2 m with a spread of almost as much. The leaves are dark green. Large pure white flowers appear in spring.

C. purpureus 'Brilliancy'
ORCHID ROCK ROSE
Produces an abundance of large rose-coloured flowers with a ruby-red spot at the base of each petal. It does very well in seaside gardens.

C. salvifolius   SAGELEAF ROCK ROSE
A good plant for ground cover on a rough bank. It is about 60 cm in height and spreads across 1 m or more. Its sage-green leaves are a fine background to the white flowers.

Clerodendrum

BLUE BUTTERFLY BUSH
DESCRIPTION. The genus includes some attractive, quick-growing shrubs and climbers growing to 1–2 m or more. Particulars of shrubby species are given below.
CULTURE. Most of the ornamental clerodendrums are to be found in the warmer parts of the world and unless otherwise stated, it can be assumed that they are tender to frost. They grow in full sun or part shade.

C. bungei   *(C. foetidum)*
CASHMERE BOUQUET
A hardy evergreen species from China with very large leaves and clusters of fragrant rosy-red flowers in summer. Its height and spread are 2 m or more.

C. fargesii   GLORY BOWER
Is probably the hardiest species, tolerating fairly severe frosts. It grows to 2 m or more, and has large leaves measuring up to 20 cm in length and fairly broad. The white flowers are not showy, but have a sweet scent. They are about 1 cm wide and are carried in loose clusters in summer. In autumn the plant is colourful when the calyces of the flowers turn crimson and it is festooned with steel-blue berries. It will grow in alkaline and acid soil.

C. philippinum
FRAGRANT GLORY BOWER
Has heart-shaped leaves of soft texture and heads of flowers measuring 10 cm across. The flowers, which appear in summer, are white with a red calyx and have a rich fragrance. This shrub grows to 2 m.

C. speciosissimum   *(C. fallax)*
RED GLORY BOWER
This species from Java grows to 1 m and has very large leaves up to 20 cm in length and almost as wide. It bears showy clusters of scarlet flowers in summer. Will thrive only in subtropical gardens.

C. trichotomum
HARLEQUIN GLORY BOWER
This hardy robust shrub may grow to 3 m in height and spread. The scented white flowers appear in summer but the plant is more attractive in autumn when it has clusters of bright blue berries subtended by red calyces.

C. ugandense   BLUE BUTTERFLY BUSH
A charming species from the warm parts of Central Africa. It is a slender plant reaching 2 m with oval, coarsely-toothed leaves. The flowers carried in loose clusters, make a lovely show in summer. Each one is 4 cm across and coloured pale and dark blue, a pretty combination of colour in a border. Prune plants back in early spring to keep them tidy and to encourage good flowering.

Clethra alnifolia

SWEET PEPPER BUSH
DESCRIPTION. A deciduous shrub from the eastern United States, which is upright in growth to 3 m. The dark-green, oval, pointed leaves are about 8 cm long, with toothed margins. In late summer and early autumn it bears terminal spires of tiny white flowers with a spicy scent. There are cultivars of this species with pink flowers. Other species of garden merit are *C. barbinervis, C. monostachya* and *C. tomentosa.*
CULTURE. They do best in cool to cold

gardens. Plant them in acid soil. Water well and mulch the plants during dry periods of the year.

Clianthus puniceus
GLORY PEA, PARROT BEAK

DESCRIPTION. This ornamental plant, native to New Zealand where it is known as Kaka Beak, is well worth a place in the garden or in a pot on a balcony or terrace. It is an evergreen, scandent shrub growing to 2 m or a little more. The leaves are divided into decorative small leaflets which give the plant a graceful appearance. The pea-like flowers, which appear in spring, hang loosely from the stems. They are brilliant scarlet in colour with prominent keels, which accounts for the name of Parrot Beak. There are forms of this with white and pink flowers as well.

CULTURE. Support the plant on a stake or a trellis as the stems are apt to fall over, hiding the flowers. Plant it in friable soil rich in humus and water well during its flowering period. It stands moderate frost. Grows in full sun near the coast but needs some shade in hot inland gardens. This plant is not easy to grow and tends to die off after a few years. It can be raised from seed.

Codiaeum variegatum CROTON

DESCRIPTION. A good-looking evergreen shrub that grows upright to 1–2 m in height. It is planted for its foliage which is glossy and somewhat leathery, and richly coloured – bronze, yellow, red, pink, rose and green. The shape of the leaves varies considerably. Crotons are quick-growing plants often raised in containers for use in the house or on the terrace or patio.

CULTURE. This plant with its many cultivars demands warmth and humidity and is therefore suitable only for gardens where winters are mild. It can be grown successfully in the open in coastal gardens but away from the coast it requires some shade.

Coffea arabica COFFEE

DESCRIPTION. A large ornamental shrub growing to 5 m, but it can be pruned back to keep it smaller. The tiny white, fragrant flowers are not showy but the plant is worth growing for its lustrous, dark-green foliage. In addition to forming a good background or screen in the garden, the coffee plant can be grown as a container plant on a large patio or terrace. It does not seem to mind having its roots restricted and can be grown successfully in a fairly small pot.

CULTURE. Does best in subtropical gardens, and is not recommended for dry regions nor for gardens which are cold. Grow it in full sun near the coast and partial shade inland. Plant in acid soil rich in humus.

Coleonema pulchrum
CONFETTI BUSH

DESCRIPTION. A quick-growing evergreen South African plant that makes a delightful show in late winter and early spring. It grows to a height of 2 m but can be trimmed back to smaller size. In fact, the plants look neater and more attractive if they are sheared back hard after their flowering period. The leaves are tiny and so are the pale-pink flowers which are carried in frothy profusion. There is also a white form, C. album. Both trim into a neat shape and can be cut to the form of a round ball, cone, pyramid or square.

CULTURE. Does well in poor soil but makes quicker growth if planted in soil to which some humus has been added. Tolerates occasional sharp but not severe frost and, once established, will endure long periods of drought and heat. Transplant it when very small. It grows well in seaside gardens.

Convolvulus cneorum
BUSH MORNING GLORY

DESCRIPTION. A delightful small evergreen shrub from the Mediterranean which grows to 1 m in height and spread. The smooth, silvery leaves are covered with silky hairs that give the plant a pleasing appearance throughout the year. In spring it bears small, delicately tinted convolvulus flowers of white flushed with palest pink. This is a good plant for the small garden and for a rock garden. It is also effective when grown in a pot on a sunny terrace.

CULTURE. Does well in friable soil that drains readily and in sandy ground, but may be grown in clay also. It will grow in warm areas, in coastal gardens and in those which have moderate frost. If it is cut to the ground by frost it usually grows up quickly again.

Coprosma repens MIRROR PLANT

DESCRIPTION. This is a fine plant for making a screen or informal hedge, to train against a wall or to grow in a large container. It is an evergreen New Zealand shrub which has become very popular in many countries of the world because of its decorative foliage and its resistance to salt in the air in coastal gardens. If not trimmed it will grow to 3 m in height with a spread of as much. No plant has shinier leaves. They seem to reflect the light – hence the common name of Mirror Plant. The leaves are dark-green and neatly shaped, oblong or oval and up to 7 cm in length. 'Variegata' (Golden Mirror Bush) has leaves edged with yellow; 'Argentea' (Silver Mirror Bush) has leaves prettily edged with white; and 'Picturata' has leaves with yellow in the middle. There are now many named cultivars with coloured leaves, and also dwarf forms.

CULTURE. When established coprosma is able to stand fairly severe frost and also long periods without water. It grows quickest when planted in soil rich in humus and watered fairly regularly. In hot inland areas plant it in semi-shade. This is a good plant to create a screen or shelter near the coast or to use to stop the drift of coastal sand. It is advisable to trim and train plants to keep them attractive in form.

Cordyline australis (Dracaena)
CABBAGE TREE

DESCRIPTION. An unusual New Zealand plant worth growing for its dramatic shape. It sends up a mass of leaves from a central core. The leaves are sword-shaped up to 1 m in length and 6–10 cm wide. As the plant matures the lower trunk becomes bare, carrying leaves at the top rather like a palm. Plant it in a large pebble or rock garden, as an accent plant, or at one side of a terrace or patio. 'Atropurpurea' has foliage of a bronze hue. Other cordylines worth growing are C. indivisa which reaches a height of 7 m and has leaves almost 2 m in length; C. stricta, an Australian species, growing to 4 m with leaves almost 1 m long and clus-

Cineraria maritima. Its silvery-grey foliage is decorative throughout the year and its gay yellow flowers are ornamental in late spring

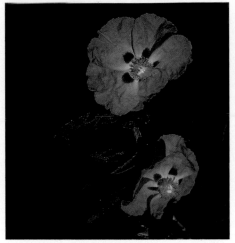

Pink Rock Rose *(Cistus purpureus)*. A good plant for hot, dry gardens

Rock or Sun Rose *(Cistus laurifolius)* is worth growing in gardens large and small

ters of lavender flowers; and *C. terminalis,* from Hawaii, which will reach 3 m in the garden, but is usually grown in containers and remains fairly small. They are grown for their unusual form and foliage rather than for their flowers.

CULTURE. All, with the exception of *C. terminalis,* tolerate severe frost and fairly long periods with little water. In hot dry areas plant them where they are in partial shade, if possible.

Cornus DOGWOOD

DESCRIPTION. The genus includes a number of species of ornamental value – trees, shrubs and ground covers. Only those of shrubby habit of growth are described here.

CULTURE. Most species stand severe cold and, in fact, do better in cold regions than in those where winters are mild. They need rich soil and an abundance of water. Not recommended for alkaline soil.

C. capitata EVERGREEN DOGWOOD
Is a robust shrub from the Himalayas. It will grow to 4 m or more if not trimmed from time to time. This species is generally evergreen but it may lose most of its leaves during a cold and prolonged winter. In late spring it bears insignificant flowers surrounded by pretty sulphur-yellow bracts. When these fade it carries large strawberry-like fruits of a dull red colour.

C. kousa KOUSA DOGWOOD
A large deciduous shrub native to Japan and Korea. It grows to 6 m in height and spread and is therefore suitable only for the large garden or park. In late spring it becomes covered with flowers surrounded by large white ornamental bracts. The foliage assumes good autumnal colours.

C. sanguinea BLOODTWIG DOGWOOD
This species is at its best where autumn and winter are crisply cold; under such conditions the leaves turn fine autumn colours and the twigs and branches become suffused with a blood-red tinge. It grows to 4 m in height. Prune plants, when necessary, immediately after flowering.

Corokia cotoneaster

BLACK COROKIA
DESCRIPTION. An interesting evergreen New Zealand shrub growing to 2–3 m with numerous angular twiggy stems that become almost black in colour as they age. The leaves are small, scarcely 2 cm in length, dark-green on the upper surface and felted pearl-grey on the underside. In spring it bears tiny, starry, yellow flowers in clusters. These are followed in autumn by orange or red berries. This plant, and two related species, *C. cheesemanii* and *C. macrocarpa,* are suitable for seaside gardens. They can be trimmed as topiary specimens or to make a low hedge.

CULTURE. Does well in sun near the coast and in part shade inland. Prefers a soil that drains readily. Will grow in alkaline or acid soil and is hardy to frost.

Correa CORREA, AUSTRALIAN FUCHSIA

DESCRIPTION. Evergreen shrubs native to Australia which grow to 1–2 m in height. The pretty little tubular flowers appear in winter and show up well at a time when few other plants are in bloom. These are delightful plants for small gardens.

CULTURE. They are not particular as to soil and grow in sand or gravel. Near the sea plant them in full sunshine; in inland gardens plant in partial shade. They will stand drops in temperature to 5 degrees below freezing.

C. alba WHITE CORREA
Reaches 1–2 m in height and has arching stems of tiny leaves and small white or pink flowers in spring. The young shoots and leaves are covered with soft down. It stands salt spray well and makes a useful low hedge in coastal gardens.

C. pulchella AUSTRALIAN FUCHSIA
Grows to 60 cm and spreads across 1 m. It has grey-green leaves and tubular rosy-pink flowers. This is a useful little shrub for the back of a large flower border.

Red Glory Bower (*Clerodendrum*) does well in subtropical gardens

Croton (*Codiaeum variegatum*) makes a fine show in a warm garden

Confetti Bush (*Coleonema pulchrum*) looks effective trimmed into a globe

C. reflexa RED CORREA
A bushy plant to 2 m with silver-grey leaves and red fuchsia-like flowers, usually prettily tipped with green or yellow. It is quick-growing and a good shrub to fill space whilst slow-growing ones mature.

Cortaderia selloana
PAMPAS GRASS
DESCRIPTION. This hardy Argentinian plant so popular in our grandparents' day is happily once more being widely grown, as it well deserves to be. It is a dramatic plant for any part of the garden − as a background to a rock garden, in a large pebble garden, near a pool or stream, or beside an entrance. The tall stems grow quickly to 3 m and more, emerging from a mass of long slender leaves. The plumes of silky flowers which appear in summer vary in colour from ivory to pale-pink and look elegant in the garden and in arrangements. They last for months when picked.
CULTURE. Pampas grows under a wide range of conditions − in acid or alkaline soil; at the coast and in hot dry inland gardens. Where winters are cold the top may be frosted down to the ground, but the plant sends out new growth early in spring to produce flowers by summer. As it is apt to spread, care should be taken to restrict its root-run. If it gets out of hand, burn it to the ground if this can be done without damaging neighbouring

plants, and then remove some of the roots. In a small garden it is advisable to plant it in a large container sunk into the ground.

Cotinus coggygria (*Rhus cotinus*)
SMOKE BUSH
DESCRIPTION. Is a bushy deciduous shrub sending up a mass of stems to a height of 3 m or more. It has oval leaves 5−7 cm long which take on brilliant shades of yellow and red in autumn. In late summer it bears clusters of tiny greenish flowers that become smoke-grey in colour as they fade. This accounts for the common name. The cultivar 'Foliis Purpureis' has leaves of deep purple that assume a reddish tinge in autumn, and 'Flame' has particularly bright autumnal colours.
CULTURE. This plant produces the finest show when grown in regions where a dry autumn is followed by a cold winter. It tolerates hot sunshine but not drought or subtropical heat. To keep the plants within bounds and to encourage fresh growth, trim back some of the stems each winter.

Cotoneaster COTONEASTER
(pronounced **Ke-tone-ee-aster**)
DESCRIPTION. Cotoneasters are useful plants for gardens large and small. The genus includes deciduous, semi-deciduous and evergreen shrubs, varying in habit from those that grow prostrate on the ground to tall plants with arching branches. They have neat,

Coprosma repens 'Variegata' has leaves margined with yellow. The shrub with red leaves is Iresine

Cotoneaster makes a splendid show in autumn and early winter

small or large leaves and flowers which are not very showy. The plants are grown chiefly because of their form and vigour, their tolerance of difficult conditions, and for the mass of colourful berries they produce from late summer to winter. Some species also have leaves that turn colour at this season. The prostrate species make a pretty ground cover and large types are excellent background shrubs. Planted close together they will form a pleasing informal hedge or windbreak. The sprays of berries are handsome in arrangements. Cotoneasters trained as standards are decorative as accent plants and are now obtainable from some nurseries.

CULTURE. Cotoneasters can be relied upon to grow well under almost any conditions. They endure severe cold, survive long periods of drought and do well in poor soil. Trim plants lightly when necessary to keep them from growing too large. Severe cutting back is likely to spoil their form and inhibit the production of berries. The removal of old branches from time to time will emphasize the beauty of the new stems.

C. adpressus   CREEPING COTONEASTER
A fine deciduous plant for a large rock garden or to cover a bank. Grows to 20 cm in height and spreads across 2 m. It has white or pale pink flowers and bright red berries. The leaves colour in autumn.

C. bullatus   HOLLY BERRY COTONEASTER
A vigorous deciduous species to 3 m with arching branches of leaves, dark green above and felted grey on the underside. Large clusters of scarlet berries follow the pink flowers. The foliage assumes rich autumn colours.

C. congestus   *(C. microphyllus glacialis)*
DWARF COTONEASTER
Plant in a rock garden, on a wall, or in a container. A slow-growing, almost prostrate plant with stems curving down. It has tiny leaves and white to pink flowers followed by crimson berries.

C. conspicuus
WINTERGREEN COTONEASTER
An evergreen reaching a height of 1 m or more. It has large white flowers in summer and scarlet berries that keep

the garden bright in autumn and winter. 'Decorus', a fine cultivar, is prostrate in growth, with dainty leaves and an abundance of long-lasting scarlet berries in autumn.

C. 'Cornubia'
A good-looking evergreen plant growing to 3 m or more, with dark green leaves up to 10 cm long, and large clusters of shiny crimson berries that persist from autumn through winter. They are seldom touched by birds. Suitable for the large garden.

C. dammeri   *(C. humifusus)*
PROSTRATE COTONEASTER
Spreads along the ground covering it with stems of bright green glossy leaves. It has masses of large white flowers in spring and showy scarlet berries in autumn. Plant as a ground cover or in a rock or pebble garden.

C. franchetii
An evergreen species to 3 m, with arching stems of sage-green leaves and orange-red berries in autumn. It is tolerant of drought and severe cold. *C. franchetii sternianus* is a handsome evergreen growing to 3 m. It has arching stems of leaves − sage-green above and silvery-grey on the underside. The berries are bright orange-red. This plant is often wrongly listed under the name of *C. wardii*.

C. frigidus
A vigorous deciduous shrub or small tree growing to 2−3 m, with large olive-green leaves and clusters of crimson berries in winter.

C. glaucophyllus
Is a semi-evergreen species with arching stems to 2 m. The leaves are large and greyish-green. Its crimson berries are carried in showy clusters right through winter.

C. harrovianus
An evergreen species reaching a height of 4 m, with large dark leaves, attractive sprays of white flowers in summer and large, pendulous clusters of red berries in autumn and winter.

C. henryanus
Is a bulky evergreen growing to 3 m. It has large grey-green leaves, small white flowers and crimson fruits. Suitable for the large garden or park.

C. horizontalis   ROCK COTONEASTER
An interesting and ornamental species of unusual form, growing to about 1 m or less, with rigid angled branches. It is deciduous and before the leaves fall they turn pretty shades of red. It is decorative in summer when in flower and in autumn when it bears masses of scarlet berries. This is a good species to train against a wall or over a bank. Some very attractive small cultivars have been produced in Australia and America. They are lower in growth and make good ground covers for a large bank. 'Variegatus' has leaves edged with white.

C. 'Hybridus Pendulus'
This cultivar is normally semi-prostrate, but can be trained to make a miniature tree with cascading stems of glossy green leaves and scarlet berries.

C. microphyllus   ROCK COTONEASTER
A fine species for the small garden or for a rock garden. Although it grows to only 1 m in height, this evergreen species may spread across as much as 2 m. It is therefore useful as a ground cover. The slender stems have tiny dark-green leaves and white flowers followed by large crimson berries.

C. pannosus
SILVER-LEAFED COTONEASTER
A graceful species which reaches 3 m in height and is evergreen or semi-evergreen. It has curving stems of white flowers in summer and clusters of coral-red berries in autumn and winter. The leaves are small, grey-green on the upper surface and felted white beneath. There is a dwarf form of this one.

C. salicifolius
WILLOWLEAF COTONEASTER
An evergreen species with arching branches up to 5 m. It has narrow leaves, dark green above and grey on the underside, and bears white flowers followed by crimson fruits in autumn. The cultivar 'Floccosus' is an outstanding cotoneaster with showy stems of berries. There is also a prostrate form, 'Repens', that grows to only 20 cm in height and spreads across 2 m.

C. thymifolius

A dwarf plant from the Himalayas, suitable for rock gardens and as a ground cover. The leaves are tiny. Pink flowers appear in spring and are followed by minute bright red berries in summer.

Crinodendron hookerianum

RED LANTERN TREE

DESCRIPTION. Under suitable conditions this evergreen plant from Chile may grow into a small tree. Generally, however, it grows to about 2–3 m. It has a rounded top of glossy, lance-shaped leaves 12 cm long and 2 cm wide, dark green on the upper surface and grey on the underside, with toothed margins. In spring it bears masses of small pendulous crimson bell-shaped flowers. In regions of high rainfall it can be grown as a hedge.

CULTURE. This plant will grow only under shady, moist conditions. It enjoys cold and needs acid soil.

Crotalaria agatiflora

CANARY BIRD BUSH

DESCRIPTION. An evergreen shrub from East Africa which grows quickly to 3 m if it is not trimmed back to keep it within bounds. The foliage is divided into soft green leaflets carried in threes. The flowers appear along the ends of the stems. They are pea-shaped and of an unusual lime-yellow shade. The main flowering time is spring and summer but the plant bears flowers during most months of the year. *C. laburnifolia*, which is native to the east coast of Australia, is another quick-growing species with greenish-yellow flowers. It, too, should be pruned back to keep it compact.

CULTURE. The Australian species will stand 10 degrees of frost, but the species from Africa is tender. Both grow well in poor soil.

Cryptomeria japonica

JAPANESE CEDAR

DESCRIPTION. In its native country, Japan, this tree may grow to a height of 30 m. It is the only species in this genus, but from it have developed many cultivars of garden value. Only those of small stature are described here. Some of these are fine conifers

for a rock or pebble garden and for growing in containers. Most of them are very slow-growing plants and may take thirty years to reach their mature size. This slow growth is an asset as they can be used effectively in small gardens and in rock or pebble gardens.

CULTURE. Plant in soil rich in humus and water well during dry periods of the year. They will stand severe frost but not drought nor subtropical conditions.

'Elegans'

A large shrub or small tree which may eventually grow to a height of 3–5 m. Its soft, feathery foliage turns coppery shades in autumn and winter.

'Elegans Nana'

Is a very slow-growing cultivar with plumose foliage, which gives it an elegant appearance. The leaves become brownish-purple in winter. The final height may be 1,5 m.

'Globosa Nana'

Grows slowly to 1 m and forms a rounded bush, sometimes broader than it is high. The foliage is lime-green.

'Lobbii Nana'

A dwarf conifer which may grow to 1 m in ten years. It has a pleasing form with clustered branchlets of dark green leaves.

'Pygmaea'

Reaches 1 m in height with a spread of a little more. Its slender branchlets of short, dark-green needle-like leaves make an effective display.

'Spiralis'

A low and slow-growing conifer of spreading form. Its leaves are spirally twisted around the stems. An unusual plant for the small garden.

'Vilmoriniana'

Forms a globular bush with a compact mass of branchlets. The dark-green leaves turn reddish-purple in winter. Its final height and spread are less than 1 m.

Cuphea ignea   CIGAR FLOWER

DESCRIPTION. A small, rounded evergreen Mexican plant for the front of a shrub border or for a rock or pebble garden. It reaches 60 cm in height and spread and has neat, narrow deep green leaves. In late spring and summer it bears masses of scarlet tubular

flowers with a dark ring at the end and a white tip. This plant makes a very pretty low, informal hedge. *C. hookeriana* is another fine species with crimson flowers tipped with yellow.

CULTURE. It is a quick-growing plant which does best in gardens where winters are mild. It grows in sun or part shade.

Cyathea   TREE FERN

DESCRIPTION. Tree ferns are of great decorative value and it is surprising that they are not more widely planted. Many of them grow naturally in New Zealand and Australia. They are delightful grouped together in a large garden or park, and a single one standing alone will enhance the small garden. Plant it next to a pool or shady patio. See also under *Dicksonia*.

CULTURE. They do best in acid soil rich in humus in an area which is not subjected to hot dry winds. They need an abundance of moisture, cool conditions and shade.

C. dealbata   SILVER TREE FERN OR PONGA

Grows to 3 m or more. The fronds are green above and silvery-white on the underside. Looks elegant when well grown.

C. medullaris   BLACK TREE FERN

This species native to New Zealand and Australia is a tall plant bearing a crown of fronds 6 m above the ground. The trunks of old plants are black and scaly.

Cyperus papyrus   PAPYRUS

DESCRIPTION. This graceful plant from Egypt was the source of the paper used for ancient manuscripts. It looks effective at the edge of a pool. As it does not grow taller than 2–3 m, it is a fine plant for the small garden as well as the large one. The rush-like stems carry rounded heads of thread-like leaves about 20 cm long at the top. They lend a certain elegance to the garden and are useful for arrangements. The plant also looks attractive growing in a pebble garden. *C. haspan* is a small plant for the miniature water garden or for pot-culture. It grows to only 45 cm in height.

CULTURE. Papyrus develops from a woody underground stem that must be

covered with or soaked in water from time to time. It can be grown in any part of the garden provided it is watered well. Under optimum conditions it spreads rapidly. Where this happens the excess roots should be dug up to keep the plant within bounds. In gardens that experience very severe frost, plant it in a pot which can be moved to a shed in winter. It should not, however, be allowed to become too dry when stored. In a small garden plant it in a container sunk into the ground, to restrict the spread of its roots.

Cytisus BROOM

DESCRIPTION. The common name of broom includes a wide range of quick-growing plants, some of which are listed under *Cytisus,* whilst others will be found under the headings of *Genista* and *Spartium.* They do not have pretty foliage and are grown chiefly for their scented, pea-shaped flowers and because of their hardiness. They vary in size considerably but all of them become rather gaunt and leggy if not trimmed back each year. In most cases it pays to cut them back to half their height immediately after their flowering season is over. Where conditions are good some species become invasive. Gardeners living in areas where harsh climatic conditions restrict the range of plants which can be grown should try all of the brooms. There are many splendid cultivars.

CULTURE. Most species thrive where few plants will flourish. They tolerate cold, long periods with little water, intense sunlight, strong wind and alkaline and sandy soil. Where the soil is

Top left
The lovely plumes of Pampas grass *(Cortaderia selloana)* are elegant in the garden and in arrangements

Bottom left
Cigar Flower *(Cuphea ignea)* is attractive in the rock garden or as a low hedge

Opposite top
In a cool misty climate Japanese maples and rhododendrons make a charming show together

Opposite bottom
Grow dwarf conifers of different shapes to brighten a slope or a rock garden

strongly alkaline, applications of iron sulphate should be made from time to time. They generally do well also in coastal gardens.

C. beanii DWARF BROOM
A charming plant for the small garden or for a rock or pebble garden. It is deciduous and almost prostrate in growth, seldom more than 30 cm in height. It spreads across much more and makes a fine ground cover on a large bank or trailing over a wall. It has yellow flowers in spring.

C. canariensis CANARY ISLAND BROOM
An upright shrub to 2 m with jade-green leaves divided into small leaflets arranged in threes, and fragrant yellow flowers in short loose spikes. It is popular as a potplant in Europe. Where growing conditions are good it may become a weed.

C. kewensis KEW BROOM
A pretty, compact species eminently suited to planting on a bank or wall, or in a rock garden. It reaches a height of 1 m and has trailing stems. In early spring it produces sprays of tiny cream flowers in abundance. Prune hard after flowering.

C. multiflorus (C. albus)
WHITE BROOM
This species, native to Portugal and North Africa, is a decorative plant for a difficult garden. It grows to 2 m or more in height and has a spread of almost as much. The arching branches of white flowers are a glorious sight in spring. A cultivar 'Lilac Time', raised in Australia, has flowers of delicate lilac.

C. praecox MOONLIGHT BROOM
An attractive broom growing to 1,5 m with stems that spray out and hang down gracefully under the weight of the creamy-yellow flowers which appear in late winter and early spring. This one makes a fine informal hedge or screen and looks splendid also standing on its own. 'Albus' is a pretty white cultivar originated in Australia.

C. scoparius SCOTTISH BROOM
The species is not recommended except in dry areas, as elsewhere it grows too easily and will spread far and wide. There are however some splendid cultivars worth planting.

They stand severe frost and do fairly well also in coastal gardens. Some are prostrate or dwarf in form, others are fairly large. The colours of the flowers are cream, yellow, rose, lilac, carmine, purple and crimson. This species and its cultivars do not grow well in alkaline soil.

Daphne DAPHNE
DESCRIPTION. These splendid little evergreen or deciduous plants are decorative when well grown, but they are not easy to grow. The different species vary in form quite considerably and are described under their names. They are grown for their pleasing foliage and scented flowers that are pretty in small arrangements.
CULTURE. They require the same kind of growing conditions as azaleas – namely, acid soil, a cool root run, an abundance of moisture, and soil rich in humus. They do best in semi-shade. Daphnes are not suited to coastal or subtropical gardens.

D. burkwoodii DAPHNE
Is a fine compact evergreen shrub to 1 m with clusters of starry, white to blush-pink, scented flowers in late winter and early spring. 'Variegata' has dark green leaves with cream margins.

D. cneorum GARLAND DAPHNE
A small evergreen plant about 30 cm high and 1 m wide, with narrow dark-green leaves and dense clusters of small fragrant pink flowers in late winter. Cultivars of merit are also available. It will tolerate slightly alkaline soil.

D. genkwa LILAC DAPHNE
A semi-deciduous shrub with slender leaves 2–3 cm long on plants 1 m tall. The silky, fragrant lilac flowers are carried in small clusters in mid-spring.

D. mezereum DAPHNE
A deciduous shrub growing to 1,5 m with oval leaves 2–6 cm long, and fragrant pink to rosy-purple flowers in winter. These are followed by red or yellow berries. This species likes lime.

D. odora WINTER DAPHNE
This species was popular for many years because it carried its sweet-scented flowers early in winter. Under good conditions it will grow to 1 m and bear

numerous pink to rose flowers in clusters. Several cultivars are prettier than the species. 'Rubra' is one of the most decorative, with crimson buds opening to pink flowers 'Aureo-marginata' has leaves edged with white, and sweet-scented pink flowers.

Deutzia BRIDAL WREATH
DESCRIPTION. Quick-growing deciduous plants that liven up the garden early in spring. They grow to 1–2 m in height but can be trimmed to smaller size. The species from which many lovely hybrids have developed are native to China and Japan. The leaves are oval and pointed, dull green and generally soft in texture, with toothed edges. The flowers are like small funnels or bells, sometimes single and sometimes double, and white or pink in colour.
CULTURE. These are hardy plants, tolerant of severe frost and fairly long periods with little water in summer and autumn. They tend to be exuberant in growth, and it is advisable to thin out stems from the base each year. Cut out some of the old ones and allow the newer ones to develop. If they appear to be growing too tall trim off the tops of the stems in late spring.
They will grow in alkaline or acid soil.

D. gracilis SLENDER DEUTZIA
Bears slender arching stems to 1 m which become a foaming mass of snow-white flowers in spring. A cultivar of this one bears rose flowers.

D. lemoinei
Grows to 2 m and is upright in habit with slender, sharply toothed leaves and showy clusters of white flowers tinged with pink. It is a lovely sight when in full flower.

D. longifolia 'Veitchii'
A large shrub with rosy-purple flowers. It fills up space but is not as decorative as the other deutzias described. It makes a good informal boundary to a large property. 'Montrose' is another fine cultivar with panicles of pale-pink flowers in spring.

D. pulchra
A pretty species growing to 2 m with somewhat leathery leaves and clusters of white flowers tinged with pink.

D. scabra

This is a robust plant growing to 2 m with oval pointed leaves and clusters of white or pale-pink flowers. It is a decorative species from which ornamental cultivars have been developed. 'Candidissima' grows to 1 m and has large, double, white flowers. 'Pride of Rochester' has pretty frilled, double flowers, mainly white flushed with pink.

Dichorisandra thyrsiflora

DICHORISANDRA

DESCRIPTION. A plant from tropical America which grows to a height of 1–2 m and has ornamental leaves as well as colourful flowers. The stems are erect and partially sheathed by broad dark green leaves. In summer and autumn it carries flowers in spikes about 15 cm long. They are of a rich shade of hyacinth-blue with a suggestion of purple. Under the right conditions it is fairly quick-growing.
CULTURE. Dichorisandra is recommended for tropical and subtropical gardens. It will not make a show where winters are cool or where frost is likely to occur. Plant it in rich soil and in partial shade, protected from hot dry winds.

Dicksonia antarctica   TREE FERN

DESCRIPTION. A handsome Australian tree fern for gardens where conditions are suitable. Plant it where it can stand alone or group it with other tree ferns under tall trees to give a woodland effect. This species is not quick-growing but it is certainly worth waiting for. It grows to 6 m and bears handsome arching fronds 2 m in length. *D. squarrosa* is a New Zealand species reaching 6 m in height with stiff leathery fronds. See also Cyathea.
CULTURE. Plant them in semi-shade in soil rich in humus. They do best in areas with cool growing conditions, and are not recommended for subtropical gardens nor those subjected to hot dry winds. Water the plants well during dry periods of the year.

Dipelta floribunda   DIPELTA

DESCRIPTION. Is a deciduous shrub from central China growing to 2–3 m, with arching branches rather like those of

the weigela. It has oval pointed leaves up to 8 cm in length. In spring it bears a profusion of pink tubular flowers with yellow throats. They are carried in clusters and have a faint, sweet scent. Winged bracts persist long after the flowers have fallen and until the seed is mature.
CULTURE. Dipelta stands severe cold and it also tolerates fairly long periods with little water. It does not, however, flower well in subtropical gardens. To keep the plants neat cut out some of the old stems at the base each year.

Disanthus cercidifolius

DISANTHUS

DESCRIPTION. A deciduous shrub from Japan, growing to 3 m, with large almost heart-shaped leaves on slender branches. The plant does not bear showy flowers but, where autumn is cold, the leaves turn the most glorious amber to burgundy tints before dropping.
CULTURE. Disanthus is a plant for few gardens. It needs acid soil with plenty of humus, a cool root run, an abundance of moisture in the air, and cool to cold winters.

Dodonaea viscosa

AKEAKE, HOP BUSH

DESCRIPTION. A large evergreen shrub that can be trained to tree form by the removal of branches coming up from the base. It grows to 5 m and has neat slender leaves rather like those of a willow, about 10 cm long. The flowers are inconspicuous but the winged fruits are quite pretty in autumn. 'Purpurea', a form with purple leaves from New Zealand, is more ornamental than the common species. Its leaves are colourful throughout the year. These are useful plants to set out along the border of a large property as they are fairly quick-growing and tolerant of poor growing conditions. They can also be planted to create shelter belts or windbreaks.
CULTURE. Hop bush is a rewarding plant in areas where growing conditions limit the number of plants which can be grown successfully. It stands severe frost, long periods of drought, poor soil and hot winds. It also grows reasonably well in coastal gardens.

Dombeya cayeuxii

PINK DOMBEYA

DESCRIPTION. An evergreen shrub of exuberant growth recommended as a space-filler in a large garden or in a new one, until the slower-growing plants have made some progress. It grows to 3 m in two years, and has large soft leaves and round clusters of pink flowers somewhat like those of a hydrangea. It flowers in autumn and winter and makes a fine show. Unfortunately the flowers do not drop when they fade and, if they are not cut off, the plant tends to look untidy in spring. Other species worth trying are *D. dregeana*, *D. natalensis* and *D. spectabilis*.
CULTURE. Dombeyas do best where winters are mild, but they will tolerate occasional moderate frost. To promote quick growth plant them in good soil and water well. Long periods of hot dry winds may damage the foliage.

Dovyalis caffra   KEI APPLE

DESCRIPTION. This is a plant for gardens where growing conditions are difficult. It is an evergreen shrub from South Africa, useful for making an impenetrable hedge about a large property. It grows to 3 m and spreads across as much or more. The stiff branches have strong thorns and are thickly covered with rather succulent glossy oval leaves 5 cm long. Male and female flowers are carried on different plants. Both are inconspicuous but, where cross-pollination takes place, the female plant bears orange-yellow fruits which make an acid jelly.
CULTURE. Once established Kei apple stands long periods of drought, drops in temperature to 5 degrees below freezing, hot winds and intense sunshine.

Dryandra   DRYANDRA

DESCRIPTION. There are about fifty species of dryandra to be found growing naturally in Western Australia. Many of them are decorative plants worth a place in gardens where conditions suit them. They are evergreen, generally robust in growth, with unusual leaves and flowers. The leaves are stiff and often saw-edged. The flowers, which generally appear from winter to spring, are useful for arrangements. They are

Dichorisandra flourishes in tropical gardens

Tree Ferns (Cyathea and Dicksonia) which are native to New Zealand and Australia are a handsome addition to the garden

Dombeya has handsome leaves and pretty flowers

Bridal Wreath (Deutzia) bears stems of dainty flowers

Daphne. A charming small plant with sweetly-scented flowers

small but carried in large dense heads surrounded by bracts at the base. Sometimes the bracts are the most attractive part of the inflorescence, and sometimes it is the gleaming styles that make the flowerhead attractive.

CULTURE. Dryandra belong to the protea family and, like other members of this family, they do best in acid soil that drains easily. They do well where summers are dry and the late autumn and winter is wet. They stand moderate frost and intense sunlight, but they are unlikely to thrive in subtropical gardens. Transplant when very small. Cut off dead flowerheads with a length of stem to keep the plants neat and compact.

D. formosa SHOWY DRYANDRA
This is one of the most attractive of the dryandras. It has long slender leaves with saw-toothed edges. The plant grows to 2–3 m and bears handsome gold and yellow flowers in late winter and spring.

D. nobilis GREAT DRYANDRA
A vigorous plant growing to 2–3 m with long, slender leaves deeply cut, and large flowerheads of golden-yellow in late winter and early spring.

D. polycephala
Sends up stems to 2 m and carries masses of flowers of sulphur-yellow in late winter. The very slender leaves are deeply saw-toothed to the midrib.

D. praemorsa
Grows to 3 m and has showy lemon-yellow flowers and holly-like leaves 5–10 cm long with spiny margins. The flowering time is late winter and early spring.

D. speciosa
This species grows to 3 m or more, and has round heads of glossy, yellow to tan styles surrounded by long, slender bracts. It flowers in winter. The narrow leaves 6–10 cm long have smooth margins.

Duranta erecta (D. plumieri)
SKYFLOWER, GOLDEN DEWDROP
DESCRIPTION. A fast-growing evergreen, native to tropical America, which reaches a height of 3 m or more. It is a plant for the large garden rather than the small one as it tends to outgrow its allotted space rather quickly. The soft green oval leaves are attractive. In summer the plant bears dainty sprays of small sky-blue flowers that make a pretty show. There is a form with white flowers, but it is not as pretty. The flowers are followed by clusters of golden berries which festoon the plant from late summer to winter. Clipped, it makes a fairly good hedge for a large property. It is also useful as a stop-gap shrub to be removed when those of slower growth have made some progress. Several specimens planted close together will provide a quick windbreak. 'Variegata' is an ornamental cultivar which has

leaves with white margins. *D. steno-stachya* is not as hardy to cold but has larger flowers.

CULTURE. Duranta is not particular as to soil and situation, growing well in full sunshine and in part shade. It does well in subtropical gardens; it also stands moderate frost and, once established, will grow with little water.

Echium fastuosum

PRIDE OF MADEIRA

DESCRIPTION. This quick-growing plant makes a splendid display towards the end of winter and early in spring, when it bears long showy spikes of flowers. It sends out many curving branches from the base to a height of 1 m and spreads across more than this. The large leaves are somewhat hairy and greyish-green in colour. The individual flowers are quite small but they are carried in spectacular candelabra-like spikes, and are of a beautiful shade of sky-blue or azure. Plant it in full sunshine near the coast and in partial shade in areas where spring is hot and dry. It looks very effective next to a white wall, or when planted near a shrub that has white flowers at the same time, e.g. *Spiraea cantoniensis.*

CULTURE. Pride of Madeira grows in clay, sand or gravelly soil and is so showy that it is surprising that it is not more generally known. It will not stand much frost, and, when grown in gardens where sharp frosts are likely to occur, particularly in August, it should be protected. The plants may die off after two or three years but as new ones develop quickly and old ones become somewhat untidy, it is a good idea to raise new ones every two or three years. It grows readily from seed.

Edgeworthia chrysantha

(E. papyrifera) PAPER BUSH

DESCRIPTION. A deciduous shrub growing to 2 m cultivated in Japan for the making of paper. It has narrow ovate

Dryandra belongs to the protea family and needs well-drained, acid soil. *(Dryandra polycephala)*

The shining orange berries of Duranta make a charming show in autumn

leaves up to 12 cm in length, green on the upper surface and grey on the underside. Before the new spring leaves emerge the plant bears a profusion of round clusters of flowers. They are tubular with a starry face, bright yellow when they open turning paler as they age.

CULTURE. Will stand 10 degrees of frost, but does well only in acid soil rich in humus. It will not thrive in subtropical regions nor where hot winds are common.

Elaeagnus   RUSSIAN OLIVE

DESCRIPTION. These are shrubs for gardens where conditions are difficult. They are large shrubs or small trees useful for making a screen or windbreak to give protection whilst more tender and slow-growing plants are small. The flowers are insignificant and are followed by berries of some ornamental value. Plant them 1 m apart for a windbreak or large informal hedge.

CULTURE. The deciduous species stands very severe frosts; the evergreen one is hardy to frosts of 10 degrees. They grow readily in any soil but to promote really quick growth, prepare holes properly, adding some compost to the soil. Once established they will endure long periods with little water.

E. angustifolia   RUSSIAN OLIVE
A pretty deciduous shrub or small tree to 4 m with small, silvery-green, willow-like leaves, and insignificant flowers followed by edible berries resembling miniature olives. Recommended as a windbreak or screen for areas with a harsh climate.

E. pungens   SILVERBERRY
An evergreen species growing to 4 m or more, with a spreading top. The edges of the dull green leaves are wavy and tinted with rusty dots. This is a wind-resistant plant which will grow at the coast. Cultivars developed from this are more decorative garden plants. 'Maculata' has leaves splashed with yellow in the centre; 'Argenteo-variegata' has leaves edged with silvery-white, and 'Aurea' has a golden margin to the leaves. These provide useful stems for arrangements.

Embothrium   CHILEAN FIRE BUSH

DESCRIPTION. When these plants thrive they make a splendid show, but they are by no means easy to grow. They occur naturally on high plateaux of Chile. *E. coccineum* and *E. coccineum* var. *longifolium* are the best known species, with spectacular scarlet flowers carried close together along the ends of the stems in early spring. *E. coccineum* var. *lanceolatum* has slender leaves and crimson flowers in showy spikes. These are evergreen plants growing to 3 m or more with beautiful glossy leaves.

CULTURE. Chilean Fire Bush stands severe cold. It needs an abundance of moisture, shade and a cool root run in acid soil rich in humus and peat. It will not do well where hot dry winds blow. In gardens where rhododendrons and Japanese maples do well, one can be hopeful of growing embothriums too.

Enkianthus campanulatus
RED-VEIN BELLFLOWER

DESCRIPTION. Is an attractive deciduous shrub from Japan which grows to 2 m or more. It is very slow in growth but is decorative from when quite small. The leaves are oval, about 5 cm in length, arranged in clusters or whorls at the ends of shoots. They turn rich shades of orange and crimson in autumn. The small, dainty, bell-shaped flowers are carried in graceful clusters towards the ends of the stems. They are creamy-white with delicate thread-like veins of red. Other species worth trying are *E. cernuus*, with pure white flowers; *E. cernuus* 'Rubens' with crimson flowers; and *E. perulatus*, which has white flowers. They all have spectacular autumn colours.

CULTURE. These are plants for special places. They require acid, peaty soil and all the conditions which suit rhododendrons. They like cool to cold growing conditions, shade and an abundance of moisture.

Epacris   AUSTRALIAN FUCHSIA
DESCRIPTION. There are thirty species which grow naturally in eastern Australia. They are related to the heaths and resemble them in foliage and flowers. Most species produce their flowers in winter, and some of them

are long-lasting when used in arrangements. The plants are inclined to sprawl or become straggly unless cut back every year or two.

CULTURE. They grow well in acid soil that drains well. In nature, they can be seen flourishing in many situations, including sandy plains and gravelly hillsides. They endure long periods with little water but do best when watered regularly during late autumn and winter. Transplant when very small.

E. impressa
COMMON FUCHSIA HEATH
A shrub growing to 1,5 m in height and spread, seen on hillslopes in south-eastern Australia and Tasmania. The small, sharply pointed leaves, only 1 cm long, are attached to the main stems, standing up at an angle. The tubular white, pink or rose-red flowers, 2–3 cm long, hang down prettily along the ends of stems. *E. impressa grandiflora* is spectacular, with large crimson flowers closely packed together at the ends of the stems. The flowering time of both of these is winter.

E. longiflora   FUCHSIA HEATH
This species grows to a little over 1 m and has slender tubular flowers coloured pink or crimson. They end in five white lobes that make a pretty contrast to the red tube. It is a spring-flowering species but has some flowers at other seasons of the year too.

Eranthemum nervosum
(*E. pulchellum*)   ERANTHEMUM
DESCRIPTION. A pretty little evergreen or semi-evergreen shrub from India which grows to 1 m in height and spread. It has elliptic leaves, tapered towards both ends, sometimes lightly toothed along the margins. The leaves are mid-green in colour and soft in texture. In winter it carries small azure flowers which make a splendid show particularly next to plants with yellow flowers. Plant it in the flower border or towards the front of the shrub border. 'Eldorado' has lilac flowers and paler leaves. There are also cultivars with tinted leaves.

CULTURE. Although it will stand mild frost it does not flower freely where winters are cool, and it is therefore recommended for tropical and sub-tropical gardens. It grows in full sun or part shade.

Erica HEATH OR ERICA

DESCRIPTION. The ericas include about 650 species, 600 of which are native to South Africa, where they occur in a small area along plains and mountain slopes near the coast along the south-western part of the country. This area has a high winter rainfall and very dry summers. Some of these ericas are to be found growing fairly high on the mountains where snow sometimes falls. These would prove the hardiest when grown elsewhere where winters are rigorous.

The flowers of ericas vary considerably in form and size. They may be bell, urn or flask-shaped, globular or tubular. The smallest ones may measure only 2 mm in length, whilst the largest flowers are 2–3 cm long. The flowers differ in texture too. Some are like porcelain, some are waxy, some sticky and some papery. The colours and flowering time of the plants vary according to species, and by planting different species, one can have some in flower almost throughout the year. The leaves of heaths or ericas are all much the same – very small, needle or scale-like, and often densely arranged on the branches. Some species make a fine show in containers. When grown in a small container the ultimate size of the plants will be much smaller than those grown in the open ground, but they flower well in pots. The small-growing species are excellent plants for a rock garden. Ericas or heaths are decorative in the garden, and they also produce charming flowers for large and small arrangements. Generally it is advisable to grow them in beds by themselves so that they can be given the kind of conditions which suit them.

CULTURE. With a few exceptions it can be taken that ericas do well only in acid soil with free drainage. In their native haunts they are generally found in sandy and gravelly soils, acid in nature. When preparing ground for them fork in plenty of acid compost and some peat. Where the soil is not acid a dusting of sulphur or aluminium sulphate over the soil once a month will help to neutralize alkalinity. Ordinary garden fertilizer and animal manure should not be applied to the soil. Established plants can endure fairly long periods with little water, but it is advisable to water them regularly from late autumn to summer. Faded flowers should be cut off to keep the plants neat and compact. Some species will stand sharp frost. They do best in a temperate climate. In hot gardens inland plant them in partial shade.

E. ampullacea
BOTTLE HEATH, CHINA HEATH
Has charming ivory to pale pink flowers carried in fours. They are flask-shaped with a starry face and look like delicate pieces of china. The plants are 60 cm high. This species flowers in spring and early summer.

E. aristata
A delightful plant in the garden and to provide material for arrangements. In spring and autumn it has slender scintillating flowers of ivory shaded pink and deep rose.

E. baccans BERRY HEATH
A vigorous species which grows quickly to 1–2 m. In late winter and early spring it becomes a foamy mass of tiny globular flowers of cyclamen-pink. It is tolerant of hot dry conditions.

E. bauera BRIDAL HEATH
This species is a captivating sight when in full flower. The flowers are tubular, closely crowded at the ends of the stems and of translucent white, palest pink and rose. They are lovely in arrangements. The main flowering time is late winter and early spring. The plant grows to 1 m.

E. blandfordia
A gay erica which grows to 1 m in height and carries numerous canary-yellow flowers closely arranged along the ends of the stems. It is at its best in spring.

E. blenna LANTERN HEATH
This species is particularly attractive as a pot plant. It has large, glossy, urn-shaped flowers of a beautiful waxy golden-orange with green at the tips. The plant grows to 60 cm and flowers in spring.

E. canaliculata PURPLE HEATH
Recommended only for the large heath garden as it grows to 2 m. It becomes smothered with tiny flowers of purple to mauve from late autumn to spring. This is one of the easiest heaths to grow. It will stand severe frost and also dry conditions.

E. carnea MOUNTAIN HEATH
A species from Central Europe, hardy to severe frost; in fact, it does best in cool regions. It grows to 30 cm and has pink or rose flowers in winter. There are several named cultivars of this one. 'Aurea' has golden foliage in spring and summer. They will grow in slightly alkaline soil.

E. cerinthoides
RED HAIRY ERICA, FIRE HEATH
This species grows wild in many parts of South Africa and is more tolerant of cold than many other species. It is one of the most striking of all the ericas with clusters of tubular coral-red flowers covered with silky hairs. The main flowering period is winter and early spring. The plant may grow to 1 m, but should be cut back hard to keep it neat and to encourage good flowering.

E. cinerea TWISTED OR BELL HEATH
A fine small heath from Europe with tiny white flowers of bell-like form arranged in dainty sprays. The colours of the species and hybrids are white, mauve, purple, pink and ruby. It endures extremes of cold. The flowering time is summer. There are numerous cultivars. 'Golden Hue' with yellow leaves is a very fine one.

E. cruenta RED HEATH
This showy heath grows to 1 m and bears tubular brick-red flowers in tiered clusters. The main flowering time is summer and autumn. Trim it lightly after flowering to keep it neat.

E. curviflora
AMBER HEATH, WATER HEATH
Reaches a height of 1 m or more, and has slender tubes of orange, brick-red or salmon-yellow. It likes moist growing conditions.

E. erigena BISCAY HEATH
A tall species from western Europe that reaches a height of 2 m or more if not trimmed each year. In late winter

In all countries of the world and since the first gardens were made in Roman times the shaping and trimming of trees and shrubs has been practised to ornament the garden

and early spring it bears rose-pink flowers. It will grow in slightly alkaline soil. Cultivars with flowers of different shades are available.

E. eugenea
A charming heath which grows to only about 60 cm in height. It has leaves that stand out at an angle from the stem. The urn-shaped corolla is about 12 mm long with reflexed segments at the end. It is generally pale pink and is partially covered by an overskirt formed by the pink calyx. This dainty species is one of the prettiest of the ericas. It stands sharp frost.

E. fascicularis TIGERHOEK HEATH
This delightful erica grows to 1 m and is a slender plant with whorls of tubular flowers towards the end of the stems. The flowers glisten and are prettily coloured, pink with green at the tip. The flowering time is autumn and winter.

E. glandulosa SPOTTED HEATH
An attractive winter-flowering species with slender tubular flowers of a pleasing apricot colour. The plant is sticky and covered with hairs. Height 60 cm.

E. glauca
CUP AND SAUCER HEATH, PETTICOAT HEATH
The common name has been given because the calyx looks like a flounced petticoat half covering the urn-shaped corolla. The calyx and corolla are subtle shades of plum colour. The plant grows to 1 m and flowers in spring. It makes a lovely potplant.

E. glauca var. elegans PETTICOAT HEATH
Has beautiful drooping flowers made up of tiered flounces of alabaster, palest pink and rose. The flowering time is mainly late winter and early spring.

E. grandiflora LARGE ORANGE HEATH
A robust and handsome plant growing to 1,5 m. Trim after its flowering period to keep it neat. The leaves are somewhat like those of a pine, but shorter. In summer tubular flowers of glowing orange appear clustered along the ends of stems.

E. grisbrookii
Bears dainty ivory-white urn-shaped flowers along the top part of the stems. The plant grows to 60 cm and flowers in winter.

E. holosericea SMALL FLOUNCED HEATH
A spring-flowering species growing to 1 m, with long sprays of fascinating flowers with a corolla of cyclamen-mauve and a pinky-mauve calyx like an overskirt partially covering it. This is a fine species for the rock garden or for growing in a pot.

E. inflata
Grows to 1 m and has fat, urn-shaped flowers of bright coral-pink to cerise in clusters at the ends of stems. The flowering time is summer. A good species for growing in a container.

E. irregularis
Is one of the few species that grows naturally in an area where the soil is alkaline. It reaches a height of 1 m and has masses of tiny, pale-pink urn-shaped flowers thickly clustered along the top parts of the stems. The flowers appear in winter and early spring.

E. lanipes
A very attractive spring-flowering species which has slender stems of urn-shaped flowers of a charming shade of pink or mauve. It is splendid for small arrangements in spring.

E. macowanii
Grows to 1 m with flowers clustered along the ends of stems, forming a loose spike. They are tubular in form and prettily coloured rose or purplish-red at the base and yellow at the tip. It flowers in spring and summer.

E. mammosa RED SIGNAL HEATH
A delightful heath that reaches 1 m in height and stands dry growing conditions better than many other species. Clusters of tubular flowers droop down daintily from the top part of the stems. The most common colour is a rich and striking shade of crimson, but there are other colour forms too – orange, pink, cyclamen, green, cream and white. The main flowering time is late winter and early spring. It stands severe frosts.

Berry Heath *(Erica baccans)* as a background to the South African Rain Daisy *(Dimorphotheca pluvialis)*

Bridal Heath *(Erica bauera)* bears captivating flowers in early spring

Lantern Heath *(Erica blenna)*. An appealing species for pot-culture or the garden

E. multiflora
A European species growing 1 m or more, with masses of small lilac to pink, bell-shaped flowers in spring. Hybrids with white and rose flowers have been originated. It is hardy to severe frost.

E. oatesii WINTER GEM
A decorative and quick-growing species that does well in containers and in the garden. It bears glossy, tubular, coral-red flowers in winter on plants 1 m tall. Is hardy to severe frost.

E. patersonia YELLOW MEALIE HEATH
This is a striking flower for small or large winter arrangements. The plant produces spikes of tubular, canary-yellow flowers on stems 60 cm tall. The name 'mealie' describes the regular arrangement of flowers up the stem, as neatly as corn on the cob.

E. perspicua PRINCE OF WALES HEATH
A spring-flowering species with very attractive plumes of glossy, tubular flowers, coloured cyclamen at the base with a white edging to the top of the tube. It grows to 1 m or more in height.

E. peziza VELVET BELL HEATH
Is a robust species growing to 2 m with clouds of minute velvety white, bell-like flowers with a faint scent of honey. It is a charming sight in late winter and early spring.

E. pinea YELLOW SUMMER HEATH
Reaches 1 m or more in height and has curved yellow tubular flowers in small clusters at the ends of the stems. The leaves are like pine needles 1 cm long. The flowering time is spring.

E. quadrangularis PINK SHOWER HEATH
A delightful heath which produces frothy masses of minute bell-shaped flowers of palest blush-pink, white or rose, on plants 60 cm tall. The flowering time is spring.

E. regia var. **variegata** ROYAL HEATH
One of the most beautiful of the many lovely South African heaths. The plant grows to 1 m and has gleaming tubular flowers with recurved lobes. They are gloriously coloured, shining white with scarlet or crimson. The main flowering time is late winter and spring.

E. sessiliflora GREEN HEATH
Decorative in the garden, as a container plant and in arrangements. This plant is deserving of a place in the garden because of the subtle ice-green colour of its flowers. They are tubular in form and carried in clusters at the ends of stems. In time the plant may grow to 1 m or more, but it can be kept back to smaller size by annual trimming after the flowering period, which is autumn and winter. It likes moist conditions.

E. taxifolia DOUBLE PINK HEATH
A summer-flowering species with little urn-shaped flowers of blush-pink with a touch of rose. It grows to 60 cm and endures long periods with little water. It is a pretty potplant as well as being decorative in the garden.

E. thunbergii MALAY HEATH
Is a charming plant for the garden or pots. It grows to 30 cm or a little more, and has tiny bowl-shaped flowers on drooping stems. The combination of colour in the flowers is unusual and striking; the corolla is bright orange and the sepals are lime-green. It flowers in spring.

E. tumida
This species endures considerable frost. The plants grow to 1 m but may become much taller if not cut back. Trimming is necessary to keep them neat and compact in form. In summer they carry pendant tubular flowers of a rich coral-red to crimson.

E. vagans CORNISH HEATH
A European species growing to 60 cm with tiny, bell-shaped flowers in spikes at the ends of stems. It flowers in summer and autumn. This species has mauve to purple flowers, but cultivars developed from it vary in colour from white to pink and deep cyclamen. It stands severe frost.

E. ventricosa WAX HEATH
Has lovely flask-shaped flowers rather broad at the base and very narrow at the throat, ending in a starry face of four lobes. They are waxy in texture and of the most delightful shade of palest pink with suffusions of rose. They are carried in dense clusters in summer. The plant grows to about 1 m in height and almost as much in spread.

There are some beautiful hybrids of this species with flowers of white, crimson and rose.

E. versicolor RAINBOW HEATH
This decorative heath grows to 1 m or more and has leaves in threes. The flowers are slender, curved, red or rose-coloured tubes tipped with lime-green. It starts flowering in summer and continues into autumn.

E. vestita WIDE-MOUTH HEATH
A good-looking plant that reaches a height of 1 m and bears very attractive tubular flowers. They are generally a rich tomato or coral-red but may be white or pink. The leaves are more attractive than in most ericas. They are pine-like and 2–3 cm long. The main flowering time is spring, but it bears some flowers at other seasons too.

E. walkeria WALKER'S HEATH
This delightful species grows to 60 cm and has densely packed conical spikes of very pretty flowers. They are of the loveliest shades of pale rose-pink, and make a fine show in a pot, in the garden and in arrangements. The flowering time is spring.

Eriocephalus africanus
WHITE WOOLLY-HEAD
DESCRIPTION. An unusual evergreen South African plant with foliage very like that of an erica — short and spiky and carried closely attached to the stems. It is of a dove-grey colour that makes a pleasing contrast to green foliage. In winter the plant bears tiny white starry flowers only about 8 mm across. When they fade, it becomes wreathed with what appears to be shining cottonwool. This is the fluffy covering of the seeds and it makes a pretty display. The stems are long-lasting and particularly suitable for dry arrangements. The plant grows to 60 cm in height and spread and is a good one for a rock garden. Cut the plants back fairly hard in late spring to keep them compact and to encourage good new growth. It does well in coastal gardens.
CULTURE. Grows well in poor soil, sand, gravel or clay. Can stand long periods with little water but should have regular moisture in late autumn

and winter to encourage flowers to develop. Stands mild to moderate frost.

Eriostemon myoporoides
LONG-LEAFED WAXFLOWER

DESCRIPTION. There are about thirty species of eriostemon native to Australia. The species described here is one of the most ornamental, growing to 1 m or more. It has slender leaves tapering sharply to the end. They are grey-green in colour and covered with tiny pellucid spots. The leaves when crushed give off an aromatic smell. The dainty flowers are carried in profusion. They are pink to rose in the bud, and open to show ivory or white starry faces with five slender petals. The main flowering period is winter and early spring. Some of the cultivars are more decorative than the species. 'Clearview Apple-blossom' has crimson buds opening to white, semi-double flowers; 'Clearview Bouquet' has pink buds and white flowers; 'Mountain Giant' is a robust one growing to 3 m with clusters of large white flowers. *E. australasius*, *E. verrucosus* (Fairy Waxflower) and *E. spicatus* (Spiked Waxflower) are other pretty species which can be found growing wild in Australia. They all have pink flowers in spring.
CULTURE. They grow in gravelly or sandy soil or clay, but prefer acid or peaty soil that is loose in texture. They should be watered in winter. The plants stand moderate frost. As they tend to become straggly with age, they should be trimmed back after flowering in late spring.

Ervatamia divaricata
(Tabernaemontana coronaria)
CREPE JASMINE

DESCRIPTION. An evergreen shrub from India that grows to a height of 2 m or more and has slender oval, pointed, glossy leaves 7–10 cm long. In late summer and early autumn it carries small clusters of waxy, ivory flowers. Each tubular flower ends in a starry face of five lobes.
CULTURE. A plant for the tropical and subtropical garden. It likes plenty of moisture throughout the year and will not do well if subjected to long periods of hot drying wind.

Erythrina CORAL BUSH
DESCRIPTION. Most erythrinas are tree-like in form but there are three very pretty ones suitable for the shrub garden. Two of them are native to South Africa. The flowers are carried in tight clusters or spikes. The individual flowers are keel-shaped and coloured tomato-red to crimson or scarlet, sometimes marked with yellow. The leaves are broad and the plants have small thorns.
CULTURE. The species described stand moderate frost, and once established, they endure long periods with little water. They like an abundance of hot sunshine and are not suitable for shady, damp gardens.

E. acanthocarpa TAMBOEKIE THORN
A deciduous South African plant which grows to 3 m, and is upright in habit. The leaves are arranged in threes with thorns on stems and leaves. In spring it bears large heads of spectacular flowers. Each one opens from a keel coloured deep crimson tipped with lime-green. Plant it in full sunshine, and, where frosts are severe, set it out near a wall which will reflect heat in winter. The flowering time is late winter and early spring.

E. blakeii BLAKE'S CORAL BUSH
Is thought to be a hybrid developed from *E. cristagalli*. It grows to 2 m or more, and in spring carries long spikes of flowers of a deep rich crimson hue. If cut down to the ground by cold it generally comes up again, but does best in hot sunny gardens.

E. humeana
DWARF CORAL TREE, DWARF KAFFIRBOOM
This species has long spikes of handsome scarlet flowers in summer. It will stand sharp frost but does not do well in cool misty areas. It is a deciduous plant and grows to 2–3 m. The leaves are divided into three broad leaflets with prickles on the underside.

Escallonia ESCALLONIA
DESCRIPTION. Escallonias are ornamental evergreen plants native to the cooler parts of South America, and one of the best of the evergreens that stand sharp frost. They vary in size but most species planted in gardens grow to 2–3 m.

Because of their neat dark-green glossy leaves, they were at one time popular as screen plants, but they are apt to grow too large for the garden of moderate size. They can, however, be trimmed back to keep them within bounds. Where space is not a limiting factor, they are well worth growing. The stems of leaves are decorative in arrangements and the flowers last for some days when picked. Some of the cultivars are smaller in growth than the species and some have pretty flowers. They flower from mid-spring to summer. The cultivar 'Apple Blossom', which grows to 1 m, is probably the most popular as an individual shrub. Other cultivars worth growing are 'C.F. Ball' with crimson flowers; 'Donard Brilliance' with rose-red flowers; 'Ingramii' with red flowers, and 'Iveyi', which has highly lustrous leaves and large clusters of white flowers.
CULTURE. Once established the cultivars will tolerate severe frost and fairly long periods of dryness too. They stand strong winds and do well in cool coastal gardens. They grow in almost any soil – acid or slightly alkaline.

E. bifida WHITE ESCALLONIA
A tall species which may be trained to form a small tree, or be planted to create a tall hedge or windbreak. It grows to 6 m if not trimmed. The dark-green finely-serrated glossy leaves are 6–10 cm long, and in summer and autumn it has large clusters of snow-white flowers. This species, which is native to Brazil, may be cut back by sharp frosts. It is also referred to as *E. montevidensis*.

E. langleyensis
Is semi-evergreen in cold areas and evergreen where winters are mild. It grows to 3 m and has long slender, arching stems of small glossy leaves. In summer it bears clusters of carmine flowers.

E. macrantha COMMON ESCALLONIA
A fairly quick-growing evergreen shrub with dark green, glossy leaves 3–10 cm long. The rose-pink flowers that appear in summer are pretty but not showy. The plant is worth growing for its attractive foliage. It makes a good dense screen or hedge 2–3 m tall.

Erica regia (Royal Heath) is a fine one for pots or the garden

Erica vestita looks delightful in arrangements and in the garden

Plant Walker's Heath *(Erica walkeria)* at the front of a rock garden or in containers

Euonymus SPINDLEBERRY

DESCRIPTION. Evergreen or deciduous plants, some of which are shrubby in habit and some of which reach tree size. They are grown for their form, foliage or berries, not for their flowers. Where berries are required several specimens should be planted to ensure cross-pollination and good fruiting. There are handsome cultivars with coloured or variegated leaves.

CULTURE. These plants are hardy to severe cold and, once established, they will survive fairly long periods with little water. They grow in alkaline or acid soil.

E. alatus WINGED SPINDLEBERRY

A deciduous species growing slowly to 2 m or a little more, with a spread of as much. It has attractive narrow dark green, finely-toothed leaves that become beautiful shades of red in autumn. The berries are purple.

E. europaeus COMMON SPINDLEBERRY

Is a deciduous shrub or small tree growing to 6 m with narrow, glossy, dark-green leaves with neat serrations along the margins. Where autumn is cold the leaves turn pretty colours before falling. The berries are rose to red. This species does not thrive in hot dry regions.

Erica taxifolia bears its charming little flowers during the summer

The unusual White Woolly-head *(Eriocephalus africanus)* produces stems that last well in dry arrangements

The Common Escallonia *(Escallonia macrantha)* is a fine evergreen shrub for cold gardens

There are many pretty forms of *Euonymus japonicus*. 'Aureo-marginatus' is one of the most decorative

The Spray Poinsettia *(Euphorbia leucocephala)* is decorative during the winter months

E. fortunei (E. radicans)

An evergreen plant of almost prostrate growth that climbs by means of rootlets or spreads across the ground making a ground cover. It has dark-green leaves with serrated edges and grows in sun or shade. Cultivars developed from this species are more suitable for gardens as they have variegated leaves and are less invasive. 'Coloratus' grows to 1 m and has leaves that turn purple in autumn and winter; 'Emerald Gaiety', 'Emerald Gold' and 'Variegatus' are low in habit, with leaves marked with white or cream. They make a good ground cover and are effective when grown on a wall or in a hanging basket.

E. japonicus JAPANESE LAUREL, EVERGREEN SPINDLEBERRY

This is a decorative evergreen species which tolerates a wide range of growing conditions. It is hardy to frost and does well in areas which are windy and in coastal gardens. The plant grows to 2–3 m and is rounded in form. The leaves are dark-green, oval, shiny and leathery and have neatly serrated margins. In winter it has red berries that split into two halves revealing bright orange seeds. It makes a useful screen plant in cool coastal gardens. Ornamental strains of this species have variegated leaves and are smaller in size. 'Aureo-marginatus' has dark green leaves with yellow margins; 'Aureo-variegatus' has leaves blotched with yellow in the middle; 'Macrophyllus Albus' has leaves with white margins; 'Flavescens' is a dwarf form with leaves margined with yellow.

Eupatorium sordidum

(E. ianthinum) GIANT AGERATUM
DESCRIPTION. A soft-wooded, evergreen shrub that grows very quickly. It has large leaves measuring up to 24 cm in length and 12 cm across. They are velvety on the surface and have well-defined projecting veins on the underside. In early spring it becomes covered with huge clusters of pretty mauve flowers, very like those of the small ageratum in form and colour. They make an impressive show particularly when near a plant that has yellow flowers at the same time. This is an excellent plant to use as a stop-gap whilst slow-growing shrubs are developing, as it will reach a height and spread of 1 m in a year. Where space is limited it should be cut back hard after it has finished flowering in spring.

CULTURE. It is tender to frost. Where frosts are not prolonged, it will often grow up quickly again even when cut down to ground level. Plant it in full sunshine at the coast and in partial shade in hot inland gardens.

Euphorbia POINSETTIA AND OTHERS

DESCRIPTION. Some very decorative plants are included under this genus name. Some are shrubs whilst others are annuals, perennials or succulents. Those described here are of a shrubby nature. The stems of most of them exude a milky sap when cut. Care should be taken as this can irritate the skin and cause pain if it gets into the eyes. In some species it is poisonous. What is referred to as the 'flower' is really an arrangement of bracts, which in many species is very conspicuous.
CULTURE. With the exception of E. venata the species described do best where winters are not very cold. They like an abundance of sunshine and stand dry growing conditions.

E. leucocephala SPRAY POINSETTIA

A quick-growing plant to 3 m, with small ovate leaves that give the plant a graceful appearance for most months of the year. In late autumn and winter it is particularly showy when the leaves fall and it becomes a frothy mass of dainty ivory-white bracts that make an enchanting show for several weeks. Stands moderate frost and dryness but it is not suitable for damp shady gardens. Recommended for the garden and for pot culture.

E. milii (E. splendens)
CROWN OF THORNS

Is a rock garden plant that flowers on and off throughout the year. It has crooked stems with long strong thorns and few leaves. The leaves are carried at the ends of the stems just below the clusters of flowers that consist of bright scarlet bracts carried in pairs. Cultivars with yellow and pink bracts are also available. Recommended for hot, dry gardens and subtropical ones; it stands moderate frost.

E. pulcherrima POINSETTIA

This evergreen or deciduous plant, native to Mexico, grows into a leggy shrub 3 m tall. The tiny yellow flowers in the centre are inconspicuous but the large scarlet bracts make a splendid show in winter. The best known form has a single layer of bracts but very handsome double ones are now grown, and also cultivars with white, yellow or pink bracts. Poinsettia thrives in hot dry places and in subtropical gardens. Where sharp frost may be experienced, plant it against a wall which reflects heat. It is a quick-growing plant. Because of its legginess it should be planted behind other shrubs that will hide the long bare stems.

E. venata (E. wulfenii) SPURGE

A pretty plant of shrubby form growing to 1 m in height and spread. It is an evergreen with masses of slender, grey-green leaves and rounded flower-heads of lime-green bracts which make an effective show in winter. They look pretty in the garden and in arrangements. This species tolerates a wide range of conditions. It does well in cool areas and stands severe frost, but it will also grow in hot dry gardens and in partial shade.

Euryops Euryops

DESCRIPTION. Quick-growing evergreen shrubs many of which are native to South Africa. Some of them are inclined to become leggy and some remain fairly compact. Most species used in the garden have decorative foliage and bright yellow daisy flowers that are ornamental in late winter and early spring. They grow very easily and deserve to be more widely planted.
CULTURE. Some species endure severe frost. They seem to do best in soil which drains readily and grow well in sandy or gravelly soils, in coastal gardens as well as those inland. They like an abundance of sunshine and regular watering from late autumn to spring when they flower. Trim in late spring or summer to keep them neat and compact in form.

E. abrotanifolius

Reaches a height of 2 m and has finely divided leaves massed at the tops of the stems. In spring its large yellow daisies stand well above the leaves.

E. acraeus   MOUNTAIN DAISY

Grows on mountain slopes in South Africa and stands considerable cold. A charming small plant that earned an Award of Merit in England. It grows to 1 m and has small silver leaves and bright yellow daisies in early summer. It is hardy to severe frost.

E. pectinatus

Is one of the prettiest species growing to 1 m and forming a rounded shrub with attractive fern-like, pearl-grey foliage. It is decorative when not in flower, and very showy in late winter and early spring when it becomes covered with neat yellow daisies.

E. speciosissimus *(E. athanasiae)*
RESIN BUSH

A tall species reaching 1,5 m in height, with leaves gracefully divided into needle-like segments and large bright yellow daisies in handsome array.

E. tenuissimus

A quick-growing plant to 60 cm with thin soft, needle-like leaves and tiny yellow daisies in winter. Cut it back hard after its flowering period is over.

E. virgineus   HONEY DAISY

Is a pretty little rounded shrub to 1 m or more, with tiny flowers carried in such masses that in winter, when it is in full flower, the foliage is almost completely hidden from view. The flowers have a honey-like scent that attracts bees from far and wide. It tolerates sharp frost.

Eutaxia obovata   EUTAXIA

DESCRIPTION. An evergreen Australian shrub growing to about 1 m, with numerous twigs covered with very small leaves. In spring the ends of the stems bear masses of small pea-shaped flowers that show up well because of their colouring. The keel of the flower is orange and the top segments are yellow. *E. microphylla* is another species worth growing. Being small it is well suited to a rock garden.
CULTURE. Plant them in soil that drains readily and in full sunshine. Once established they stand quite considerable frost and long periods with little water.

Exochorda racemosa
PEARL BUSH

DESCRIPTION. A deciduous shrub from China which grows to 2–3 m but can be kept smaller by annual trimming in late spring or summer. It has oval leaves and bears white flowers in spring. Before the flowers open, the buds appear to be strung along the stems like a row of pearls – hence the common name. The open flowers are decorative – almost like the blossoms of a fruit tree. They are effective in arrangements as well as in the garden.
CULTURE. It grows in regions that have severe frost and is not recommended for subtropical or very dry areas. Plant it in acid soil in light shade.

Fabiana imbricata
MOCK HEATH, CHILE HEATH

DESCRIPTION. This is not really a heath as its common name suggests. It is a member of the potato family, but it is very similar to a heath in growth and foliage. The plant reaches a height and spread of 2 m or a little more, and has tiny wedge-shaped leaves and slender tubular white flowers with reflexed segments at the mouth. The cultivar 'Violacea' has mauve to lilac flowers. The flowering time is summer.
CULTURE. It grows in regions that experience severe frost but does not do well in hot dry regions or subtropical gardens.

Fatsia japonica   *(Aralia sieboldii)*
JAPANESE ARALIA

DESCRIPTION. A Japanese plant worth growing because of its ornamental foliage. The leaves are large, dark green, glossy and deeply cut, giving them a fan-like appearance. They may measure as much as 40 cm across. The plant, which is evergreen, grows to 3 m in the open ground but may remain smaller when grown in a container.
This is a good plant for a shady patio or terrace. It also looks effective when grown indoors, but it may be planted in the garden under trees which will protect the leaves from bright sunlight. There is a form with variegated leaves.
CULTURE. Plant it in soil rich in humus and water well and regularly throughout the year to encourage growth of the stems and leaves. It stands moderate frosts. In cool coastal gardens it will not be damaged by sunshine but inland, where the sun is bright, it should be planted in the shade.

Felicia amelloides   *(F. aethiopica)*
FELICIA, BLUE DAISY, AGATHEA

DESCRIPTION. Shrubs with pure blue flowers are rare, and this South African plant with pretty blue flowers is a valuable addition to gardens large and small. It grows to only 30 cm in height and forms a spreading mound of charming small, daisy-like flowers of clear sky-blue. If the flowers are sheared off in early summer when they fade, the plant will produce another mass of flowers before the weather turns cool in autumn. The flowers which measure about 3 cm across are carried well above the foliage and make a sparkling show. Grow it in the flower border, in the rock garden, in hanging baskets or in the front row of the shrub border. It does well in coastal gardens.
CULTURE. It thrives in sandy soils and in clay, likes an abundance of sunshine and tolerates mild frost. Once established it will stand three or four months of dry growing conditions.

Forsythia   FORSYTHIA, GOLDEN BELL

DESCRIPTION. Deciduous shrubs that make a splendid show in late winter and early spring when the leafless branches become covered with yellow flowers. The flowering stems are fine for arrangements. Soft, oval pointed leaves appear in tufts at the ends of stems as the flowers fade. To keep plants neat and to encourage good flowering cut out a few of the older branches at ground-level when necessary. The most popular species are *F. intermedia*, *F. suspensa* and *F. viridissima*, but there are now named cultivars of great merit. The species grow to 2 m or more, but some of the cultivars are only 1 m in height and spread. 'Arnold Giant', 'Beatrix Farrand' and 'Lynwood Gold' are the names of three exceptional cultivars.

Crown of Thorns (*Euphorbia milii*) does well in hot, dry gardens

Poinsettia (*Euphorbia pulcherrima*) yields showy flowers

Forsythia likes cold growing conditions

CULTURE. These are plants for cold gardens. They enjoy damp and snowy conditions and do not flower well in regions which do not have frost. They are not particular as to soil but should be watered well throughout the year, especially in winter.

Fortunella japonica

(*Citrus japonica*) ROUND KUMQUAT
DESCRIPTION. A decorative evergreen Japanese plant grown as a shrub or grafted as a standard. It is effective in the garden and when grown in a large container. This near-relation of the orange has pretty, dark-green leaves with a slight gloss and ornamental fruits like a miniature orange, 3–4 cm in diameter. The plants grow to 2 m in height. The fruit makes a delicious preserve. A form 'Variegata' has leaves and fruit striped with cream. *F. margarita* (Oval or Nagami Kumquat), which comes from China, has fragrant white flowers followed by small orange fruits that are tasty in marmalade and preserves.
CULTURE. Kumquats will grow in regions with frosty winters but they are unlikely to flower and fruit well in a cold garden. They do best where winters are mild and the air warm and humid.

Fuchsia FUCHSIA

DESCRIPTION. These delightful and colourful plants have been popular for generations, not only in the garden but as pot plants for the house, terrace or patio. It is not surprising therefore that each year sees the introduction of new cultivars.

Fuchsias vary in their habit of growth. Some are dainty, trailing plants suitable for hanging baskets and small pots on walls; some are shrubby in habit growing to 1 m or more in height and spread, whilst others are tall and can be trained as standards or to decorate a trellis. The shapes of the flowers vary, too. Some are tubular, others have a funnel-shaped or bowl-shaped corolla; some are single and others are double. Some are only 1 cm long whilst others measure up to 6 cm in length.

The colour variations are many. The sepals, i.e. the top parts that are usually turned back or reflexed, are white, red or pink, but the corolla may be white, pink, rose, red, mauve, violet, apricot or tangerine.

These are delightful plants to grow in a woodland garden to produce colour from late spring right through to autumn.
CULTURE. Fuchsias grow very well, quickly and easily if given just a little attention. They like soil rich in humus and do best in dappled shade. Dense shade will limit their flowering and strong sunlight and dry winds will damage the plants. They like to be kept moist throughout their flowering period, and, in areas where the air is dry, it is advisable to put a thick mulch of straw over the ground and to water

them as often as possible from above, as moisture on the leaves and in the air encourages good flowering. Fertilize plants in mid-summer, if necessary, using a general garden fertilizer, applying it in very small quantities. If they are planted in good compost in the garden no fertilizing should be required.

Frequently fuchsias tend to grow too quickly and it is advisable therefore to pinch out the growing tip occasionally during the flowering season. This will force the development of basal side stems and so prevent the plant from becoming too tall and leggy. Generally they need to be trimmed back fairly hard in spring, cutting back most of the previous year's growth. This will ensure a compact and free-flowering plant. In areas that have severe frost, the frost may kill much of the previous year's growth. In this case merely tidy up the plants. They will grow out quickly and vigorously again in spring and flower by summer.

Galphimia glauca

(*Thryallis glauca*)
GOLD SHOWER, THRYALLIS
DESCRIPTION. A small evergreen shrub native to warm regions of Central America. It has a height and spread of 1 m or a little more. The ovate leaves are grey-green on the underside and have a single tooth on each side near the base. In summer it carries sulphur-yellow flowers in clusters at the ends of

Fuchsias are appealing plants for shady places

stems. It is a pleasing little shrub for the front of a shrub border or as a background in a flower border. CULTURE. Is suitable only for warm coastal gardens or inland where winters are mild. Water well during dry periods of the year.

Gardenia GARDENIA

DESCRIPTION. Evergreen small and large shrubs varying in height from 1–3 m, with attractive foliage that is highly or slightly glossy. Their white, sweetly-scented flowers have made them popular garden subjects for many generations. The flowers are pretty in arrangements.

CULTURE. Gardenias can be grown under a wide range of climatic conditions but they are rather particular as to soil. They like acid soil which drains readily. Prepare fairly large holes with plenty of acid compost and peat. In areas where the water is alkaline, sprinkle a tablespoonful of aluminium sulphate, sulphur, iron sulphate or iron chelates on the soil around them once a month to neutralize the effect of the water. Yellowing of the leaves is often a sign that the soil is not sufficiently acid and that such medication is required. Near the coast they grow

Honey Daisy *(Euryops virigineus)*. A quick-growing shrub for hot, dry gardens which have moderate frost

A Fuchsia hybrid of fine form and colour

well in full sun but where the sunlight is intense it is advisable to plant them in partial shade. They endure moderate frost once they are established, but they undoubtedly do best in warm moist gardens, not subjected to long periods of hot dry winds.

G. jasminoides *(G. florida)*
DOUBLE WHITE GARDENIA
Is a charming shrub native to China that does well in tropical and temperate gardens and in pots in a sheltered position. It grows to 1,5 m and has dark-green glossy leaves, decorative throughout the year. The white scented flowers that appear in summer are 5 cm across. There are forms with single or double flowers. Cultivars known as 'Florida', 'Magnifica', 'Mystery', 'Professor Pucci' and 'Veitchii Improved' are highly ornamental plants. 'Radicans', a low-growing form reaching a height of only 30 cm, is pretty in a rock garden or pot.

G. thunbergia WILD GARDENIA
A slow-growing South African plant that does best in warm coastal gardens, but it tolerates some frost. It reaches a height of 3 m when mature, and bears handsome highly-scented flowers in summer. Each flower consists of a long tube which, in the bud-stage, looks like a neatly furled umbrella. The bud opens to a beautiful waxy, starry face, and when the flowers fade they give place to oval grey fruits the size of small apples. This species is more tolerant of alkaline soil than the Chinese ones.

Garrya elliptica
CATKIN OR SILK TASSEL BUSH
DESCRIPTION. Where conditions suit it this plant will grow to 3 m, but it generally remains smaller than this. It is an evergreen with oval leaves with waxy margins, dark green on the upper surface and grey on the underside. The flowers are carried in pendant catkins. The male catkins are long and slender and the female ones rather short and not as attractive. For this reason nurseries propagate only plants with male flowers. They are greenish-yellow and appear in winter.
CULTURE. This plant does best in cool gardens. Where hot drying winds pre-

vail, plant it in partial shade and water it abundantly throughout the year.

Genista BROOM
DESCRIPTION. A genus of large and small shrubs, some of which are well worth planting, particularly in regions where difficult conditions limit the variety of plants which can be grown. The brooms are almost leafless plants, but they are nevertheless of perennial interest because of the succulent greenness of their stems. The flowers are shaped like a sweet-pea and usually yellow in colour.
CULTURE. These are admirable plants for hot dry gardens subject to sharp frosts. They are also tolerant of a wide variety of soils — sand, gravel or clay, and they do well in slightly alkaline or acid soil. They should be pruned back after their flowering period is over.

G. aetnensis MOUNT ETNA BROOM
This species is a good plant for gardens where aridity and frost inhibit the growth of many other shrubs. Its almost leafless stems have a fresh appearance throughout the year. It grows to 4 m and has slender arching and drooping stems which become covered with small yellow, pea-shaped flowers in late winter and early spring.

G. hispanica SPANISH GORSE
A hardy small shrub growing to 1 m or more, with spiny stems and a sparse covering of tiny leaves only 1 cm long. In mid-spring it carries golden-yellow flowers all along the stems. After flowering is over cut the shrub back hard to keep it compact. This is a better species for the small garden than the others which tend to grow too large.

G. monosperma BRIDAL WREATH BROOM
A decorative robust plant for the large garden. It grows to 4 m, but it should be trimmed back annually after flowering, to keep it to half this size and to encourage fresh new growth. In spring it becomes covered with a foaming mass of tiny white fragrant flowers on slender, arching stems.

G. pilosa
A prostrate-growing species which makes a good ground cover in difficult places. It grows to a height of 30 cm and has stems that tend to root where

they touch the ground. The yellow flowers make a splash of colour late in spring.

G. tinctoria
A hardy erect shrub to 1 m which bears an abundance of bright golden-yellow flowers in mid- to late spring. 'Royal Gold' is a splendid small cultivar, and 'Humifusa' is a prostrate one that makes a gay ground cover for a dry bank.

Gordonia axillaris GORDONIA
DESCRIPTION. A large winter-flowering evergreen plant that may attain a height and spread of 3 m or more. It can, however, be trimmed to keep it to smaller size. Where conditions are not to its liking it will probably not grow to more than half of this. The lustrous oblong, dark-green leaves, 10–15 cm in length, make it an attractive plant even when it is not in flower. In late autumn and winter it bears single ivory flowers rather like a single rose, with a cluster of showy yellow stamens ornamenting the centre of the flower.
CULTURE. Gordonia belongs to the same family as the camellia and likes the same kind of growing conditions: acid soil and an abundance of moisture. It is not a plant for subtropical or coastal gardens. When established it will stand sharp frost.

Grevillea
AUSTRALIAN SPIDER FLOWER, GREVILLEA
DESCRIPTION. Evergreen Australian plants, of which there are more than 200 species. They belong to the protea family. They vary in form from almost prostrate plants to tall trees. As they differ also in foliage and flower, descriptions are given under the species names. The common name of Spider Flower has been given to them, not because they attract spiders, but because of their long curved styles that bear some resemblance to a spider's legs. The leaves are effective in arrangements and the flowers of some species last for a long time when picked.

Most species are more suitable for the large garden than the small.
CULTURE. Although grevilleas do best in acid soil that drains readily, many of them will grow in soil which is slightly

alkaline. A sprinkling of alum or sulphur over the soil around the plants will often help to neutralize alkalinity sufficiently to promote their growth. They do well in sandy and gravelly soils and some species stand considerable frost. Hot sunshine and dry winds in summer do not affect them, but they do not thrive or flower well if left dry during winter and spring, which is the time when many of them flower. Many species stand 5 or more degrees of frost and some species also flower well in coastal gardens and in warm humid ones.

G. aspleniifolia FERN-LEAF GREVILLEA
Can be found growing on slopes from Sydney to the Blue Mountains. This species, which has a height and spread of 2 m, likes more moisture and tolerates more cold than most of the others. Its leaves are very slender, 15–20 cm long and sharply indented, making them somewhat like a fern in appearance. They are popular for adding to flower arrangements. The brick-red flowers carried in fairly small heads about 5 cm long make a fine show in spring.

G. banksii
Attains a height of 3–4 m and has attractive leaves deeply divided into slender segments – dark-green on the upper surface and silvery-green on the underside. The ornamental, bright crimson cylinders of flowers appear from late spring to summer. *G. banksii* 'Forsteri' is a robust cultivar suitable for the large garden.

G. bipinnatifida FUCHSIA GREVILLEA
A low-growing species from Western Australia. It has unusual and attractively divided leaves, deeply cut into segments, and rose-red flowers from spring to summer. It stands moderate frost.

G. caleyi CALEY GREVILLEA
A species growing to 2–3 m which stands moderate frost. The leaves are narrow and deeply cut into slender segments. The flowers carried in clusters are rose to red. Water the plants regularly throughout the year to encourage good flowering. It does well in coastal gardens.

G. excelsior FLAME GREVILLEA
A robust species from Western Australia which grows to 3–6 m. It has leaves like pine needles, and showy spikes or cones of orange to flame flowers. It tolerates heat, frost and long periods with little water.

G. fasciculata PROSTRATE GREVILLEA
This species grows to a height of only 60 cm but spreads across a great deal more than this, and is a good plant for a rock garden or to cover a large dry bank. The leaves are slender, about 4 cm in length, dull green on the surface and rusty in colour on the underside. The flowers of tangerine-red appear from autumn to spring.

G. juniperina JUNIPER GREVILLEA
Is a robust plant growing to 2 m or more, which stands considerable frost. It has dark green, needle-like foliage and scarlet flowers in spring.

G. lavandulacea LAVENDER GREVILLEA
The common name is due to the fact that the leaves are small, slender and grey-green in colour, somewhat resembling those of lavender. The plant is low-growing, seldom more than 1 m in height, but it spreads across 2 m. The flowers vary in colour from rose-pink to deep red. They make a sparkling show in winter and early spring. This species, and forms derived from it, are good ones for covering dry banks and for coastal gardens where the soil is poor and sandy.

G. macrostylis
MOUNT BARREN GREVILLEA
Is a large species growing to 3 m in height, with small leaves divided into sharply-pointed, wedge-shaped segments, and crimson and yellow flowers in showy clusters in spring.

G. petrophiloides ROCK GREVILLEA
This is another grevillea that does well in regions where poor soil, aridity and frost make it difficult to grow many plants. It reaches a height of 1–2 m and spreads across more than this. The leaves are divided into needle-like segments. In late winter and spring the plant becomes covered with showy spikes of rose-coloured flowers.

G. 'Porinda Canberra'
Grows to 1,5 m or more, with a spread of as much and has neat dark green foliage. The coral-red flowers show up beautifully against the leaves from early winter through to spring, and on and off during other seasons of the year, too. Stands severe frost.

G. 'Porinda Constance'
A handsome robust plant growing to 3 m, with leaves somewhat like an olive, but smaller in size. The arching stems are a fine sight in winter and early spring when embellished with orange-red flowers. Will grow in cold areas.

G. 'Porinda Leanne'
Grows to 2 m and has apricot flowers in spring and at other seasons. This is a decorative cultivar for regions which have severe frost and periods of drought.

G. rosmarinifolia *(G. ericifolia)*
ROSEMARY GREVILLEA
Is a robust shrub growing to 2 m with a spread of as much. The leaves are slender, dark green above and grey-green on the under surface, rather like those of rosemary in form and colour. In autumn and winter it carries heads of bi-coloured flowers of crimson and yellow. The cultivar 'Jenkinsii' has larger flowers of deeper colour.

G. wilsonii WILSON GREVILLEA
A winter-flowering species 1,5 m in height and spread, with slender pointed leaves and clusters of bright scarlet flowers in winter. It stands drought, heat and frost.

Grewia occidentalis
CROSSBERRY, FOUR CORNERS
DESCRIPTION. An evergreen South African plant which reaches a height of 2 m or more, and is fairly fast in growth where conditions are good. It has deep green, finely serrated oval leaves about 7 cm long. In spring it carries star-like cyclamen or pink flowers 2–3 cm across with a centre of showy stamens. The flowers have five narrow petals and five long sepals of the same shade. Planted close together, it makes a good informal hedge. The fruit is formed from four balls in cross-formation –

The sweet-scented Gardenia *(Gardenia jasminoides)* produces its lovely flowers in spring and summer

Grevillea *(Grevillea banksii)* is one of the most attractive of Australian plants

Hebe has pretty spikes of flowers and good-looking foliage

hence the common name of crossberry or four corners.

CULTURE. Plant in good soil with plenty of compost added, and water well during summer. Where the sunlight is intense grow it in light shade. It stands only mild frost.

Hakea HAKEA

DESCRIPTION. This genus includes more than a hundred species of evergreen shrubs and trees native to Australia, particularly the western part. The flowers of most of them are not highly ornamental, but the species described are good ones for planting to form a hedge, screen or windbreak around a large property.

CULTURE. They grow extraordinarily well in a variety of soils – alkaline as well as acid, and in sand, gravel or clay. They endure long periods with little water and stand severe frost. Transplant when very small as otherwise they may not take.

H. laurina
SEA URCHIN OR PINCUSHION HAKEA
Is a fairly quick-growing shrub or small tree 3–6 m tall, with fairly narrow pointed leaves 10–15 cm long. In late winter it bears 'pincushions' of crimson flowers with projecting ivory styles tipped with gold. The flowers are aptly named. They look like sea urchins or pincushions full of pins. It makes a good hedge if trimmed, but can be trained to tree form, too. In regions

where frosts are severe, protect young plants in their first year. This species has become popular in the south of France.

H. multilineata GRASS-LEAF HAKEA
Is a vigorous plant growing to 3 m which occurs naturally in Western and South Australia. The leaves are up to 20 cm long and very slender, with clear parallel veins. It has spikes of scarlet flowers in spring.

H. saligna
WILLOW-LEAF OR HEDGE HAKEA
A quick-growing species which responds well to clipping and will form a tall, dense good-looking hedge in three or four years. The young foliage is tinged with bronze. Once established it stands long periods of drought and 10 degrees of frost. If left untrimmed it will grow to 6 m and can be trained to form a tree. The leaves are 4–10 cm long and slender.

Halimium lasianthum

(Helianthemum formosum) SUNROSE
DESCRIPTION. Is a pretty evergreen summer-flowering shrub from Portugal, growing to 1 m in height and spread. The leaves are olive-green, oval and pointed. The cup-shaped flowers are very like those of cistus. They are 4–5 cm across and bright yellow in colour with a maroon blotch at the base of the petals. This is a fine plant for the large rock garden or to clothe a dry bank. Three other pretty

species are *H. atriplicifolium, H. halimifolium* and *H. ocymoides.*

CULTURE. It grows quickly in poor soil and stands heat, frost and aridity. It also does well in coastal gardens.

Hamamelis mollis WITCH HAZEL

DESCRIPTION. The twigs of this deciduous plant were once much used as rods for water divining, which probably accounts for its common name. It is not a very showy shrub but a good one for cold gardens. It grows to 2–3 m and is loosely branched. The young shoots are hairy. The leaves, which are oval with a rough green upper surface and grey on the underside, turn yellow in autumn. The plant bears its curious fragrant yellow flowers in winter. The flowers consist of four very narrow curved petals emerging from a brown calyx. They are useful for winter arrangements.

CULTURE. The plant and its flowers will stand intense cold. It will also tolerate fairly warm weather but not subtropical conditions nor dry wind. Plant it in soil that is slightly acid and rich in humus. It does well in partial shade.

In the large garden a screen of trees with a foreground of shrubs makes a pleasing backdrop to the scene

Hamelia chrysantha HAMELIA

DESCRIPTION. This little shrub is evergreen or semi-evergreen. It may grow to 2 m in height but is usually smaller than this. In summer it carries little clusters of tubular flowers of yellow and orange. It is fairly quick-growing. CULTURE. Grows well in sun or light shade. Does best in coastal gardens where winters are mild. Not recommended for frosty areas.

Hebe HEBE, VERONICA

DESCRIPTION. This is a large genus of ornamental evergreen plants, members of which grow in different parts of the world, but most of the attractive garden species are native to New Zealand. There are also many cultivars now available. Hebe varies in size from low-growing, almost prostrate plants to large robust shrubs. They are worth growing because of their attractive foliage as well as for their flowers. Some species provide pretty flowers for arrangements. The leaves of some species are oval with rounded or pointed tips, and a well-defined central vein. They are pale to dark green and slightly glossy. Their flowers, carried in colourful clusters often like a small bottlebrush, are decorative in the garden for a long time. Others have cord-like leaves rather like a cypress. These are delightful plants for the rock or pebble garden and for making an informal border. They are grown for their leaves rather than for their flowers. The main flowering period is summer. CULTURE. They will stand moderate to severe frost provided they have an abundance of moisture in the soil or the air. Plant in soil rich in humus and mulch during dry periods of the year. To keep the plants neat and compact trim them back lightly after their flowering period. They do well in coastal gardens but should not be planted in subtropical gardens nor in regions which have long periods of hot dry winds and little moisture. Where the sun is intense plant them in semi-shade.

H. 'Andersonii Variegata'

This is a very decorative hebe which grows to 1 m or more, and has long leaves with ivory margins and long spikes of lavender-blue flowers in summer.

H. armstrongii WHIPCORD HEBE

A rounded foliage-plant growing to 1 m with leaves very different from most of the other species. They are very small and pressed against the stem, giving the impression that the plant is related to cypress. Its stems of foliage are effective in arrangements.

H. 'Blue Gem'

A hardy little plant that stands intense cold but not long periods with little water. It does well at the coast. It has glossy leaves and bears blue flowers in summer.

H. buxifolia BOXLEAF HEBE

Grows to 1 m and has very small leaves densely crowded on the stems, and small clusters of white flowers in summer. It makes a good formal or informal hedge.

H. cupressoides CYPRESS HEBE

A slow-growing plant to 1 m with tiny moss-green leaves closely arranged along the stems, rather like those of cypress. The plant looks effective in a container or rock garden and makes a pleasing small hedge.

H. hulkeana LILAC HEBE

Is 1 m in height and spread and has dark green, glossy oval leaves with sharply serrated margins, and clusters of lavender flowers useful for arrangements as well as being pretty in the garden.

H. 'Inspiration'

A fine cultivar raised in New Zealand with pretty foliage and dainty mauve flowers on plants 1 m tall. It is a pretty one for the small garden.

H. salicifolia WILLOW-LEAF HEBE

A tall-growing species reaching a height of 3 m with narrow, dark-green leaves and clusters of white, mauve or purple flowers in summer.

This species makes a good hedge in a large garden. 'Variegata' has leaves with broad cream margins and pink flowers.

H. speciosa SHOWY HEBE

Grows to 1–2 m and is rounded in form, with foliage of dark green and spikes of rosy-purple flowers in late spring and summer. The flowers are pretty in arrangements. Several ornamental cultivars of this species are available: 'Blue Boy', 'Midsummer Beauty', 'Pink Pearl' and 'Sapphire' are particularly attractive ones. H. speciosa 'Tricolor' is a fine cultivar with glossy variegated leaves and long spikes of rosy-purple flowers in summer. It grows to 60 cm in height and spread.

Heliotropium arborescens
(H. peruvianum)

HELIOTROPE, CHERRY PIE

DESCRIPTION. This little evergreen is an old favourite. It grows to 1 m in height and spread, and has soft stems and rough, deeply veined, oval leaves. The plant is grown for the scent and colours of its flowers. They are tiny but carried in pretty rounded heads that look like miniature posies, and are of pleasing shades of lilac and lavender to purple. The flowering time is winter and early spring. Heliotrope makes a good pot plant if trimmed in summer to keep it neat and compact. Beautiful named cultivars are now available. CULTURE. Heliotrope is tender to frost and does best in warm humid gardens. In regions where hot dry winds prevail plant it in a protected and shady position. Where winters are dry, water it well to encourage good flowering.

Hibiscus rosa-sinensis

HIBISCUS

DESCRIPTION. This evergreen shrub from tropical China is so well known in all parts of the world where the climate is temperate that it needs little description. It grows to 3 m or more in height and spread but can be kept back to much smaller size. In fact it should be cut back lightly each year in late winter or very early spring to encourage good flowering. This is a quick-growing shrub with a long flowering period from spring right through to autumn. The leaves are handsome, broad at the base, pointed at the tip, lustrous and deep green in colour. The original species has large scarlet trumpet-shaped flowers. Hybrids and cultivars have flowers of many different colours from palest creamy-yellow through apricot shades to bright canary-yellow, and from palest pink to deep rose and crimson. Many of them have double flowers. The cultivar 'Autumn Leaf' has shiny leaves tinged with bronze. A form with variegated leaves and small scarlet flowers is a new and ornamental introduction. Hibiscus makes a colourful hedge in a large garden.

CULTURE. Hibiscus stand a wide range of growing conditions. They are undoubtedly at their best in warm subtropical gardens but, once established, will tolerate mild to moderate frost. If plants are cut back by frost they often send out new shoots that flower the following summer. In regions with dry summers the plants should be watered well at this time of the year to encourage good flowering.

Hibiscus syriacus

ALTHEA, ROSE OF SHARON
DESCRIPTION. An upright deciduous shrub which is not as decorative as the ordinary garden hibiscus, but it is a good shrub for cold gardens. It may reach a height of 3 m but can be kept down to smaller size by annual pruning in winter. This winter pruning is recommended as it seems to encourage more prolific flowering in late summer and autumn. The leaves are broad, almost triangular and sometimes lobed, and quite attractive. The flowers (single or double) make a fine show. Their colours vary from pure white, through many shades of pink and rose to carmine and ruby-red, and from palest mauve to deep purple.

CULTURE. Once established this plant stands severe cold, heat and fairly long periods with little water.

Holmskioldia sanguinea

CHINESE HAT BUSH, PARASOL FLOWER
DESCRIPTION. Is a rangy plant of slender form with stems reaching to 2–3 m in height. The oval leaves are about 10 cm long. The flowers are carried in loose clusters in autumn. They are a pleasing unusual shade of brick-red. Cultivars with mustard and yellow flowers are available, too. Each flower consists of a short curved tube emerging from a large rounded coloured calyx, which looks rather like a Chinese hat in shape.

CULTURE. It grows in areas with mild frost and tolerates aridity, but does not do well in damp shady places. To keep the plants neat and shapely, cut off the stems which have flowered.

Hovea HOVEA

DESCRIPTION. A genus of evergreen shrubs native to Australia where they can be found in a variety of soils. They have pea-shaped flowers of mauve or blue on plants that vary in height according to species.

CULTURE. They are hardy to moderate frost and, if cut back by frost, usually put forth new shoots very quickly. They do best in gravelly, well-drained soil.

H. elliptica   KARRI BLUEBUSH, HOVEA
Is 2 m or more in height and has slender stems and narrow oval leaves 5–7 cm long, and clusters of purple-blue flowers in spring. It does best in partial shade.

H. longifolia   LONG-LEAF HOVEA
Grows to 2 m in height and spread and has long slender leaves and purple-blue flowers in spring.

H. pungens   DEVIL'S PINS
A small plant with narrow leaves with prickly tips. Flowers of blue or violet are carried in profusion in spring. This species needs a warm situation and well-drained soil.

Hydrangea macrophylla

(H. hortensis)
HYDRANGEA, CHRISTMAS FLOWER
DESCRIPTION. A deciduous shrub of rounded form growing to 1–2 m in height and spread. Some of the newer cultivars remain small in stature. The old-fashioned large-growing types need space to develop as severe pruning will limit the number of flowers they bear. The leaves are attractive, broadly oval with deeply serrated margins, and the plants produce handsome heads of flowers for a long period during summer. Hydrangeas are one of the easiest of flowering shrubs to grow, and one of the most rewarding in the garden because of their long flowering period. They do very well in containers and provide ornamental flowers for arrangements. Each flowerhead is made up of a mass of tiny flowers surrounded by circular bracts which make the whole head attractive. When cutting flowers for arrangements make sure that most of the tiny florets are open, showing their stamens, as otherwise the flowerhead is likely to fade very quickly. After picking stand the bottom 2–6 cm of the stems in boiling water for about ten seconds, and then leave them in a container of water 20–30 cm deep for several hours. Thereafter arrange them in water in which some alum has been dissolved, using one teaspoon of alum to each litre of water. If this is done they should remain fresh-looking for two or more weeks.

Lacecap hydrangeas are not as popular as they once were, but they are certainly worth growing. Their heads are flat – not domed – with a ring of ray florets on the outer edge of the inflorescence and fertile flowers in the middle.

CULTURE. Hydrangeas require reasonably good soil. They will not grow in highly alkaline soil. They also need regular and thorough watering throughout their growing period, which is from late winter or early spring until they lose their leaves, when less water is required. They stand severe frost but where such frosts occur it is advisable to put down a thick mulch in autumn, and to prune the plants in spring rather than in winter in order to prevent frost-damage to new shoots. In coastal gardens they will grow and flower well in full sunshine, but in inland gardens where the sunlight is intense and the air dry, they should be planted in shade or partial shade.

Gardeners who find it difficult to grow hydrangeas successfully in the garden should try planting them in large containers filled with good soil and compost. Few plants are more effective when grown in tubs, and they often flower better when their roots are somewhat restricted than when grown in the open ground.

The colours of the flowers depend largely on the type planted and the nature of the soil. In alkaline soil they may be shades of pink, whilst in distinctly acid soil they will become blue. Where plants are grown in containers it is possible to treat the soil and produce plants with pink and blue flowers side by side. Gardeners who have alkaline soil and who wish to have blue flowers should grow the plants in tubs of acid compost. It is possible to treat the soil by sprinkling about a tablespoon

Heliotrope does best in gardens where winters are mild

Hibiscus produce their fascinating flowers for many months of the year

Hydrangeas with variegated leaves are decorative plants to lighten a shady part of the garden

of aluminium sulphate, sulphate of iron or sulphur on the ground around each plant, but this is not as effective in producing blue flowers as planting in acid compost. Special preparations for changing the nature of the soil in order to have blue flowers are also obtainable from firms which deal in horticultural supplies.

In regions where the soil is acid, pink flowers may be produced by dusting a little lime on the soil in late winter or early spring.

A general misconception about hydrangeas is that there are only a few different ones. In fact, there are several ornamental species and numerous named cultivars – which differ in vigour of growth and in the size of the plant, the flowerheads and the individual florets that make up each head. In a neutral soil they may be pink to deep rose in colour, pale or dark blue or white. In a limy soil the pinks will remain pink whilst the blues may turn pink or shades of mauve, and in acid soil the pinks become blue or shades of blue or mauve. The following are the names of a few good cultivars:

'Admiration' (low–rose); 'Altona' (tall–blue); 'Alpenglühn' (low–rose); 'Amethyst' (medium–blue); 'Armand Draps' (low–pink); 'Benelux' (medium –pink); 'Blue Prince' (tall–blue); 'Carousel' (tall–deep pink); 'Europa' (medium–pink); 'Flambeau' (low–red); 'Germaine Moullere' (tall–white); 'Goliath' (tall–blue); 'Hamburg'

(medium–blue); 'Maréchal Foch' (medium–dark blue); 'Sensation' (medium–deep rose); 'Westfalen' (low–blue).

To ensure good flowering, some care should be taken when pruning the plants. This may be done from late summer to early spring. Where severe and late frosts are usual, prune in spring. If too many stems are allowed to remain, the plant will produce flowers of poor quality. On the other hand, if too much of the current year's growth is cut off there will be too few flowers. No hard and fast rules can be laid down with regard to the pruning of hydrangeas as the types vary considerably in growth. If there are too many stems coming up from the base cut some back to two or three buds or eyes, shorten others and leave the stems that have not flowered untrimmed, to produce early flowers.

To encourage larger heads apply a monthly dressing of liquid fertilizer or manure, using a general garden fertilizer if pink flowers are wanted and a special acid-soil fertilizer for blue flowers.

H. paniculata 'Grandiflora'
PEEGEE HYDRANGEA
A robust, deciduous species for the large garden; it grows rapidly to 4 m. It has large leaves and very large white flowerheads of almost conical form, which make a splendid show in mid-summer.

H. quercifolia OAKLEAF HYDRANGEA
Is 2 m or more in height with handsome, deeply lobed leaves, 20 cm long, that become bronzed or rusty-red in autumn. It bears creamy-white flowers in conical heads. Prune back hard in winter. This species stands more sun than *H. macrophylla*.

Hypericum
HYPERICUM, ST JOHN'S WORT
DESCRIPTION. The genus includes a large range of shrubs and perennials native to different countries. Most of them grow readily anywhere and some species can become weeds. Here only the good garden species are described. They are evergreen or semi-evergreen with pretty foliage of soft green that is ornamental throughout the year. The oval leaves are arranged opposite each other on the stems. The cup-shaped flowers of pale to deep yellow are enhanced by prominent stamens that ornament the centre of each flower. They bear most of their flowers in summer, but may have some throughout the year. Hypericums are attractive anywhere in the garden, and are also ornamental when grown in containers. In recent years new cultivars have become more popular than the species. The following are three of merit: 'Hidcote', 'Rowallane', and 'Sun Gold'. CULTURE. These plants stand severe cold, and when mature they will also tolerate long periods with little water, but they flower best when watered reg-

ularly and well. They grow in full sunshine and in partial shade, preferring partial shade in hot gardens inland. A light trimming in late winter or early spring will keep the plants neat.

H. calycinum
An evergreen or semi-deciduous species growing to only 30 cm in height, spreading as it roots, to cover a large area. This species makes a good ground cover for sun or part shade. It does not mind poor soil or competition from the roots of trees. Spade it back every two or three years to prevent it from invading territory other than its own. It has large golden flowers in summer.

H. forrestii *(H. patulum forrestii)*
A fine hardy species that will reach more than 1 m in height and spread. It bears a profusion of large golden flowers in summer. Where autumn is cold, the leaves turn colour.

H. leschenaultii
A highly ornamental evergreen species 2 m tall, with a profusion of large flowers in summer. It is a good plant for the large garden.

H. moserianum GOLD FLOWER
Reaches a height of 1 m and has arching stems tinted rose when young, and clusters of yellow flowers in summer. The cultivar 'Tricolor' has small green leaves splashed with white and edged with pink. It makes a pretty container plant, and the stems of colourful leaves are attractive in arrangements.

Hypocalymma robustum
SWAN RIVER MYRTLE

DESCRIPTION. This decorative little evergreen shrub from Western Australia is a member of the myrtle family. It grows to 1 m in height and spread, and has slender shining leaves only 2–3 cm long on twiggy stems. The young growth is bronze in colour. In late win-

Hydrangeas are most rewarding shrubs in the garden and in containers for a show indoors or on the shady patio or terrace

The oak-leaf hydrangea *(Hydrangea quercifolia)* bears handsome heads of ivory flowers for a long period

ter and spring it is wreathed in pink flowers similar to peach blossom, with fluffy stamens which add to their attractiveness. The flowers make a pretty show on the plant and look charming in arrangements. *H. angustifolium* is another decorative species with ivory or pink flowers.

CULTURE. Plant it in well-drained soil in a sunny place. It grows in sand or gravel but may not thrive in heavy clay. It does well in sun or semi-shade and will endure long periods of drought. Transplant when very small.

Hypoestes aristata RIBBON BUSH

DESCRIPTION. An evergreen South African shrub growing to 1 m or more in height and almost as much in spread. The pointed leaves are broad at the base and the little flowers are clustered close to the stem between the leaves. Each flower consists of a narrow tube opening to two lips. The central segment at the top is white spotted with purple; the others are mauve. The segments curl, looking like pieces of looped ribbon. The flowering time is autumn.

CULTURE. This is a quick-growing shrub that does best in partial shade, in soil rich in humus. It thrives in subtropical gardens but can stand moderate frost. Where frosts are severe, plant it in a sheltered corner.

Impatiens BALSAM

DESCRIPTION. Quick-growing, evergreen or semi-deciduous shrubs with a height and spread varying from 30 cm to 2 m. They flower for many months of the year but are at their best in spring and summer. The flowers open to a flat, round face of unequal petals, with a curved spur projecting from the back of the flower. They are of a slightly glossy or velvety texture and of lively colours. The leaves vary according to species. There are numerous named cultivars of great merit.

CULTURE. Balsams do best in tropical and subtropical gardens and in shade or partial shade. They are tender to frost and, where winters are cold, it is advisable to grow them in containers that can be sheltered during the cold months of the year. They do well in seaside gardens provided they are protected from wind. It is advisable to cut

plants back after their flowering period, or early in spring, to keep them neat and compact.

I. holstii BALSAM
A shrubby little evergreen plant with soft stems sometimes tinged with rose, growing to 60 cm or more. It has soft green ovate leaves with neatly serrated margins. The flowers that appear in spring and summer are scarlet and 3–5 cm across. It makes a charming potplant. Cultivars have flowers of different colours – white, pink, salmon, cerise and shades of orange.

I. oliveri AFRICAN BALSAM
A tall species from tropical East Africa growing to a height of 2 m or more. The soft, ovate, shining green leaves with neatly serrated edges measure up to 20 cm in length. They are carried in whorls and are in themselves decorative. The flowers of palest lavender have a shimmering surface. It stands moderate cold but not dryness. Because it is quick-growing it is a useful stop-gap shrub to plant between slow-growing ones. It does well in seaside gardens, blooming in sun or shade. In warm gardens it is inclined to grow too large.

I. sultanii BUSY LIZZIE
A charming shrublet with a height and spread of 30–60 cm. The soft stems are clothed with pretty ovate leaves. Where the climate is temperate it produces flowers for many months of the year. The colours of the flowers are red, white, pink, cyclamen, cerise and flame. It does well in pots, flowering prolifically in a small pot that keeps the roots confined. Delightful new cultivars with double flowers like miniature roses and others with variegated leaves are now available.

Iochroma cyaneum (*Jochroma*)
JOCHROMA
DESCRIPTION. Is a large shrub or small tree growing to 3 m with a rounded or spreading top. It is evergreen in warm regions and semi-deciduous where winters are cool. This is a useful plant for a quick screen or to plant as a stop-gap whilst slower plants are reaching maturity. It has large oval leaves pointed at the tips, up to 15 cm in length, and pale-green in colour. In summer it bears large clusters of glossy,

tubular flowers of a rich shade of purple-blue. They are of an exceptional colour and very attractive.

CULTURE. This plant should not be tried in gardens where winters are severe. It tolerates some cold but not very low drops in temperature. It grows well in sand, clay or gravelly soil and, once established, will survive fairly long periods with little water. As strong wind is likely to break long stems, it is advisable to cut it back a little each winter.

Iresine herbstii BLOOD-LEAF

DESCRIPTION. A small, quick-growing evergreen shrub planted for the beauty of its leaves. They are oval in form, 3–5 cm in length and of well-defined colours – either rose to ruby with burgundy splashes and lighter veins, or lime-green with yellowish veins. The stems of the plants are also brightly coloured rose or yellow. They are at their best in summer and autumn. The plant is decorative in the garden and in pots on a terrace or patio, or indoors. As it grows very quickly from cuttings, new small plants can be raised in pots for moving to any part of the garden for a quick show of colour. Mature plants grow to 1 m, but they tend to sprawl and should therefore be cut back to ground-level each winter to force new growth and keep the plants compact.

CULTURE. Iresine will stand cool but not frosty winters. It does best in semi-shade except at the coast where it grows well in full sunshine. Make cuttings in spring or summer. In cold areas grow it in containers which can be put under shelter in winter.

Isopogon dubius (*I. roseus*)
ROSE CONEBUSH
DESCRIPTION. Is the best-known species of a genus that includes several attractive shrubs native to Western Australia. It is an evergreen growing to 60 cm with deeply divided leaves and heads of flowers like pincushions about 3 cm across. They are made up of numerous very slender pin-like perianth tubes of rosy-red emerging from a central cone. The plant is a charming sight in spring. Other pretty species are *I. anemonifolius* and *I. anethifolius* with yellow flowers;

I. cuneatus and *I. divergens* with mauve to purple flowers.

CULTURE. This genus is a member of the protea family and likes acid soil that is friable and has good drainage. Plants should be watered well when forming buds and flowers but do not mind being dry at other seasons of the year. They tolerate moderate frost. Transplant when very small.

Ixora coccinea   IXORA

DESCRIPTION. A shrubby quick-growing plant which reaches 1 m in height and spread. It is an evergreen with oval deep green leaves and round clusters of scarlet flowers in summer. Each flower is a slender tube ending in a starry face. This is a useful plant for quick effect. Planted close together it makes a pleasing informal low hedge. Individual shrubs can be shaped to a rounded form.

CULTURE. Ixora is native to warm countries of the East and it will not stand much frost. This is a pretty shrub for subtropical gardens where it receives the warmth and moisture which promote its best development. In cold areas it should be grown as a potplant in a sheltered place.

Jasminum   JASMINE

The genus includes a diversity of plant forms – shrubs, climbers, twiners and ground covers – from different regions of the world. The species here described are shrubs. These are quick-growing plants that do not mind being cut back to keep them within bounds.

CULTURE. The shrubby jasmines described below are all frost-resistant, and established plants stand long periods with little water. They are therefore invaluable for a difficult climate.

J. humile   ITALIAN JASMINE
This evergreen species may send out long shoots to 3 m, but it can be kept trimmed to about 1 m in height and spread. The leaves are divided into three to seven oval pointed leaflets 3–5 cm long. In mid-summer it carries small clusters of fragrant, bright yellow flowers only 1 cm across. *J. humile* 'Revolutum', with larger flowers, makes a more impressive show.

J. mesnyl   (J. primulinum)
PRIMROSE JASMINE
A cheerful evergreen plant for the garden where cold and drought limit the number of plants which can be grown. Train it as a climber against a wall or down a bank, or trim to shrub size, or use as a hedge-plant. The soft, lance-shaped leaflets arranged in threes are ornamental throughout the year, and in winter it is gay with bright-yellow flowers.

J. nudiflorum   WINTER JASMINE
A deciduous species for the cold garden, with willowy stems which grow to 4 m if not trimmed. In winter its golden-yellow flowers strung along the bare green stems make a good show. Use it as a shrub, to trail down over an ugly dry bank, or grow it as a hedge plant.

J. parkeri   DWARF JASMINE
An evergreen that makes a good ground cover and which is small enough also for the rock garden. It grows to 30 cm and spreads across more than this. The tiny oval leaflets are only 3–6 mm long. In summer it bears small yellow, scentless flowers in profusion.

Juniperus   JUNIPER

DESCRIPTION. Some are large trees, some are shrub-like in habit and some are almost prostrate in growth. Many of them are ornamental and deserve a prominent place in gardens where conditions suit them. They are conifers with needle or scale-like foliage. Some of them have leaves of variegated colours and some have foliage which is metallic blue in hue. Some grow in columnar fashion, whilst others spread horizontally. These spreading types are good ones to plant in a rock garden, or in a container on a terrace or patio. They are slow-growers and therefore excellent plants for small gardens.

CULTURE. Junipers tolerate a wide range of climatic conditions. They grow in regions with very cold winters and some of them stand hot dry winds and intense sunlight, but they are not at their best in subtropical gardens. In hot dry areas it is advisable to plant them in partial shade. They grow in alkaline or acid soil.

J. chinensis 'Aurea'   GOLDEN JUNIPER
A tall, slender conical shrub which may eventually reach tree size, with a height of 6 m and a spread of 2 m across at the base. It is a fine accent plant as its form can best be appreciated when it stands alone. The tips of its leaves are attractively tinged with gold. As the leaves tend to scorch, plant it where it is protected from drying winds and full sun all day long.

J. chinensis 'Japonica'
A compact, shrubby type with prickly, jade green foliage. The stems spray out horizontally at the ends. When mature it may be 1,5 m in height and 2 m in spread.

J. communis 'Compressa'
This is one of the best of the conifers for the rock or pebble garden or for a small garden. It is columnar in form and looks like a miniature tree 1 m tall. Plant two or three near each other as it is not easy to grow and one or more may fail to reach maturity. Needs protection from hot, dry wind.

J. communis 'Depressa Aurea'
A decorative cultivar with horizontal branches of prickly leaves that are golden-yellow for most of the year and bronze in winter. It needs sun to colour well, but may scorch if subjected to very intense sunlight. Final height and spread about 3 x 4 m.

J. communis 'Repanda'
Grows into a handsome mound 2 m high and wide. The mid-green leaves may turn bronze for a short time in winter. It does well in light shade.

J. conferta   SHORE JUNIPER
A vigorous species which grows naturally along the shore in parts of Japan. It makes a good, robust ground cover and looks effective clambering over a wall or hanging over the sides of a large tub. The prickly leaves are light green, and the height and spread is about 1–2 m.

J. davurica 'Expansa Aureospicata'
A dwarf form with horizontal branches of small sage-green leaves arranged in thick clusters. Golden tufts of leaves appear here and there on the plant. The ultimate height is about 60 cm and the spread may be 2 m if not trimmed.

Chinese Hat Bush or Parasol Flower (*Holmskioldia sanguinea*). A quick-growing plant where winters are mild

Hypericums are fine plants for the small garden

Althea (*Hibiscus syriacus*) grows well in cold gardens

J. horizontalis CREEPING JUNIPER

This juniper sends out horizontal stems at ground level. These may root on their own and help the plant to spread as a ground cover. It should have some of the leading branches cut back to encourage a thicker mat of side stems to form. Stands severe cold. The leaves of cultivars derived from this vary from green to metallic blue. 'Glauca' is the neatest, but the following are also handsome when well grown: 'Bar Harbor', 'Montana', 'Plumosa' and 'Wiltonii'.

J. x media

This cross has produced some excellent cultivars for large gardens. 'Gold Coast' is a semi-prostrate plant with gold-tipped leaves densely arranged; 'Mint Julep' is an American hybrid with rich mint-green leaves on a wide-spreading but low-growing plant; 'Pfitzeriana Aurea' is wide-spreading with terminal shoots tinged with gold in summer; 'Pfitzeriana Glauca' has glaucous grey leaves; 'Plumosa Albovariegata' has green and yellow foliage on arching stems.

J. procumbens 'Nana'

CREEPING JUNIPER
A compact plant which hugs the ground, sending up vertical stems of apple-green leaves to a height of 30 cm. It makes a good ground cover.

J. sabina SAVIN JUNIPER

The species is a robust plant with strong horizontal branches. It is suitable for the large garden or park. There are several cultivars of more compact growth. 'Arcadia', 'Cupressifolia', 'Blue Danube' and 'Tamariscifolia' are recommended.

J. virginiana 'Globosa'

A dwarf juniper with a rounded form of closely packed, plume-like stems covered with densely arranged bright-green leaves.

J. virginiana 'Grey Owl'

Too large for the garden of moderate size but useful in a large garden or for landscape work. This is a vigorous plant with wide-spreading branches clothed with foliage of soft silvery grey.

J. virginiana 'Sky Rocket'

Tree-like in form and of extremely slender growth, it may reach 6 m but be no more than 30 cm in breadth. A good accent plant in the small garden. The leaves are greyish-green.

Justicea carnea

(*Jacobinia carnea*) JUSTICEA, JACOBINIA
DESCRIPTION. This plant, sometimes referred to as Brazilian Plume Flower, is a quick-growing, evergreen shrub reaching a height of 1,5 m, but it can be trimmed back to keep it smaller. It has large attractive dark-green leaves, broad at the base and pointed at the apex, with clear veins. In spring and summer the plant bears very pretty cone-shaped heads of flowers of a charming shade of coral or dusty pink. There is also a cultivar with pretty yellow flowers.

CULTURE. Justicea is a decorative plant for subtropical gardens and for regions where winters are not very cold. Mild frost may cut it back to the ground but it grows up quickly again. In regions with severe frost it is advisable to plant it in a container that can be kept under shelter during winter. Trim the plants back in late winter to keep them from becoming straggly. It likes acid soil rich in humus and plenty of moisture, and does best in partial shade.

Kalmia latifolia

MOUNTAIN LAUREL, CALICO BUSH
DESCRIPTION. This is a beautiful evergreen shrub growing to 2–3 m or more where conditions are favourable. It grows well only in a few places. It has decorative glossy leaves, oval in form and 5–10 cm long, and from late winter to mid-spring it bears round clusters of cup-shaped flowers of a delicate shade of shell-pink. This is a plant for the keen gardener who is prepared to take some trouble to ensure its growth.
CULTURE. Kalmia is related to erica (heath) and will grow only in soil which is distinctly acid. It is native to the north-eastern part of the United States and does well in cold regions provided it has an abundance of moisture and plenty of humus. Plant it in shade or partial shade.

Balsam or Busy Lizzie does best in shade. It is a pretty plant for the warm garden and for growing indoors

Jochroma (*Iochroma cyaneum*) produces clusters of shining flowers in summer

Justicea (*Justicea carnea*) – an ornamental shrub for dappled shade

Kerria japonica KERRIA

DESCRIPTION. A deciduous shrub growing to 1–2 m with slender branches that spread out gracefully from the centre of the bush. The leaves are broad at the base and pointed at the tip with serrated margins and prettily pleated along the veins. In cold districts they turn yellow before dropping. In late winter and early spring the bare stems bear five-petalled flowers of deep yellow measuring about 4 cm across. There is also a form with double flowers like pompons. Group it with other shrubs to add to the colour in late winter and early spring, or set plants close together to make an informal hedge.
CULTURE. Kerria is not for subtropical gardens. It needs frost for its best development. In gardens where the sunlight is intense, plant it in partial shade. Water well during winter to encourage good flowering. Prune plants hard after flowering by cutting out branches that have flowered, leaving the newer ones to grow on and bear flowers the following year.

Kolkwitzia amabilis BEAUTY BUSH

DESCRIPTION. A pretty deciduous shrub from China that grows upright to 3 m, with stems that tend to arch out at the end, giving it a graceful appearance. The small soft, pointed leaves are pale green with slight serrations. In spring clusters of little funnel-shaped flowers appear in profusion all along the ends of the stems. They are rather like those of an abelia in form, and coloured palest pink with a suffusion of yellow in the throat. Although the flowers are less than 3 cm in length they nevertheless make a pretty show. Plant it alone behind smaller shrubs or set several together to form a tall screen.
CULTURE. Beauty Bush stands severe cold but not long periods with little water. It does best in acid soil but grows also in alkaline soil, in full sun or partial shade. When the plant becomes too large cut out some of the stems which have flowered, soon after the flowering period is over.

Kunzea KUNZEA

DESCRIPTION. A genus of evergreen Australian shrubs some of which are very showy. It is part of the myrtle family and closely related to callistemons and leptospermums. The kunzeas have heath-like leaves and small flowers with ornamental stamens. The flowers are carried in clusters or spikes.
CULTURE. Plant them in soil which drains readily as they do not thrive in heavy clay. They stand moderate frost and dry conditions.

K. ambigua WHITE KUNZEA
A bulky plant which has a height and spread of 2–3 m. It makes a fine show, festooned with white flowers from mid- to late spring.

K. baxteri BOTTLEBRUSH KUNZEA
A spectacular plant when in flower. It grows to 2 m in height. In late winter and early spring it carries masses of flowers which look like miniature bottlebrushes made up of ruby-red stamens tipped with gold.

K. capitata
A species suitable for the small garden. It grows to 1 m and bears pink to cyclamen or magenta flowers in spring.

K. muelleri YELLOW KUNZEA
This is a hardy little plant which is suitable for the rock garden. It grows to 60 cm in height and spread, and bears dainty yellow flowers in spring.

K. parvifolia CRIMSON KUNZEA
Is one of the most decorative of the kunzeas. It grows to a little more than 1 m and becomes gay with a profusion of magenta flowers in spring. When once established it stands dry conditions.

K. pulchella (*K. sericea*)
SILKY KUNZEA
Makes a brilliant splash of colour in spring when it becomes covered with scarlet flowers like small bottlebrushes. The leaves are silky, and grey rather than green in colour. It does best in regions of moderate rainfall.

Lagerstroemia indica

PRIDE OF INDIA

DESCRIPTION. This tree is popular in many parts of the country and deservedly so because of the decorative flowers it bears in summer and the vivid autumn tints of the leaves before they fall. New dwarf forms of the tree, suitable for the shrub garden are now available. The colours of the flowers include shades of pink ('Petite Pinkie'), rose-red ('Petite Embers') and purple ('Petite Orchid').

CULTURE. It tolerates severe cold and hot dry weather, but where frosts are sharp it is advisable to give the plant some protection during the first year of growth. Once established, it thrives with little additional watering. In humid regions it may get mildew for which a general fungicide should be applied in spray or powder form.

Lantana montevidensis

(*L. sellowiana*) TRAILING LANTANA

DESCRIPTION. This plant should not be confused with the shrubby lantana which has been declared a noxious weed in South Africa because of its tendency to seed itself and spread over wide areas of the country. This one is a trailing plant that makes a fine ground cover, but it will clamber over any support near by – such as a low wall or fence, and will drape itself prettily over a bank. It looks decorative too, when grown in a container. The dark-green leaves are about 3 cm long with serrated edges. The plant becomes festooned with round heads of small mauve to purple flowers rather like those of a verbena in form. They make a splendid show in spring, but the plant bears some flowers throughout the year, particularly if it is sheared off after the first blooming is over.

CULTURE. This lantana will stand moderate frost but it does not like damp, shady conditions. It is a splendid plant for gardens where the soil is poor and the sunlight intense. It will also endure long periods with little water.

Lavandula   LAVENDER

DESCRIPTION. Has been popular for generations because of the scent of its flowers and leaves. It is native to the Mediterranean region but flourishes in many parts of the world. Lavender grows with cheerful abandon in a container and it is therefore suitable for a sunny balcony, terrace or patio. It looks attractive also when grown as a low informal hedge, provided it is trimmed regularly to keep it from becoming leggy at the base. Plant it along a path, in the rock garden, or amongst other shrubs at the front of a shrubbery. The main flowering period is summer.

CULTURE. Lavender stands sharp frosts but does not do well in hot humid regions. Plant it in soil that drains readily. It does not mind sand or gravel, but stiff clay seems to inhibit its growth. It likes full sunshine and, once established, will tolerate long periods with little water. Cut plants back fairly hard after flowering to keep them shapely and to encourage new basal growth.

L. dentata

TOOTHED OR FRENCH LAVENDER

Grows to 1 m and has very narrow bright green leaves with square-toothed margins. The pale purple flowers are carried in short spikes. To make an effective low hedge, set plants 30–45 cm apart and tailor when small to produce bushiness at the base.

L. spica

COMMON OR ENGLISH LAVENDER

Will grow to 1 m and is bushy with tiny grey leaves with smooth margins. The lavender-coloured flowers are carried high above the foliage in long spikes. This is the one from which scent is made. There are several attractive cultivars smaller in size than the species. The most popular are 'Compacta Nana', which grows to 20 cm, 'Nana Atropurpurea', – also known as 'Hidcote'– growing to 30 cm, and 'Munstead', which reaches a height of 45 cm and has deep, lavender-blue flowers.

L. stoechas   SPANISH OR BUSH LAVENDER

A bushy plant with highly aromatic leaves and dark purple flowers in dense spikes ending in a tuft of purple, petal-like bracts. It makes a pretty informal hedge.

Lavatera assurgentiflora

LAVATERA

DESCRIPTION. A rangy shrub native to the eastern seaboard of the United States. It reaches a height of 3 m and has lobed, maple-like leaves 8–15 cm long, hairy on the underside. In spring, and on and off through the year, it produces saucer-shaped, rosy-cerise flowers. It is quick-growing.

CULTURE. This is not a highly ornamental plant but it is a useful one for seaside gardens as it stands wind and salt spray. It also tolerates drought when established.

Lebeckia   LEBECKIA

DESCRIPTION. These evergreen South African shrubs vary in habit of growth and foliage. They are exceptionally pretty from late winter to mid-spring and well worth a place in gardens large and small.

CULTURE. They grow in sandy or gravelly soils and once established they endure long periods with little water and considerable frost. They do best where the sunshine is intense and are not recommended therefore for cool, shady gardens.

L. cytisoides   WILD BROOM

This species bears a faint resemblance to Spanish broom, but it is more ornamental in form and foliage. The stems are soft and arching, and the leaves, arranged in threes, are a pretty shade of green. It has a height and spread of 1–2 m. In late winter and early spring it carries sprays of sweet-scented, pea-shaped flowers of bright yellow.

L. simsiana   DWARF LEBECKIA

A sprawling plant that grows to a height of 60 cm and spreads across much more. The long, needle-like leaves are soft in texture and grey-green in colour. The stems arch up prettily from the ground and bear at the ends long spikes of brilliant yellow flowers with a faint scent. This one is a splendid plant for the rock garden or for the middle of a flower border.

Leonotis leonurus

LION'S EAR, WILD DAGGA

DESCRIPTION. Is a quick-growing shrub or herbaceous perennial native to Africa. It is upright in habit reaching a height of 2 m and has rough, pointed, dull green leaves 5 cm long. The hooded tubular flowers are carried in whorls one above the other up the stem. The species generally grown has bright orange flowers, but there is a form with ivory-white flowers also. The main flowering time is autumn and winter.

CULTURE. Grows well in poor soils and in hot dry areas. It also does well in warm humid gardens. Where frosts are sharp it may die down to the ground but it generally grows up to flower again the following autumn. Cut it back hard after the flowers fade to keep the plant neat and compact.

Leptospermum TEA TREE

DESCRIPTION. The genus includes many decorative shrubs and small trees, most of which are native to Australia and New Zealand. The common name of Tea Tree is said to have been given because Captain Cook made an infusion from the leaves of *L. scoparium* to prevent scurvy in his crew. The leaves are tiny and slender, green or sometimes grey-green in colour. The flowers are seldom more than 1 cm wide but carried in great profusion. Some are single and some double. The main flowering period is late winter and early spring. The flowers last fairly well in arrangements. The plants look attractive standing alone but make a better show when those with flowers of different colours are grouped close together. They can be planted near one another to make an informal hedge and can be grown successfully in containers, too. New dwarf cultivars are excellent for the rock garden or for growing in a pot. Most species grow in coastal gardens.

CULTURE. They do best in acid soil that drains readily but they can be grown in soil which is slightly alkaline. If the leaves become yellow apply alum (aluminium sulphate) or sulphur to the soil (a tablespoon to a square metre) and water it in. This will help to neutralize alkalinity. They grow easily and survive moderate frost and long periods of dry weather in summer. Plants tend to become woody with age unless the tops are cut down lightly each year after flowering. Very often established plants die off for no apparent reason. This may be due to soil conditions which do not suit them. It is more likely to happen in alkaline soil or

heavy clay that does not allow for good drainage. Transplant plants when small.

L. citratum

Has a graceful habit of growth and slender little leaves with a distinct lemon scent when crushed. In spring it bears a profusion of white flowers. It is not as pretty as some of the named cultivars but it is a useful shrub for windy seaside gardens.

L. flavescens 'Citriodora'

Grows to 3 m or more and has upright branches that arch out near the top. The tiny leaves are dusty green and the flowers white. The leaves have a lemon scent when crushed.

L. laevigatum AUSTRALIAN MYRTLE

This species is robust and has been used for generations to make a high hedge or windbreak. It has, however, been declared an 'invader plant' and should therefore no longer be grown.

L. rotundifolium

ROUND-LEAFED TEA TREE

Grows to 3 m and has small oval dark green leaves and masses of pretty pale pink flowers 3 cm across, in spring.

L. scoparium

NEW ZEALAND TEA TREE, MANUKA

The original species is no longer a popular plant but numerous forms, varieties and cultivars developed from this have become popular in many countries of the world.

'Boscawenii'

A dwarf form to 60 cm with single white or pale-pink flowers and bronze-tipped foliage. Plant in a rock or pebble garden.

'Flore Pleno'

Has lovely double, pale-pink flowers on bushes 1 m in height and spread. Recommended for the small garden.

'Keatleyi'

Grows to 3 m in height and bears a profusion of large, blush-pink flowers with a dark rose centre.

'Lambethii'

Is 2 m in height and has large single pink to rose flowers. A robust and handsome cultivar.

'Nanum'

A low-growing shrub to 30 cm with tiny leaves and single flowers of light pink or rose. A splendid plant for the rock garden or for pot culture.

'Nichollsii'

Grows to 2 m and has showy crimson flowers. A fine one for the large or small garden.

'Red Damask'

A handsome one that grows to 2 m or more, and has double flowers of ruby-red and leaves tinged with rose. It flowers in winter and spring.

'Robert Tarrant'

A decorative form with double pink flowers on plants almost 2 m tall. It makes a good informal hedge.

'Roseum Flore Pleno'

A charming cultivar with pale-pink double flowers like little rosettes on plants 2 m tall.

'Ruby Glow'

This rewarding shrub is upright in growth to 2 m. It bears double crimson flowers in great profusion.

'Snow Flurry'

Grows to 2 m and has leaves tinged with red, and double white flowers. It flowers prolifically in spring but has some flowers at other seasons too.

L. squarrosum (*L. persiciflorum*)

PEACH-FLOWER TEA TREE

A quick-growing Australian species reaching 3 m with a spread of almost as much. It has large pink flowers which are much like those of a single peach.

Leschenaultia biloba

BLUE LESCHENAULTIA

DESCRIPTION. A twiggy shrub from Western Australia growing to about 60 cm in height and spread. It has slender green leaves sparsely carried on the stems and, in spring, it becomes covered with five-petalled flowers of clear sky-blue. Flowers of a true blue are rare in nature and this plant is a valuable addition to the horticultural world because of the distinctive blue of its flowers. There are other species of leschenaultia with scarlet or crimson flowers, but they are not as attractive.

CULTURE. It grows naturally in full sun in sandy or gravelly soil that drains readily. Transplant when very small

Beauty Bush (*Kolkwitzia amabilis*) has delicately coloured flowers in late winter and early spring

Leptospermum scoparium 'Red Damask'. One of the prettiest cultivars

Leucadendron discolor provides long-lasting flowers for arrangements

and water the plants well in late autumn and winter. They endure long periods with little moisture in summer and early autumn.

Leucadendron LEUCADENDRON
DESCRIPTION. A genus of the protea family which includes several shrubs and one tree worth cultivating in gardens. Their natural habitat is the south-western part of South Africa where the rains fall in winter and the summers are hot and dry. Male and female flowerheads are carried on different plants, the female flowers being on the whole more decorative than the male. Leucadendrons are grown for the distinctive colouring of the involucre of leaves surrounding the flowers rather than for the flowers themselves. These top leaves become tinted yellow, gold, pink and rose in late winter and spring and make the mountain slopes of their natural habitat a field of glowing colour. They are now being widely cultivated because the stems look effective and last long when cut for arrangements.
CULTURE. Leucadendrons need an acid soil that drains readily. They do not thrive in heavy clay on a flat site where water cannot drain away quickly. On the other hand, they are not suitable

for drought-stricken areas as they need an abundance of water during late autumn and winter. They should be trimmed back lightly late in spring to keep them from becoming too large. Plants tend to become woody with age and should be replaced with new ones every few years.

L. album
This is not a very ornamental plant but is included because it grows in alkaline soil and in coastal gardens, and it stands quite severe frost. It reaches 1,5 m and has very slender leaves.

L. daphnoides
Grows to 1 m or more, and makes an impressive show in late winter and early spring with its large heads of involucral leaves, which are yellow tinted with rose and crimson.

L. discolor
Is one of the most decorative of the leucadendrons. It grows to 2 m and has ornamental leaves at the top arranged like a cup. They are sulphur-yellow outlined with crimson or rose with a central cone of the same shades.

L. eucalyptifolium
Reaches 2 m in height and makes a glorious display with its bright-yellow leaves which surround the yellow flowerheads like a halo. It is a graceful plant for the garden and produces fine stems for arrangements.

Leucadendron tinctum is at its best in late winter

The Golden-yellow Pincushion or Kreupelhout (*Leucospermum conocarpodendron*) does well in coastal gardens

The colourful foliage of different conifers and shrubs adds interest to this garden

L. floridum

A charming small species with dainty flowerheads carried in profusion in early spring. The colouring is subtle – pale lime-green combined with soft creamy-yellow and silver. The plant grows to 1 m or a little more in height and spread.

L. loranthifolium

A robust plant which grows to 2 m in height and spread. It stands long periods of heat and dryness in summer and grows well in poor gravelly soils. The leaves are an unusual metallic blue in late winter and early spring.

L. modestum

A species suitable for the small garden as the plants do not grow to more than 1 m. They have slender yellow leaves surrounding the central head of yellow flowers, making a pretty show in early spring.

L. platyspermum

Reaches a height of 2 m and is upright in habit of growth. The female flowerhead with its central cone of emerald, surrounded by a halo of jade green or sulphur-yellow leaves, makes a handsome show.

L. salignum *(L. adscendens)*

A gay shrub growing to 2 m or more which glows with colour in late winter and early spring. The involucral leaves turn pale or deep yellow, sometimes prettily edged with rose, or they may become a deep fiery crimson. The colouring seems to be more intense in areas with sharp frost than in coastal regions.

L. sessile *(L. venosum)*

This species which grows to about 1 m becomes yellow or crimson in late winter when the top leaves turn colour. It makes a pretty show in the garden and in arrangements.

L. tinctum *(L. grandiflorum)*

Although the plant may become straggly with age the flowerheads, with their surrounding colourful leaves, make a splendid show in late winter and early spring. The colours vary from misty yellow through apricot to glowing tones of rose and crimson – pretty outdoors and in vases.

Leucospermum PINCUSHION

DESCRIPTION. This South African member of the protea family is like some of its Australian relatives in that it produces splendid and showy flowerheads that last long on the plants and in arrangements. The relationship between this genus and the Australian banksia is apparent. In both cases the small flowers are carried tightly clustered together in large heads. Each flower consists of a very slender tubular perianth that splits and rolls back. As this happens, the styles that have been enclosed within the perianth tube emerge to make the charming 'pincushion' effect in the case of the leucospermum, and the showy bottlebrush head in the case of the banksia. There are many species in each genus and it would be very easy to become an enthusiastic collector of both banksias and leucospermums. In the garden of average size, there is, however, generally space for only one or two species. Many of them provide rewarding flowers for arrangements from autumn to summer.

CULTURE. Most species prefer acid soil with good drainage. Once established they stand fairly sharp frost provided they are not dry at the same time. They can endure months with little moisture during summer and early autumn. Not suitable for subtropical gardens nor for cool misty ones where there is insufficient bright sunshine.

L. catherinae CATHERINE WHEEL

In spring this species produces large flowerheads that open to show long, curved projecting styles arranged rather like the spokes of a wheel, which accounts for the common name. They are subtly coloured from soft apricot to rose with a silver glint. The plant grows to 1,5 m but can be kept smaller by the removal of the faded flowerheads.

L. conocarpodendron GOLDEN-YELLOW PINCUSHION, KREUPELHOUT

A magnificent species for the large garden or park. It grows to 3 m and becomes woody with age. The flowerheads which measure up to 12 cm across make a wonderful show with their glistening, golden-yellow styles

and ornamentation of silver hairs. It does well in coastal gardens.

L. cordifolium *(L. nutans)* PINCUSHION

From late autumn to spring this species carries decorative flowerheads, varying in colour from apricot to a beautiful shade of coral-red. There is a yellow form but this is rare. The plant grows to 1,5 m in height with a much greater spread, but if the faded flowers are cut with a long stem, the plant can be kept to smaller dimensions. A mature plant carries as many as 300 to 400 flowerheads at a time and, as each one is 12 cm across, a plant in full flower is an arresting sight. This is probably the best species to grow for the cutflower trade, not only because it carries so many flowers but because the flowers last for three weeks in arrangements. Plants tend to become woody and one should be prepared to set out new ones every six to nine years. Beautiful cultivars of different colours are now available.

L. cuneiforme GLOSSY PINCUSHION

Grows to 1,5 m and bears flowerheads 5 cm across of a combination of yellow, apricot and coral-red. The flowers are invariably in pairs, and a plant in full bloom is a splendid sight. It will grow in soil that is slightly alkaline.

L. glabrum GLOSSY PINCUSHION

This species bears handsome flowers on plants 2 m tall. The flowerhead is domed and attractive at all stages, from bud to the fully open flower. The buds are coral-pink tipped with silky, pearl-grey hairs, and when the flower opens the crimson perianth tubes roll back to reveal glistening styles of apricot to coral, with tips of lime-green, yellow or rose.

L. grandiflorum RAINBOW PINCUSHION

A robust plant for the back of a large border. It grows to 2 m in height and almost as much in spread. In spring it carries flowers of a combination of apricot and coral-red, which show up well against the grey-green of the leaves.

L. lineare NARROW-LEAFED PINCUSHION

The flowers of this species are very similar to those of *L. cordifolium*, but the leaves are very slender and give the whole plant a lighter appearance. The flowers are usually paler. It grows to 1,25 m in height and spreads across a good deal more. The flowering time is spring.

L. mundii
Grows to 1 m or more in height and spread, and has flowers that change in colour as they mature, so that a bush may have flowers of several shades on it at the same time, from golden-yellow to cadmium-orange and crimson. Flowers in late winter and early spring.

L. oleifolium (L. crinitum)
TUFTED PINCUSHION
This species is very like *L. mundii*. They have flowers of the same colours, generally carried in pairs, and they are both most colourful in late winter and early spring.

L. patersonii PATERSON PINCUSHION
This is an exceptionally handsome member of the genus. It bears a distinct resemblance to the popular *L. cordifolium*, but is more upright in growth, attaining a height of 3 m or a little more. Mature plants may develop a tree-like form. The flowers are very similar to those of *L. cordifolium* but are more domed, and its leaves and seeds are larger. An outstanding characteristic of this leucospermum is the fact that it occurs naturally in alkaline soil and is therefore suitable for gardens where the soil is of this nature, whereas most of the other members of this genus prefer acid soil.

L. prostratum CREEPING PINCUSHION
A useful ground cover in gravelly soil. It bears miniature 'pincushions' of flowers in great profusion in late winter and early spring. They combine shades of apricot, orange and coral-red.

L. reflexum ROCKET PINCUSHION
Another apt name for this plant could be Smoke and Flames, for the leaves are the soft grey shade of smoke, and the crimson flowers look like spurts of flame against the blue of the sky. This is a handsome shrub for the large garden or park or to line a long avenue. The plant grows to 2–3 m in height and spread and its silvery-grey leaves are decorative throughout the year. In the late winter and early spring it produces its sensational flowers which are apricot to orange in the bud. As the flower matures the whole head changes to flame colour, and the styles uncurl and reflex, giving the head the appearance of a rocket taking off.

L. tottum PINK PINCUSHION
This is probably one of the best of the pincushions for the garden of average size. The plant grows to 1 m or a little more, and has neatly formed heads of flowers that vary in shade from salmon to a soft dusty pink. It has the additional advantage of flowering in late spring, when the other species are past their best.

Ligustrum PRIVET
DESCRIPTION. Deciduous or evergreen shrubs or trees. They have for generations been widely used for making low or high hedges or windbreaks. They are also useful for formal planting. Clipped topiary specimens planted on either side of an entrance or in containers on a terrace add attraction to the garden. Privets have neat leaves, oval in shape and varying in size according to species. If left untrimmed, they bear clusters or spikes of small, white flowers in late spring and early summer. The flowers are followed by blue-black berries which attract birds from far and wide. When making a hedge set plants very close together and trim them back hard to make them thick at the base. The leaves of the variegated types are decorative in arrangements.
CULTURE. Privets can be relied upon to grow under a wide range of climatic conditions. They will endure severe frost, long periods with little water, drying winds and poor soil. To promote quick growth it is advisable to improve poor soil by the addition of humus, and to water regularly until plants are two or three years old. They grow in full sunshine or partial shade. The plants can be transplanted when fairly large. They tend to rob the soil of nutrients and may affect the growth of other plants near them.

L. ibota
A small species growing to 6 m with neat oval leaves of soft green. If not trimmed back annually it grows into a pretty little shade tree. Close-planted and clipped regularly, it makes a good low formal hedge.

L. japonicum
JAPANESE PRIVET, WAXLEAF PRIVET
Is an evergreen reaching 3–6 m or more with oval leaves rounded at the ends, measuring 4–10 cm in length, mid-green on the upper surface and paler below. This is a fine species for trimming into topiary specimens – pyramids, globes or other shapes – or for making into small standard trees. A cultivar known as 'Rotundifolium' has almost round leaves and grows to only 2 m while 'Texanum' reaches a height of 3 m. 'Aureum' (Golden Japanese Privet) has leaves with a yellow margin.

L. lucidum GLOSSY PRIVET
If not trimmed, this species will grow into a tree 9 m tall. It is generally trimmed to form a windbreak or dense hedge. Where severe frost limits the number of evergreens that can be grown this species should be tried, as it is a decorative plant whether grown as a tree, a windbreak, a formal hedge or a topiary specimen. The leaves are fairly large – 10 to 15 cm long, broadly oval and pointed, slightly glossy and fairly dark green. They are somewhat leathery, quite different from those of *L. japonicum*, which are soft. Some gardeners prefer the variegated forms of this species. *L. lucidum* 'Tricolor' has leaves bordered with creamy-white and *L. lucidum* 'Aureo-variegatum' has leaves bordered with yellow. These variegated forms grow less vigorously than the species – seldom reaching a height of more than 3 m.

L. ovalifolium CALIFORNIAN PRIVET
Is evergreen in regions with moderate winters but loses most of its leaves where frosts are very severe. It makes a good hedge. The roots of this species can inhibit the growth of small plants near it. The popular Golden Privet is a form of this species listed as 'Aureum'.

121

Glossy Pincushion (*Leucospermum glabrum*) has handsome heads of flowers

Narrow-leafed Pincushion (*Leucospermum lineare*) is splendid in the garden and in arrangements

Tufted Pincushion (*Leucospermum oleifolium*). An unusual shrub for the large garden

Paterson Pincushion (*Leucospermum patersonii*). A robust spring-flowering plant

Plant the Creeping Pincushion (*Leucospermum prostratum*) on a wall or bank

Rocket Pincushion (*Leucospermum reflexum*) at the back, with *Leucospermum cordifolium* and *Mimulus glutinosus* in front

It has leaves with a broad yellow edge. It makes a very good specimen plant trimmed to any shape.

L. sinense CHINESE PRIVET
A deciduous or semi-evergreen shrub or small tree to 6 m with large clusters of white flowers in spring. It does well in dry and frosty gardens. 'Variegatum' has leaves with ivory margins.

L. vulgare COMMON PRIVET
Is an evergreen or deciduous shrub growing to 4 m if not clipped. It has light green leaves. A dwarf form of this known as 'Lodense' is more suitable for formal low hedges as it grows to only 1 m in height and spread.

Lithodora diffusa

(*Lithospermum diffusum*) LITHOSPERMUM
DESCRIPTION. An evergreen shrub of prostrate habit, seldom more than 30 cm tall. It is spreading in habit and looks lovely trailing over a wall or bank, or peeping out from between rocks in a rock garden. The leaves are narrow and hairy. Little starry flowers of clear plumbago blue appear in profusion in late winter and early spring.
CULTURE. This charming little plant thrives only in acid soil and under rather cool conditions. In a hot garden it should be planted where it is sheltered from intense sunlight and dry winds.

Lonicera HONEYSUCKLE

DESCRIPTION. This genus of plants includes evergreen and deciduous shrubs and twining or climbing plants. They are quick-growing and therefore useful as a stop-gap planted between slow-growing plants. Some species are worth growing also because of their scent. The shrubby forms described here need trimming as they become older to keep them neat and compact.

The mauve trailing Lantana (*Lantana montevidensis*) makes an effective show draped over a wall or bank

CULTURE. Honeysuckles are remarkably adaptable as regards climate and soil. They endure sharp frost and will perform fairly well in poor soil – be it slightly alkaline or acid. Plant them in full sunshine near the coast and in partial shade where the sunlight is intense.

L. etrusca 'Superba'
BUSH HONEYSUCKLE
A quick-growing, semi-deciduous bushy plant to 2 m with a spread of almost as much. To keep it small and compact, cut the stems back immediately after its flowering period. The leaves are oblong or oval, 3–6 cm long – the upper pairs united at the base. The flowers carried in whorls are yellow suffused with red. This species is sometimes wrongly called *L. gigantea superba*.

L. fragrantissima
WINTER OR CORAL HONEYSUCKLE
An evergreen or semi-evergreen species growing to 3 m that is easily kept to smaller size by annual trimming. It has dark-green oval leaves, 2–5 cm long. Inconspicuous creamy-white flowers with a rich perfume are carried in pairs in the axils of the leaves in winter. When trimming, cut out old growth at the base leaving the new stems to grow on and produce the following year's flowers.

L. nitida   BOX HONEYSUCKLE
An evergreen grown for its compact form and neat foliage. It is a fine plant to trim into a low hedge or shape as a formal specimen plant standing alone. Untrimmed, it will grow to 1,5 m. The dark-green oval leaves are shiny, and only about 1 cm long. Untrimmed plants produce insignificant scented creamy-white flowers in summer. It does well in seaside gardens as well as those at high elevations. The cultivar *L. nitida* 'Aurea' has variegated leaves. It looks attractive in a container or in a rock garden. Slow-growing.

L. pileata   PRIVET HONEYSUCKLE
An evergreen shrub to 60 cm growing horizontally. It makes a good ground cover for a bank. The scented flowers are insignificant but the leaves are attractive. They are oval and dark green.

L. tatarica   TARTARIAN HONEYSUCKLE
Deciduous shrub growing into a bushy plant 3 m in height and almost as much in spread, with oval cordate leaves about 5 cm in length, and masses of ivory or pink flowers in axillary pairs in spring. It makes a good background plant in a large garden and does well in part shade.

Luculia   LUCULIA, PINK SWA
DESCRIPTION. The genus includes two beautiful species from the East that deserve to be better known and more widely grown. Not only are they decorative in appearance but the flowers have a delightful scent, reminiscent of lilac. They flower in autumn.
CULTURE. These desirable plants require soil rich in humus and moist, misty climatic conditions. They tolerate mild frost but they should be protected during their first two winters. Transplant when very small, taking care not to disturb the soil around the roots, and pinch out the growing tip to encourage bushiness at the base. Where the sunlight is intense for most of the year plant them in filtered shade or where they have only the morning sun. Luculia are not easy to raise but well worth the effort required to get them to grow.

L. grandiflora   LUCULIA
Is a semi-deciduous or evergreen plant growing to 4 m if not trimmed. It has large leaves up to 30 cm long with red stalks and midribs, and huge clusters of snow-white flowers. A plant in full flower will scent the entire garden.

L. gratissima   PINK SWA
An enchanting plant from the Himalayas which will grow to 3 m under congenial conditions, but it can be kept smaller by trimming so that it does not become too large for the small garden. It is evergreen with broadly oval leaves 10–20 cm long, and clusters of scented, phlox-like flowers of a charming shade of shell-pink. It stands fairly sharp frost when well established, provided it is not subjected to dry conditions.

Mackaya bella   MACKAYA
DESCRIPTION. An evergreen South African plant growing to a height of 2 m. It is slow-growing except in warm, humid regions. It has glossy oval pointed leaves up to 6 cm long, and delicately coloured flowers rather like those of a tecoma in form. They are funnel-shaped at the base ending in a face made up of five reflexed segments of unequal size. The colour is palest mauve with veins etched in deep maroon. This is a pretty plant for a shady part of the garden.
CULTURE. It will stand occasional frost but does not thrive in cold gardens. Recommended for tropical and subtropical regions, and for warm coastal gardens.

Magnolia liliiflora   (M. purpurea)
TULIP MAGNOLIA
DESCRIPTION. A deciduous shrub growing slowly to a height of 3 m or a little more. It sends up many stems from the base and is an effective plant even when small as it flowers freely. It has fairly large ovate or obovate leaves which come out only after the flowers begin to fade. The handsome flowers appear in late winter and show up beautifully against the bare stems and the winter sky. They are tulip or chalice-shaped, mauve on the outside and white, or white flushed with mauve inside. A darker form which flowers a little later is known as *M. liliiflora* 'Nigra'. Both are desirable plants for the garden. Plant them behind low evergreen shrubs which will hide the base of the bare stems in winter but allow the flowers to show above.
CULTURE. This magnolia enjoys cold conditions and will not thrive in tropical or subtropical gardens. Where severe frost may cause damage to the flowers, plant it so that it is sheltered from the early morning winter sun. It grows in full sunshine, but, where the sunshine is intense for most of the year it does better in partial shade. Plant in acid soil and water well, particularly during winter and early spring.

Mahonia MAHONIA

DESCRIPTION. Evergreen shrubs grown for their attractive foliage, which is decorative in the garden and in arrangements.

CULTURE. Mahonias are not for hot, dry gardens nor subtropical ones. They like cool to cold growing conditions and do best in acid soil with plenty of humus added and in a shady position under trees. They should be watered during dry periods of the year.

M. aquifolium OREGON GRAPE

Is an erect plant reaching 2 m in height with leaves divided into pairs of tiny, glossy leaflets rather like those of holly. The young growth is tinged with bronze. The golden-yellow spikes of flowers appear in spring and are followed by purple berries that make a good jelly. The dwarf form 'Nana' is more suitable for small gardens. It makes a good ground cover under trees in a cool garden.

M. japonica (M. bealei)
LEATHERLEAF MAHONIA

Grows to 2 m and has large leaves divided into numerous leathery, spiny, broadly oval leaflets jade-green in colour. In late winter and early spring it bears long racemes of small lemon-yellow flowers, with the scent of lily-of-the-valley. These are followed by purple berries. It makes a good tub plant for a shady place.

M. lomariifolia

Is the most attractive of the mahonias. It has stems of leaflets of sculptured design. They are spiny and glossy, and arranged symmetrically along the central stem, rather like the leaflets of a sword fern. In winter long spikes of golden-yellow flowers appear at the ends of stems. These are followed by blue berries relished by birds. Grow it in shade or partial shade in the ground or in a container. This species may tolerate alkaline soil but not dry conditions.

M. pinnata CALIFORNIAN HOLLY GRAPE

Grows to 2 m and has crinkled, spiny leaves. It is not as decorative as the other species but it stands cold, heat and drought.

Malvaviscus arboreus
WAX MALLOW

DESCRIPTION. A quick-growing evergreen shrub that reaches a height and spread of 2 m. It has large, velvety, heart-shaped leaves with toothed margins. In summer it carries small scarlet flowers which look somewhat like an unopened hibiscus flower. They are not particularly showy, but the plant is worth growing for the foliage effect, and also because it is a useful stop-gap shrub for the new garden to provide something green and verdant whilst slow-growing shrubs are small.

CULTURE. It grows best in tropical and sub-tropical gardens but will stand moderate frost, too. In hot dry areas it will not grow quickly unless watered fairly regularly.

Megaskepasma erythrochlamys MEGAS

DESCRIPTION. This formidable botanical name is that of a decorative evergreen shrub from Venezuela. It is quick-growing and, where space is limited in the garden, it should be trimmed back to keep it small. It grows to 3 m in height and spread, but flowers well if cut back annually to keep it half this size. The large oblong pointed leaves are 10 to 25 cm long, with a corrugated surface. The two lipped flowers are white or palest pink and not very showy. They emerge from spectacular crimson bracts carried in long spikes which make a splendid display in autumn, against the green of the leaves.

CULTURE. This is a rewarding shrub for tropical and subtropical gardens. It does well in warm coastal regions but does not thrive in areas where winters are cool or where it is subjected to long periods with little humidity. Plant in shade in inland gardens.

Melaleuca
BOTTLEBRUSH AND OTHERS

DESCRIPTION. The genus includes more than one hundred species, all except one of them native to Australia and Tasmania. They are closely related to the callistemons. Both have flowers with prominent stamens which give them the appearance of a bottlebrush, and for this reason both are sometimes referred to by this common name. In some species of melaleuca the flowers form round balls. In the callistemons the stamens are not joined as they are in the melaleucas. The genus includes trees as well as shrubs. The leaves are small and neat, sometimes needle-like and sometimes rather like those of an erica.

CULTURE. These are useful and colourful plants with a tolerance of a wide range of growing conditions. Some of them stand moderate to severe frost. Many species also grow well in areas subjected to dry winds and long periods of drought. Protect plants from frost when young. They like acid soil and may not thrive where the soil is highly alkaline. They generally do well in coastal gardens and inland. Cut plants back lightly when necessary to prevent them from crowding out neighbouring plants.

M. diosmaefolia

A species from Western Australia which grows to 3 m or more. It has pleasing foliage and bears small cylinders of greeny-yellow flowers in spring and summer. It does well in seaside gardens.

M. elliptica GRANITE HONEY MYRTLE

This robust species grows quickly to a height of 3 m. It is a handsome shrub with grey-green leaves and crimson to scarlet flowers in spring and summer. It stands fairly severe frost.

M. hypericifolia

A handsome background shrub which grows to a height of 3 m or more. It has drooping stems of slender leaves somewhat like those of hypericum, and showy cylinders of orange-red flowers in late spring. Stands coastal wind and some frost.

M. incana GREY HONEY MYRTLE

An outstanding species growing to 2 m or a little more, with pleasing, silvery-grey leaves densely arranged on arching, weeping branches. It is ornamental even when not in flower. The yellow cylinders of flowers appear in spring.

M. lateritia ROBIN REDBREAST BUSH
An attractive bushy plant growing to
2 m, with tiny leaves on graceful
branches and showy cylinders of
flowers in spring and early summer. It
is hardy to sharp frost.

M. nesophylla PINK MELALEUCA
Is a vigorous species which does
exceptionally well in poor sandy soil,
in hot dry places and in coastal gardens. It is tender to frost when young.
The plant may grow to 6 m if not
trimmed. It can be trained to tree-form
by cutting out lower stems. The grey-
green leaves show up the balls of
mauve to cyclamen flowers which
appear in summer.

M. pentagona
A species from Western Australia with
a height and spread of 2 m or more. It
has small sharp leaves and cyclamen-
mauve flowers in tiny heads. It does
well in seaside gardens.

M. radula
Is a pretty species of slender habit
reaching a height of 2 m with narrow
leaves on arching stems. Heads of
mauve or lilac flowers with golden
anthers add to the beauty of the plant.
The main flowering time is spring.
Prune it after flowering to keep it neat.

M. steedmanii
A delightful small species from Western Australia which grows to 1–2 m. It
has narrow oval leaves and crimson
bottlebrush flowers with golden
anthers. Does well in dry gardens. The
flowering time is spring.

Melastoma malabathricum
MELASTOMA
DESCRIPTION. A rangy shrub rather
similar to Lasiandra in appearance. It
is of upright growth to 2–3 m, with

Golden Privet stands considerable frost and
some dryness

Luculia is one of the most enchanting of the
shrubs that flower in autumn

long stems clothed with elliptic-oblong leaves, rather rough and hairy. During summer and autumn it bears handsome flowers of a rich magenta hue with prominent stamens and anthers that show up well in the centre of the flowers.

CULTURE. Recommended only for gardens where winters are mild. It does well if watered regularly and thoroughly. Trim plants back if they become leggy.

Melianthus major   HONEY BUSH

DESCRIPTION. A South African plant grown for its decorative foliage. The large jade-green leaves are beautifully divided into leaflets with ruffled and serrated margins. It grows to 1,5 m and has many sturdy stems rising from the ground. It is particularly handsome in spring when it carries burgundy-coloured flowerheads on long stems. After the flowers fade, the stems bear large green seed capsules. Unfortunately the plant gives off an unpleasant smell when touched.

CULTURE. This is a quick-growing plant. Once it is established it stands fairly long dry periods but not much frost. It grows in full sun but, in inland gardens, it does best in filtered shade.

Michelia figo   *(Magnolia fuscata)*

BANANA MAGNOLIA, PORT WINE MAGNOLIA
DESCRIPTION. An evergreen shrub or small tree from China growing to 3 m with a conical or rounded top. It has oval, pointed leaves of medium green with a glossy upper surface. In early spring it bears burgundy-coloured flowers. Before opening these are enclosed in brown bracts. In the evening the flowers give off a very strong scent of fruit salad, with banana predominating. The plant is neat but the flowers are not showy. It is worth growing, however, for the fresh and delightful scent of the flowers that pervades the garden after sunset. It is quite an attractive plant for a container on a patio or terrace.

CULTURE. Plant it in soil rich in humus and in partial shade. Banana magnolia will stand only light frost.

Micromyrtus ciliata
FRINGED HEATH MYRTLE
DESCRIPTION. A low-growing evergreen, Australian shrub suitable for the small garden or a rock garden. It has a height and spread of 60 cm and small leaves neatly arranged along the stems. In late spring it bears masses of tiny flowers. The buds are rose, opening to a white face. It makes a delightful show when in full flower.

CULTURE. Plant it in soil which drains readily. Once established, it stands moderate frost and long periods with little water. In very cold areas mulch the soil around plants, and water in winter. Transplant when very small.

Mimetes
MIMETES
DESCRIPTION. A genus of evergreen South African shrubs, members of the protea family, which make an attractive show in early spring. They grow to 1,5 m in height with upright stems. The leaves are slightly leathery in texture and symmetrically arranged on the stems, overlapping one another. In spring the leaves at the top change colour, becoming suffused with crimson, pink and lime-yellow. The small flowers emerge from between these colourful leaves and add to the beauty of the plant with their shining tufts of silky hairs. The stems are pretty in arrangements as well as in the garden.

CULTURE. Mimetes will not do well in subtropical regions nor those subjected to severe frost and dryness at the same time. They will stand moderate frost but only if they are kept moist. The plants tolerate a long dry period in summer and early autumn but need water from late autumn to spring to encourage flowering. Plant them when very small in acid soil.

M. argenteus
The flowerhead is not as colourful as in other species but the glistening silver leaves make this a unique plant – effective when grown near those with dark green leaves. It reaches a height of 1,5 m but it is not easy to grow.

Tulip Magnolia *(Magnolia liliiflora)* has beautiful flowers of sculptured form. They appear when the plant is bare of leaves and highlight the garden from mid- to late winter

This Mahonia *(Mahonia lomariifolia)* is an evergreen shrub of unusual form with decorative flowers in spring

Megas *(Megaskepasma erythrochlamys)* creates a bright show in a warm garden

M. cucullatus *(M. lyrigera)*

A handsome species 1,5 m in height and spread. Groom the plant each year after flowering to keep it compact. The top leaves on the stems remain yellow and crimson for a long time in late winter and early spring. The flowers, ornamented with silky white hairs, peep out from between them adding to the charm of the display.

M. hirtus

This species seems to like marshy ground. It does well in coastal gardens if watered adequately. The flowerhead, with its gaily coloured background of red and yellow, ends in a small tufted top somewhat like that at the top of a pineapple.

Mimulus glutinosus

(Diplacus glutinosus) MONKEY FLOWER
DESCRIPTION. The common name, derived from *mimo* meaning monkey, describes the shape of the flower. This is a quick-growing evergreen reaching a height of 60 cm. It has slender leaves, slightly glossy and dark green, and flowers of yellow, apricot or terra-cotta. Each flower is made up of a funnel opening to a face made up of two sections, the upper divided into two lobes and the lower into three. Cultivars of merit are 'Aurantiacus' with apricot flowers; 'Puniceus' with flowers of wine-red, and 'Mrs Scholes', which bears terra-cotta flowers. They flower in late spring and early summer. This is a pretty little shrub for the front of a shrub border or to plant in a border of annuals and perennials.
CULTURE. It stands only mild frosts, and in areas with a cold winter it should be planted in a protected position. To encourage good flowering cut the plants back after they have flowered.

Murraya paniculata *(M. exotica)*

ORANGE JASMINE
DESCRIPTION. A quick-growing evergreen 1–2 m in height and more in spread. It has leaves divided into three neat, dark-green, glossy oval leaflets about 3–5 cm long that are decorative throughout the year. In summer it carries clusters of cup-shaped, five-petalled white flowers which resemble orange blossom in appearance and

scent. Planted close it will make a dense informal hedge or screen.
CULTURE. This shrub is native to the East Indies and does well in tropical and subtropical gardens, but once it is well grown, it stands moderate frost. Plant in soil rich in humus and water well during dry periods of the year. It grows in full sun or part shade.

Mussaenda

MUSSAENDA, FLAG BUSH
DESCRIPTION. Evergreen or partly deciduous shrubs native to the warm parts of Africa and the Pacific Islands. They are quick-growing and bear small colourful flowers. Their main attraction is in the enlarged leaf-like sepals that highlight the bush for the whole of summer and early autumn. Only one of the sepals behind each flower enlarges, and these stand out well, looking like a host of small flags – which accounts for the common name. The plants reach 1,5 m in height and more in spread. They should be trimmed once a year to keep them tidy.
CULTURE. Although one species will stand mild frost, they undoubtedly do best in warm, humid areas and are recommended for subtropical and tropical gardens. Elsewhere they can be grown as container plants, brought out of shelter to grace the terrace or patio in summer. They should be watered during dry periods of the year.

M. erythrophylla RED FLAG BUSH

An attractive shrub from tropical Africa with oval, rounded leaves of bright green. The yellow flowers are carried in little clusters. As the flowers fade, the enlarged sepals turn brilliant scarlet. This species does well only in subtropical gardens.

M. frondosa WHITE FLAG BUSH

Has pale-green foliage, bright orange-yellow flowers and large flag-like white sepals which ornament the plant for a long period. Beautiful hybrids with pink sepals are now available. This species stands mild frosts and does well in semi-shade.

Myoporum NGAIO

DESCRIPTION. The genus includes evergreen trees and shrubs native to Australia and New Zealand. They are use-

ful as screen plants in coastal districts where winds are strong, or as background plants in dry regions where frosts are not extreme.
CULTURE. Transplant when young, spacing plants only 1 m apart if a quick, dense screen is required. Although they grow in poor soil the addition of humus to the soil and regular watering will speed up growth.

M. desertii TURKEY BUSH

Is not a decorative plant but of value in hot dry gardens to provide plant cover. It grows to 2 m and has small leaves and white bell-shaped flowers followed by insignificant small yellow berries that are relished by wild turkeys in its native land. It stands moderate frost.

M. insulare BOOBIALLA, MANITOKA

A useful species growing to 3 m with bright green leaves and inconspicuous white flowers followed by small maroon berries. A good hedge or screen plant in coastal gardens and in dry hot areas inland.

M. parvifolium CREEPING BOOBIALLA

This is a prostrate-growing plant, only 30 cm in height. It creeps, rooting itself as it grows. In spring it bears small white flowers that are followed by small purple berries. It makes a good ground cover and is also grown as a pot plant.

Myrtus MYRTLE

DESCRIPTION. A large genus of shrubs and small trees from many parts of the world. The best species for the garden are evergreen plants with decorative foliage. The leaves are generally neat, oval and pointed, dark green and lustrous. Some species bear pretty flowers followed by berries. They vary in height, many species growing to 3 m, whilst some of the cultivars are less than 1 m tall. The tall species make a good windbreak or screen but can look effective too when grown alone as specimen shrubs. They do well in coastal gardens.
CULTURE. Myrtles will stand cold growing conditions. Plant them in soil rich in humus, and water until established. Well-grown plants may not die during a drought, but the plants slow down if continually subjected to long periods without water. They are fibrous-rooted

plants and can be transplanted when fairly large, provided the top growth is cut back.

M. bullata
This species from New Zealand grows to 3 m or more in height and has small oval leaves tinged with bronze. It will not thrive in dry areas.

M. communis COMMON MYRTLE
Grows to 6 m but is usually cut back to form a hedge or screen, 2–3 m in height. It has oval and pointed leaves, bright green and glossy, and about 5 cm long that give off a pleasant aromatic scent when crushed. White flowers with showy stamens appear in summer and are followed by deep purple berries. It grows well in partial shade and stands drought. Dwarf cultivars of this species are more suited to small gardens. 'Variegata' is an excellent one which grows to 2 m and has leaves edged with ivory.

M. ugni CHILEAN GUAVA
Grows to 2–3 m and has neat leathery dark-green leaves 1–3 cm long, and white flowers followed by small fruits that look like miniature guavas. They make a tasty preserve. It is a good hedge plant. 'Variegata' is a cultivar with leaves edged with cream.

Nandina domestica
JAPANESE OR CHINESE SACRED BAMBOO
DESCRIPTION. This is an unusual and ornamental plant to grow next to a pool, or in a container on a terrace or patio. It can also be used for indoor decoration. Although it looks like a small bamboo, this plant is not a bamboo, but related to the berberis. It grows to 2 m sending up numerous stems from the ground. In a cold climate it may lose some of its leaves but where frosts are not very severe it is evergreen. The leaves are prettily divided into pointed, oval leaflets 3–5 cm long, giving a charming, almost fern-like pattern. The new leaves are tinged with bronze and red. Where frosts are sharp the leaves turn scarlet in autumn. Small ivory-white, waxy flowers are carried in clusters in summer. If fertilization takes place the flowers are followed by bright scarlet berries in autumn. Dwarf forms known as 'Nana Compacta' and 'Pygmaea' are more

suitable for indoor pot-culture and for rock or pebble gardens. They grow to only 45 cm in height and are particularly lovely when the leaves turn colour. It is said that in Japan this plant is grown near the house so that if anyone dreamed of disaster the dreamer could rush out at once and tell the story to the plant. By doing this the disaster would be averted.
CULTURE. Plant it in acid soil, rich in humus. It stands frost and also long periods with little water. Grows in partial shade but colours best when it has sun.

Nerium oleander OLEANDER
DESCRIPTION. An evergreen of great merit in areas where growing conditions are difficult. The plant reaches a height of 3 m or more, and develops many arching stems from the base. In the garden of average size it is advisable to cut out some of the stems every few years. This keeps the plant down to reasonable size, and encourages the development of new flowering stems. It has narrow, lance-shaped leaves somewhat leathery and slightly glossy, of a pleasing mid-green. Cultivars with variegated leaves are also available. Some have single flowers and others have double ones. The flowers arranged in pretty clusters appear all through the summer. They are shades of pink, rose, salmon, cyclamen, crimson and white.

All parts of the plants are poisonous and children should be trained at an early age to recognise the plant and to avoid chewing twigs, leaves or flowers. Twigs should not be put on barbecue fires as even the smoke from burning twigs may cause irritation. Although poisonous, one never hears of anyone having being poisoned by them, but this is no reason for not taking precautions. For generations oleanders have been grown in many parts of the world as roadside shrubs and trees.

This is an excellent shrub for background planting, for growing on the strip dividing major roadways, for street and avenue planting, and as a tall hedge or windbreak. It looks most attractive when grown as a tall standard.
CULTURE. They like strong sunlight, can endure severe frost, and once established, will also survive long periods of

drought. They are not particular as to soil, growing well in alkaline or acid soil. They do well in coastal gardens where the humidity is not high.

Notospartium carmichaeliae
PINK BROOM
DESCRIPTION. This New Zealand shrub is a very pretty sight in summer when it carries its pink to cyclamen pea-shaped flowers on slender, arching stems. It grows to 3 m but can be tailored to a smaller size.
CULTURE. It is quick-growing and once established will stand sharp frost and fairly long periods with little water. To encourage good flowering, water the plants regularly in spring. It does well in sandy and alkaline soil.

Nylandtia spinosa
(Mundia spinosa) TORTOISE BERRY
DESCRIPTION. A South African plant that is rather like gorse in manner of growth. The slender stems are sparsely clothed with small leaves hardly as large as those of an erica. The stems end in a sharp spine. Towards the end of winter and early in spring the whole plant becomes a filmy mass of tiny misty-mauve pea-shaped flowers. After the flowers fade it bears a profusion of scarlet berries that are apparently relished by tortoises, which abound in the area in which it occurs. This is a shrub for the windy, seaside garden where only a limited number of shrubs will survive. It has a height and spread of 1–2 m.
CULTURE. It grows in sandy and poor gravelly soils, and endures long periods with little water and moderate frost.

Nymania capensis
CHINESE LANTERN
DESCRIPTION. Is an evergreen or semi-deciduous South African plant that grows in drought-stricken areas. It reaches a height of 2 m and is upright in habit. The flowers are inconspicuous but are followed by large balloon-like seedpods about 4 cm across that look rather like Chinese paper lanterns. They are prettily coloured from lime-green to bright coral-red and light up the shrub in late winter and early spring. The leaves are very small and leathery.

Opposite top
Shrubs and trees make a pleasing
background to a border of flowers, and
they give the garden a lush and verdant
appearance when the annuals and
perennials die down

Opposite bottom
Choose shrubs with colourful foliage as
they brighten the garden for most months
of the year

Above
The golden tinge of the leaves of Sambucus
make a delightful background to the plants
in front

Right top
The repetition of colour of the same shrub
creates a dramatic effect

Right bottom
A curving grass path invites one to wander
through this shrub garden

CULTURE. Recommended for hot dry gardens and for areas where the soil is alkaline. This is a slow-growing plant that stands moderate frost and poor soil.

Ochna serrulata (O. atropurpurea)
CARNIVAL BUSH, OCHNA
DESCRIPTION. An evergreen or semi-deciduous shrub native to Southern Africa. It grows slowly to 3 m and has foliage that is decorative for most of the year. The neat leaves are oval and pointed, with finely serrated margins. In early spring they are bronze and highly lustrous, turning darker green as they mature. Golden-yellow cup-shaped flowers with five petals gaily ornament it in spring, and when these fall the plant remains colourful as the calyces turn deep crimson and show up the seeds, which become jet-black as they ripen. Close-planted, ochna makes a pretty hedge. Individual specimens take kindly to trimming as specimen shrubs or container plants.
CULTURE. This is a slow-growing plant which does better in subtropical gardens than in cold areas. In hot inland gardens plant it in partial shade, and water well during dry periods of the year. It will survive mild frosts.

Olearia OLEARIA, DAISY BUSH
DESCRIPTION. Evergreen shrubs and small trees many of which are native to Australia and New Zealand. Some species are grown for their foliage and others for their charming, daisy-like flowers. Many species do well in seaside gardens.
CULTURE. Most species will endure considerable cold and some drought. Where the sunlight is intense and hot winds blow for much of the year, try growing them in partial shade and water them well. They grow in alkaline soil. Trim straggly plants in late winter or early spring.

O. angustifolia
LONG-LEAFED DAISY BUSH
A New Zealand species growing to 3 m or more which can be trimmed annually to keep it smaller. The narrow leaves are about 12 cm long, slightly glossy, green on the upper surface and grey underneath. White daisies with a purple centre adorn the plant in late spring and early summer.

O. chathamica CHATHAM DAISY BUSH
Similar to *O. angustifolia*, but smaller in size and with smaller leaves. The daisies are pale mauve or white suffused with mauve. It stands severe cold but needs moisture.

O. cheesemanii
This large New Zealand shrub grows to 2–3 m in height and spread. The leaves have undulating margins, are dark green on the upper surface and grey-green on the underside. In spring small white daisies cover the plant in such profusion that the leaves are hardly visible.

O. phlogopappa (O. gunniana)
TASMANIAN DAISY BUSH
Has narrow green leaves on plants 1 m or more in height and spread. In spring it becomes covered with small daisies that may be purple, mauve, white, pink or blue. Prune plants back after flowering to keep them neat.

O. tomentosa (O. dentata)
Grows to 1,5 m in height and spread and has leathery leaves with serrated margins. Its flowers are mauve.

O. traversii SILVER AKEAKE
This large shrub or small tree is grown for shade and shelter in coastal gardens in the south of England and in New Zealand. Its flowers are insignificant. The plant reaches a height of 6 m and is fairly quick-growing even in sandy soil. The leathery leaves are green on the upper surface and pearl-grey on the underside.

Orphium frutescens ORPHIUM
DESCRIPTION. A delightful South African plant of shrubby habit, worth a place in gardens large and small. It seldom grows to more than 45 cm in height and spread, and produces its pretty glistening cyclamen-pink flowers in early summer. This is a time when few shrubs are in flower. It is an ideal plant for the front of a shrub border, for a wall or bank and for a rock or pebble garden. The leaves are slender and the flowers have five obovate shiny petals with a sticky texture. They last well on the plant and in arrangements.
CULTURE. Transplant when very small or grow *in situ* from seed. It stands mild frost and dry conditions for a short time, but does best if watered well and regularly.

Osmanthus OSMANTHUS
DESCRIPTION. Evergreen shrubs or trees, generally with tough or leathery foliage sometimes toothed and sometimes smooth. The flowers are fragrant but not showy. These are useful plants for making a hedge or windbreak where growing conditions are difficult.
CULTURE. Osmanthus stand severe frost and long periods with little water. They grow best in acid soil and partial shade but do fairly well also in regions where the soil is slightly alkaline.

O. delavayi DELAVAY OSMANTHUS
A slow-growing plant from western China. It reaches 2 m in height and has arching stems of dark green, oval leaves about 3 cm long with serrated margins. In late winter and early spring it bears sprays of scented tubular flowers with starry faces.

O. fragrans SWEET OLIVE
Reaches a height of 3 m. Can be trained as a tree or grown as a hedge or screen. Cut plants back hard when young to encourage bushy basal growth. The slender leaves are oval and pointed, 6–10 cm long, somewhat leathery and slightly glossy. The insignificant flowers have a fruity fragrance; they are used in China for scenting tea. Where sunlight is intense plant it in partial shade.

O. ilicifolius HOLLY OSMANTHUS
Grows to 3 m and has oval, olive-green leaves something like those of the English holly, with spines not quite as pronounced. The flowers are insignificant but fragrant and useful for arrangements. They appear in spring and are followed by blue berries. Small cultivars with attractive foliage are available. 'Aureomarginatus' has leaves splashed with gold, and 'Rotundifolius' is a more compact plant with rounded leaves.

Paeonia suffruticosa

TREE PEONY

DESCRIPTION. Peonies are divided into two broad classes – those of herbaceous growth and those that are bushy in form. When these grow well they are amongst the most beautiful of all flowering plants. Tree peonies were treasured plants in Japan and China a thousand years ago. Some specimens there are thought to be more than 200 years old. They are popular in gardens in Europe and well worth taking some trouble to grow. The plants are deciduous, growing to a height of 2 m or a little more. They have pretty foliage and large round, single or double flowers somewhat like an old-fashioned rose, with prominent stamens. The flowers are held well above the foliage. Most of the plants grown are hybrids of *P. suffruticosa* and *P. lutea*, with lovely flowers of pink, rose, saffron, salmon, apricot, mauve, purple and crimson.

CULTURE. Peonies are not for subtropical regions nor for those which have hot dry winds. They enjoy cold but must have moisture in the ground and in the air. They flower well only when properly established and should not be moved. It is therefore important that the ground be prepared thoroughly before planting. Make holes 60 cm wide and deep and add a couple of shovels of old manure and compost to the soil returned to the holes. Set the plants fairly deep in the soil. In areas of intense sunshine shade them from afternoon sun or plant them where they get only filtered light during the hottest part of the day. They do best in regions with cold winters and cool misty summers. Peonies like a soil which is slightly alkaline and a dressing of lime once or twice a year will help to promote better growth.

Pelargonium

GERANIUM, PELARGONIUM

DESCRIPTION. The common name of 'geranium' is often used for these decorative pelargoniums, but as the name geranium really applies to other plants, it is as well to learn to differentiate between them. The real geraniums have flowers made up of petals of equal size, usually arranged in a bowl or saucer-like fashion. Pelargoniums, on the other hand, have flowers made up of five petals of unequal shape. The leaves also are very different. Those of the pelargonium are lobed or indented often as broad as they are long, sometimes very like those of the ivy, whereas the leaves of geraniums are much more delicately formed and cut.

There are more than 200 species of pelargoniums and there are many cultivars grown in different countries of the world. Pelargoniums were very popular during the 19th century. They then fell from favour for some years. They are now much in demand, and new introductions have found a prominent place in gardens in the Northern and Southern Hemispheres.

These are delightful plants for any part of the garden and for growing in containers on a balcony, window-ledge, patio or terrace. Some of them are bushy in habit whilst others grow in a trailing fashion and are decorative plants for hanging baskets and for growing on a wall or bank. Some have smooth, almost leathery leaves with a glossy surface; some have leaves marked with a band of brown, red, darker green or yellow, whilst others have leaves that are soft in texture and covered with soft hairs. Some have leaves with an aromatic scent, whilst others have leaves with a strong scent of lemon or peppermint. Some have tiny flowers whilst others have very large ones. Some have single flowers and some have double ones.

Many nurseries now list pelargoniums under different cultivar names and gardeners who are keen on growing a wide range of these flowers should consult a book or catalogues on pelargoniums. The 'azalea-flowering' pelargoniums have large flowers of the same shape and colouring as azaleas, carried in similar rounded heads. *Pelargonium angulosum* is an exceptionally decorative species.

CULTURE. Because they grow so easily, gardeners are inclined to give their pelargoniums no attention at all and are then disappointed at having poor results. These plants will grow in poor dry soil but they will not produce an abundance of flowers unless they have fairly regular attention. Plant them in soil to which some compost has been added. They do better in light soil than in heavy clay that may become waterlogged. Water the plants regularly and trim them after their flowering period is over.

Plants that are not trimmed tend to become tall and leggy, rather untidy in appearance and not very prolific in bloom. It is an excellent idea to pinch out the tips of the young plants in early spring to encourage them to become bushy in growth. They produce most of their flowers in spring, but will also carry some flowers at other seasons, too.

In regions with severe frost, pelargoniums should be grown in pots which can be moved into a sheltered corner during winter. From spring to autumn the pots can be sunk into the ground in the garden. They grow very well in full sun near the coast but generally do better in light shade when grown in hot areas inland. They stand long periods with little water, but may not flower well if dry in spring.

P. peltatum IVY-LEAFED GERANIUM
This is the parent of the so-called 'climbing geraniums'. It has long stems which can be trained up a support and it looks decorative clambering over a tree stump or cascading over a wall or bank. The common strain of this species is of a charming soft shade of pink but cultivars of other shades are obtainable.

P. zonale ZONAL GERANIUM
These are often grown for the beauty of their leaves. They have rather succulent smooth leaves, or else soft hairy ones with a distinct band of a contrasting colour. Many of them bear pretty flowers too. The names of numerous lovely cultivars will be found listed in nursery catalogues.

Pentas lanceolata PENTAS

DESCRIPTION. Is a pretty plant for the small garden, the front of a large shrub border or to plant amongst flowers. It is a quick-growing evergreen or semi-deciduous shrub that reaches a height and spread of 60 cm or a little more. The leaves are oval and pointed, rough in texture and medium green in colour. In summer it carries round heads of

Monkey Flower (*Mimulus glutinosus*) produces dainty flowers from mid-spring to the end of summer

small tubular flowers with a starry five-petalled face. These are pink, rose, crimson or white. They look effective in the garden and are long-lasting when picked for arrangements.
CULTURE. Pentas is not hardy to severe frost but endures moderate frost quite well. Once established it will also survive fairly long periods with little water, but it flowers best if watered regularly. To keep plants neat and compact groom them after their flowering period is over.

Pernettya mucronata PERNETTYA
DESCRIPTION. An evergreen shrub from Chile growing to 1 m with a spread of more than this. The stems are wiry and sparsely covered with tiny oval, pointed, dark green leathery leaves. 'Bell's Seedling' is the best known cultivar with urn or cup-shaped flowers of white or pale pink in spring. These are followed by crimson, white, pink or purple berries which make a pretty show against the green of the leaves. They are poisonous and not eaten by birds.
CULTURE. Suitable for gardens with cold winters and cool summers. It must have acid soil with plenty of humus. Mulch plants each year in summer to keep the soil cool and add to the humus content, and give an occasional

Mimetes (*Mimetes cucullatus*) is colourful in spring

Olearia bears an abundance of small daisy-like flowers in late winter and early spring

Red Flag Bush (*Mussaenda erythrophylla*) carries its red 'flags' in autumn

The Common Myrtle (*Myrtus communis*). A hardy shrub or small tree flowering in spring

Nandina has attractive flowers, foliage and berries

dressing of alum (aluminium sulphate) or sulphur to maintain acid conditions. It does best in filtered shade.

Persoonia pinifolia

PINE-LEAFED GEEBUNG

DESCRIPTION. This is an evergreen Australian shrub belonging to the protea family. It grows erect to 2–3 m and has arching stems covered with fine soft, pine-like foliage, which gives the stems a pleasing feathery appearance. In summer it bears numerous yellow tubular flowers all along the ends of the stems. These are followed, in autumn, by green berries. This plant is attractive for a long period of the year. CULTURE. It grows naturally in areas with moist conditions and is not recommended for hot dry gardens. Plant it in acid soil which drains readily.

Petrophile linearis PETROPHILA

DESCRIPTION. In spring this evergreen Australian shrub of the protea family bears pretty clusters of tubular flowers of dusty pink. It grows to 1 m and has very narrow leaves, tapered towards the stems. *P. biloba* has long stems of similar flowers. They are attractive on the shrub and in arrangements. Other species worth growing are *P. diversifolia* and *P. sessilis* both of which have yellow flowers.
CULTURE. Plant in well-drained acid soil. They like sunshine but must have some moisture in late autumn and winter. They endure moderate frost.

Chinese Lantern (*Nymania capensis*) festooned with seedpods

Plant pelargoniums in pots or in the garden

Oleander (*Nerium oleander*) stands frost, drought and heat

Some pelargoniums are worth growing for their pretty foliage

Phaenocoma prolifera
PINK EVERLASTING

DESCRIPTION. This is an evergreen South African plant that grows to 60 cm. It has angular twiggy stems clothed with tiny grey-green leaves. In spring it bears flowers with silky, papery petals, rather like those of an everlasting. The buds are a warm shade of rose. The scintillating flowers are palest pink shading to rose. They are delightful in arrangements, being literally everlasting. The main flowering time is early spring, but it carries some flowers in summer too.

CULTURE. Plant it in sandy or gravelly, well-drained soil. It grows well in coastal gardens and inland, provided it has an abundance of sunshine and water in winter. It stands moderate frost. Transplant when very small.

Phebalium glandulosum
PHEBALIUM

DESCRIPTION. About thirty species of phebalium grow naturally in Australia, most of them in the eastern part of the country. This is an evergreen shrub to 1 m with very small narrow leaves carried on twiggy stems. Bright-yellow, starry flowers appear in spring. Two other species worth trying are *P. bullatum* (yellow flowers), which stands drought, and *P. dentatum* (pink flowers), which prefers good soil and some shade.

CULTURE. When established they will endure fairly severe frost and hot, dry summers. Plant when very small in soil which drains readily.

Philadelphus MOCK ORANGE

DESCRIPTION. Deciduous shrubs growing to 2–3 m with graceful arching stems. The leaves are soft, broad at the base and pointed at the tip. Large white, saucer-shaped flowers with round petals appear in late spring and early summer. These are splendid plants for making a screen or informal hedge or for background planting.

CULTURE. They survive cold winters and can tolerate dryness in summer also. They grow well in soil that is slightly alkaline and in acid soil too. In hot gardens inland plant them in partial shade. When plants become too large cut out some of the older stems at the base.

P. coronarius SWEET MOCK ORANGE
Grows to 3 m and has serrated leaves of soft green. In late spring and early summer it makes a gay sight, festooned with clusters of ivory or white flowers which give off a sweet fragrance. 'Aureus' has leaves that are yellow in spring and turn lime-green later.

P. purpureo-maculatus
Reaches a height of 2 m and has graceful, arching stems with soft oval leaves. The lightly fragrant flowers 4 cm across are white with a maroon spot at the base of each petal. 'Belle Etoile', one of the most decorative of the mock oranges, is derived from this species.

P. virginalis
This is a hybrid growing to 2 m or more, with double white flowers in late spring. The following are the names of some pretty cultivars: 'Avalanche', 'Enchantment', 'Mont Blanc', 'Virginal' and 'Virginal Aurea'.

Phlomis fruticosa
JERUSALEM SAGE

DESCRIPTION. An evergreen herbaceous shrub from the Mediterranean which grows quickly to 60 cm or a little more in height. It spreads across 1 m, sending up stems from the ground. The leaves are woolly in texture, wrinkled and yellow-green in colour. In spring it bears whorls of decorative, hooded flowers of sulphur-yellow. Plant it towards the front of a shrub border or at the back of a flower border. It does well when grown in a container, too.

CULTURE. Although it is a prettier plant when grown in good soil, it does well under adverse conditions. It can stand sharp frost and also long dry summers. It grows in acid or alkaline soil, in seaside gardens and inland.

Phormium tenax
NEW ZEALAND FLAX

DESCRIPTION. An evergreen plant from New Zealand which has become popular in many parts of the world because of its unusual form and its adaptability with regard to growing conditions. It consists of erect-growing, sword-shaped leaves arranged in a circular fashion. The leaves of mature plants may be 2 m long. The flower stem, which rises to 3 m, carries sprays of brick-red or crimson flowers near the top. Cultivars with leaves of different colours are available. 'Atropurpureum' has maroon-red leaves; 'Rubrum' has burgundy leaves and 'Variegatum' has green leaves with white stripes. Plant them in any part of the garden, making sure that enough space is left for the development of the long leaves. Owners of small gardens should procure the small-growing cultivars such as 'Rubrum'. *P. colensoi* 'Tricolor' (Whaririki), is a delightful one with leaves prettily marked with cream, yellow and green.

CULTURE. Phormium tolerates a wide range of conditions. It stands severe frost and long periods with little water and grows in poor soil at the coast and inland.

Photinia PHOTINIA

DESCRIPTION. The genus includes attractive evergreen and deciduous shrubs and trees, some with pleasing foliage, some with pretty flowers and some with both. They are useful as background plants or to form a large hedge or tall screen.

CULTURE. Photinias grow well in regions with moderate to severe frost, and do well also in districts subjected to long periods of drought and hot dry winds. Plant them in good soil and water them well in winter and spring. To keep plants from growing too large, thin out some stems at the base every three or four years, and trim back top growth annually as this encourages the development of new bronze leaves.

P. fraseri
A spreading evergreen reaching 3 m suitable for the large garden or park. Its new leaves are tinged with bronze. Old foliage is dark green on the upper surface and paler beneath, and slightly shiny. The stems of leaves are useful for arrangements.

P. glabra JAPANESE PHOTINIA
A quick-growing, evergreen shrub to 3 m or more, with lush oval leaves 7 cm long. The new growth has pretty bronze highlights. This species is easily kept down to 1–2 m by annual pruning in late spring, after the flowers have faded. Large clusters of white flowers appear in late winter and early spring.

The two cultivars 'Rubens' and 'Red Robin', which have richly coloured new growth of coppery-red, are even more attractive than the species. They should be trimmed back regularly to encourage the repeated formation of colourful new leaves.

P. serrulata CHINESE PHOTINIA
This is a splendid large, evergreen shrub or small tree for gardens with cool to cold winters. It grows to 6 m or more, but can be kept to smaller size by annual trimming in winter. The beautiful large, oval leaves 16–20 cm long with finely serrated margins, are dark green on the upper surface and pale on the underside. The plant is at its best in spring, when it produces lustrous new leaves of a deep copper colour at the same time as its large flat heads of ivory-white flowers. The flowers are followed by orange-red berries relished by birds. Once established it tolerates sharp frost and dry weather. A variegated form with leaves marked with creamy-white is smaller in stature and more suitable for the small garden. It grows in alkaline soil.

P. villosa
A deciduous species which will grow to 3 m or more in height and spread, if not trimmed once or twice a year. The new foliage is yellow or tinted with pink, turning dark green when mature. In autumn the leaves become bright red before falling. White flowers appear in spring and are followed by scarlet berries in autumn.

Phygelius capensis
CAPE FUCHSIA, RIVER BELLS
DESCRIPTION. Is a quick-growing little shrub which sends up numerous stems from the ground to a height of 1 m. It has soft leaves, broad at the base and pointed at the apex, with finely serrated margins. The flowers arranged along the tops of the stems are tubular in form and salmon to bright coral in colour. The flowering time is late spring and early summer. Plant it in a shady flower border or at the front of a shrub border.
CULTURE. Cape Fuchsia will stand moderate frost but does not thrive in regions subjected to long periods of drought. It does best in partial shade.

Phylica pubescens
PHYLICA, FLANNEL BUSH
DESCRIPTION. A quick-growing evergreen South African shrub reaching a height and spread of 1 m or more. It has small pointed leaves neatly arranged along the stem, and both the stems and leaves are covered with silky hairs which glisten in the sunlight. The ends of the stems make an unusual show in late winter and early spring, when the growth at the top becomes shining lime-green in colour, scintillating as it waves in the breeze. Phylica is decorative in the garden, in containers and when used for arrangements. It lasts for a long time in vases.
CULTURE. Plants can stand a long dry period in summer but need to be watered regularly and well from mid-autumn to late spring. Plant it in acid soil. Cut plants back lightly in late spring to keep them compact and to prevent them from becoming woody at the base. As it is prettiest when young, it is advisable to set out new plants every four or five years. Transplant it when very small.

Phyllanthus nivosus SNOW BUSH
DESCRIPTION. A dainty evergreen shrub grown for the beauty of the foliage. The plant has pliable slender stems growing to 1 m in height and spread. The oval leaves are soft in texture and have a transparent appearance. They are coloured white, ivory and green. Another form has foliage splashed with pink, rose and white. They can be trimmed into a neat round shape or allowed to grow in their own gracefully spreading fashion. This is a pretty plant for warm coastal gardens.
CULTURE. It is tender to cold and suited only to tropical and subtropical gardens. Plant it in good soil and water abundantly, as dryness and wind are apt to spoil the leaves.

Phyllostachys BAMBOO
DESCRIPTION. Bamboos look graceful standing at the side of a stream or pond. In the small garden it is advisable, because of their tendency to spread, to plant them in a container sunk into the ground. On a large property they make an effective screen plant. The dwarf species are attractive growing in a container, in a rock or pebble garden, or standing in a large tub on a terrace or patio.
CULTURE. Although many of the bamboos occur naturally in warm humid regions of the world, several species stand severe frost provided they are not allowed to become too dry. Those described are hardy to sharp frost. In hot dry gardens plant them in partial shade. Should they spread too far, dig up some of the roots.

P. aurea GOLDEN BAMBOO
Is a Japanese species which spreads unless kept in check. It grows to 2–3 m or more, and has sturdy stems with variegated foliage. The leaves are 4–10 cm long and less than 1 cm wide. This species makes a good tub plant.

P. bambusoides GIANT BAMBOO
Should be planted only on large estates, as the stems grow to 10 cm in diameter, and the plants become very tall and are apt to spread quickly. The young spring shoots are edible. 'Castillonis' is a decorative cultivar growing to 3–6 m. The stems are yellow, marked with dark green vertical bands which make an effective contrast. The leaves are 6–15 cm long, 1–2 cm broad and plain green, or striped with yellow.

P. nigra BLACK BAMBOO
Grows to 3 m or a little more and has stems 3–4 cm in diameter. These are coloured olive or purple-black. It sends out runners underground which root easily and it must therefore be kept in check.

Physocarpus opulifolius 'Luteus' GOLDEN NINEBARK
DESCRIPTION. This is a deciduous shrub that reaches a height of a metre or more and spreads across as much. It has attractively lobed leaves, double-toothed, lime-green in spring and turning green later. The clusters of tiny pinkish-white flowers are not outstanding but the plant is worth growing for its foliage. The flowers are followed by clusters of inflated pods that sometimes become tinged with red in autumn.
CULTURE. This plant is from North America and it stands considerable cold but needs to be watered regularly. Plant it in soil rich in humus, in semi-shade rather than in full sun.

Jerusalem Sage (*Phlomis fruticosa*) grows well in coastal gardens

Picea glauca 'Conica'

DWARF ALBERTA SPRUCE

DESCRIPTION. This is a very slow-growing plant that may reach a height of 2 m after many years of growth. It is of a delightful pyramidal shape and has light green leaves which are decorative throughout the year. Where conditions suit it this conifer will make a charming specimen planted alone on a lawn or at an entrance.

CULTURE. Dwarf Alberta Spruce needs cool growing conditions and an abundance of water. It enjoys frost, provided that it is not subjected to dry conditions at the same time. It will not thrive in warm gardens.

Pieris

PEARL FLOWER, LILY-OF-THE-VALLEY BUSH

DESCRIPTION. The genus includes three very handsome species indigenous to North Burma and Japan. These are evergreen shrubs with leathery, glossy leaves and clusters of small, white urn or bell-shaped flowers in spring. The new leaves of burnished copper tones are even more ornamental than the flowers. Plant them in a woodland set-

Pentas (*Pentas lanceolata*) yields pretty flowers for summer arrangements

The flowers of Mock Orange (*Philadelphus coronarius*) have a delicate fragrance

Flannel Bush or Phylica *(Phylica pubescens)* is an unusual shrub for the small garden

ting or in containers in partial shade protected from hot wind.

CULTURE. All species need acid soil rich in humus and cool to cold growing conditions. They require the same kind of soil and climate as rhododendrons and should be grouped with such plants.

P. formosa var. **forrestii** *(P. forrestii)*
RED-LEAF PEARL FLOWER, CHINESE PIERIS
A lovely plant 2 m in height. It has glistening leaves almost 10 cm long that are copper to crimson when young, with salmon highlights, becoming deep green as they mature. It bears striking large heads of tiny urn-shaped flowers in spring. Plant it in filtered shade to encourage good growth and flowering. Two spectacular cultivars are 'Jermyns' and 'Lord Wakehurst'.

P. japonica *(Andromeda japonica)*
LILY-OF-THE-VALLEY SHRUB,
JAPANESE PEARL FLOWER
Grows to 3 m and has highly glossy, oval pointed leaves carried in groups close together towards the ends of the branches. They are beautiful throughout the year. In late winter and early

New Zealand Flax *(Phormium tenax)*. Plant it in the large rock or pebble garden

Chinese Photinia *(Photinia serrulata)*. A handsome plant for a large garden

spring the plant bears its charming little ivory urn-shaped flowers in drooping panicles. This species is more tolerant of severe frost than *P. formosa* var. *forrestii*. 'Bert Chandler' and 'Blush' are two fine cultivars.

P. taiwanensis
This fine evergreen grows to 3 m and is ornamental throughout the year, particularly in spring when it has red leaves and ivory-white flowers.

Pimelea   RICE FLOWER
DESCRIPTION. A genus of about eighty species of evergreen shrubs, native to Australia that are related to the Daphne. They vary in height and spread, have very small leaves, and bear flowers in rounded clusters in spring and summer.
CULTURE. Plant them in acid soil with plenty of compost and water well during winter and early spring. They will stand fairly long periods of dryness in summer. Transplant when small, and groom plants lightly after their flowering period to prevent them from becoming straggly. The species described stand sharp frost when established.

P. ferruginea   ROSY RICE FLOWER
Grows to 1 m and has twiggy stems of tiny, slender leaves and round, rose-pink pincushions of minute flowers in spring. It grows in full sun near the coast but seems to do better with some shade in hot areas inland.

P. ligustrina   TALL RICE FLOWER
This one reaches 2 m in height and has dense heads of small white flowers in summer. It grows quickly and needs regular grooming to keep it tidy.

P. physodes   QUALUP BELL
Not easy to grow, and appears to do best in soil that drains readily. It grows to 1 m and has drooping heads of fragrant flowers enclosed by large purple-red bracts.

P. rosea   PINK RICE FLOWER
Bears pretty round clusters of tiny pink flowers with a tubular base and a starry face of four segments. It grows to 1 m in height and flowers in spring. The oval leaves are only 1 cm long, dark green on the upper surface and paler beneath.

P. spectabilis
SHOWY RICE FLOWER, BUNJONG
Grows to 1 m or a little more, has small, linear pointed leaves and rounded heads of ivory to rose-pink flowers. Each floret is tubular in form with a starry face.

Plectranthus   SPUR FLOWER
DESCRIPTION. The genus includes shrubs and perennials from various parts of the world. The species described are shrubby evergreen plants native to South Africa, excellent for quick colour in a shady situation. They have large leaves and pretty clusters of flowers in autumn.
CULTURE. They grow in poor soil and reach a height of 1 m in a year. It is advisable to cut them back in late winter or early spring to prevent them from becoming too large for their allotted space, and to keep plants compact and encourage flowering. This can be done by trimming off shoots all over the plant, or by cutting out some of the older growth at the base, leaving newer stems to develop. At the coast they grow in full sun, but in gardens away from the sea, where the sunlight is strong, it is advisable to plant them in shade. They do not stand severe frost. In areas with cold winters plant them in large containers which can be stored under cover until spring.

P. ecklonii   PURPLE SPUR FLOWER
Grows rapidly to 1,5 m in height and spread, and has broadly oval leaves, rough in texture, dark green on the upper surface and paler on the underside. They give off an unusual herb-like smell when touched. In autumn it carries splendid large spikes of purple-blue flowers that are ornamental for a long time.

P. fruticosus   PINK SPUR FLOWER
A very quick-growing shrub for a shady corner. It grows to 1 m or more, has quadrilateral stems and leaves with a rough texture. They are dark green on the upper surface and rosy/maroon on the underside, with maroon leafstalks covered with silky maroon hairs and veins. The leaves are almost heart-shaped with saw-tooth margins. Small flowers of dusty pink carried in large clusters make a pretty show in late summer and autumn.

Plumbago auriculata
(P. capensis)   PLUMBAGO
DESCRIPTION. This is an attractive, quick-growing evergreen or semi-deciduous shrub which tolerates difficult growing conditions. If not trimmed, it grows to 2 m or more, and tends to sprawl. Annual pruning in early spring not only keeps the plant neat, but it also makes it bushy at the base and encourages good flowering. Plumbago makes a pretty hedge when clipped regularly, and a decorative informal one when trimmed once or twice a year. It can be tailored to different shapes – globe, pyramid or square – and, as a topiary specimen in a tub it looks effective at the entrance to a drive or on a terrace. The pliable stems carry neat soft leaves that are oval and pointed. In summer it becomes covered with phlox-like flowers of sky-blue. A white form is known but it is not as attractive as the blue.
CULTURE. It thrives in almost any kind of soil, and once established will endure long periods of drought. Severe frost will cut it to the ground but it often grows up quickly again to flower the following summer. It does well in coastal gardens and in hot ones inland.

Podalyria   PODALYRIA
DESCRIPTION. Two pretty South African species are worth trying in gardens where frosts are not severe. They are evergreen, quick-growing plants with pleasing foliage and pretty pea-shaped flowers with a delicate scent. The flowering time is late winter and early spring.
CULTURE. They do well in clay, sand or gravelly soil and in any situation, standing bright sunshine and partial shade. Once established they tolerate cool winters provided the soil is moist, but they are likely to succumb to prolonged periods of sharp frost. Water them from autumn to spring and leave them dry in summer.

P. calyptrata   SWEET PEA BUSH
This species, which grows to 3 m, can be trained to tree form but it sends out stems from near the base and is therefore usually regarded as a shrub. The leaves are fairly small, oval, soft in texture and opalescent-green in colour.

The charming pinky-mauve flowers give off a very sweet scent which pervades the whole garden. There is a form with white flowers but it is not as pretty. In small gardens it is advisable to trim the plants back lightly after their flowering period is over. It is decorative when trained as a tree for the small patio where space is limited.

P. sericea
SILVER SWEET PEA BUSH, SATIN BUSH
A small shrub growing to 1 m in height and spread. It has silvery stems and masses of small oval leaves clothed with glistening hairs, which make them look as though they have been fashioned from burnished silver. In winter it bears pea-like flowers of a delicate shade of pinky-mauve. When these fall the plant becomes festooned with large silver seedpods which are more decorative than the flowers.

Polygala POLYGALA
DESCRIPTION. There are more than 500 species of polygala, varying considerably in appearance and habit of growth. Two ornamental, evergreen South African species are described here. These have hitherto been more widely grown in Australia than in their native country. The flowers are pea-shaped with an attractive tuft of silky hairs emerging from the keel. The flowering time is late winter and early spring.
CULTURE. They are quick-growing plants which like acid soil, but they also grow well in regions where the soil is slightly alkaline. They stand moderate frosts and long dry summers. Water them in winter in the summer-rainfall region.

P. myrtifolia
LARGE-FLOWERED POLYGALA
Is 2 m in height and spread, has pale green oval leaves and flowers like a sweet pea, coloured a rich shade of purple, delightfully marked with paler shades. The flowering time is spring.

P. virgata PURPLE BROOM
A tall, slender graceful plant 2 m high and about 1 m wide. It is somewhat like Spanish broom in its manner of growth. Very slender leaves are sparsely carried along rush-like stems. In late winter and early spring it bears spikes of flowers of glowing purple that last for a long time. Each flower is prettily trimmed with a silky purple fringe.

Pomaderris kumeraho
GOLDEN TAINUI
DESCRIPTION. A pretty evergreen shrub native to New Zealand. It grows to 2 m and has ovate leaves 5–10 cm long, olive-green on the upper surface and pale grey on the underside. In spring it bears rounded flowerheads about 20 cm across. The individual golden-yellow flowers are very small but they are carried in profusion and show up well against the green of the leaves.
CULTURE. It grows in light, gravelly or sandy soil and takes sharp frost. Water well in winter and spring. It is wind-resistant and suitable for coastal gardens.

Portulacaria afra
SPEKBOOM, JADE PLANT, ELEPHANT'S FOOD
DESCRIPTION. An evergreen South African plant of value in gardens where a scarcity of water and intense sunlight makes it difficult to grow a wide range of plants. It will grow to 2 m, but is easily kept down to smaller size. Planted close together and trimmed from time to time it makes a good low or medium-size hedge. The stems and leaves are succulent. The leaves measure only about 1 cm in length, and, in times of drought when grazing is in short supply, these are fed to stock. A single specimen grown in a pot makes an attractive feature on a patio. There is also a more decorative form with red stems and variegated leaves tinged with yellow. Clipped and trimmed, it can be trained to form an effective quick piece of bonsai.
CULTURE. This succulent plant stands rigorous conditions. It grows where the rainfall is meagre and it stands moderate to sharp frost, intense heat and poor soil. Grows in alkaline as well as acid soil.

Potentilla fruticosa
FINGER BUSH, POTENTILLA
DESCRIPTION. A hardy deciduous shrub 1 m in height and spread. The leaves are divided into 3–7 small oval leaflets, pale to grey-green in colour. In late spring and summer it bears saucer-shaped, five-petalled flowers of bright yellow that look somewhat like a small single rose. It is effective in front of a shrub border or planted at the back of a flower border. Cultivars have flowers of white to orange. 'Abbotswood' – 1 m with greyish green leaves set off by white flowers; 'Gold Star' is a low spreading plant; 'Katherine Dykes' has arching branches more than a metre across with fernlike foliage and clear yellow flowers; 'Princess' is about a metre wide with pink flowers, and 'Royal Flush' is 60 cm high and wide with rosy-pink flowers with bright yellow centres.
CULTURE. These plants stand the most severe frost and hot sunshine. Although they prefer acid soil they will grow in an area where the soil is slightly alkaline. They do well in full sun and partial shade. After flowering cut out some of the old growth at ground-level.

Prostanthera MINT BUSH
DESCRIPTION. The genus includes more than seventy evergreen Australian shrubs, most of which have foliage with an aromatic scent. The leaves are very small, often only 1–2 cm long. The plants vary in size quite considerably. They need some grooming to keep them neat and compact and to prevent them from becoming leggy at the base. Some species tend to die off after a few years. They make a pretty show in spring when they flower. The flowers are tubular, ending in two lips – the upper one divided into two lobes and the under one, into three.
CULTURE. Transplant when very small into soil which is loose in texture, and preferably a little on the acid side. Water them during winter. Most species can stand a dry summer and autumn, and fairly severe frost.

P. incisa MINT BUSH
Grows upright to 2 m and has small leaves with clearly toothed margins. In spring it bears a profusion of lilac to rosy-mauve flowers.

Plumbago is one of the prettiest of the summer-flowering shrubs

P. induta

A rewarding plant that has become popular as a garden subject within recent years. It has silver-grey leaves and large flowers of a misty lavender shade.

P. nivea   SNOWY MINT BUSH

Grows to 2 m and bears masses of snow-white flowers which make a fine show in spring.

P. ovalifolia   OVAL-LEAFED MINT BUSH

Reaches a height of 2 m or more but should be trimmed back to keep it neat and compact. It has slender oval, greyish-green leaves and bears masses of purple flowers in spring.

P. rotundifolia

ROUND-LEAFED MINT BUSH

If not trimmed this species will grow to 3 m. The rounded leaves are less than 2 cm in length and give off a strong mint scent when crushed. In late winter and

Top left
Red-leaf Pearl Flower *(Pieris)* needs acid soil and a cool moist climate

Bottom left
In winter the Sweet Pea Bush *(Podalyria calyptrata)* bears a profusion of sweetly-scented flowers

Opposite
In this charming garden colourful shrubs enhance the beauty of the pool and Japanese lantern

early spring it carries an abundance of purple flowers. A more suitable form for the garden of ordinary size is *P. rotundifolia* 'Rosea', which grows to 1 m and has pink to rose flowers.

Protea PROTEA

DESCRIPTION. These handsome South African plants are closely related to some of the Australian shrubs and trees, such as banksia, dryandra, grevillea, hakea and waratah. The plants vary in size from those which grow a few centimetres above the ground, carrying their flowers at ground-level, to tall plants the size of small trees. The leaves vary in size, form and colouring. The flowers are carried crowded together in large or small heads, surrounded by large ornamental bracts which look like petals. These may enclose the flower-head almost entirely or they may stand out forming a halo around the flowers. The colour and texture of the flowers and bracts differ from species to species. These plants need little care and attention to keep them neat and tidy. Generally cutting off the faded flowers with a good length of stem will keep them trim. The flowers last well on the plants and in arrangements, and as they appear mostly from autumn to spring, when flowers are scarce, they are a valuable addition to the garden. They are now being widely grown to provide winter flowers for the cut-flower trade.

CULTURE. Proteas do best in well-drained acid soil. This does not indicate, however, that they like dry growing conditions. It means that they grow better in loose soil, which is sandy or gravelly in texture and which allows water to run through readily, than they will in an impermeable clay. Before planting prepare soil by adding humus. The natural habitat of most proteas is a region of South Africa which has dry summers and a fairly high rainfall from autumn to spring. Some species stand severe frost, but, as their flowers may be spoiled by frost, gardeners in regions of dry frosty winters should plant them where they are protected from the early morning winter sun and water them well in winter. Avoid disturbing the roots of these plants by deep cultivation.

P. acuminata
(P. cedromontana) CEDARBERG PROTEA
A small protea which grows to 1 m and has long slender leaves and a flower-head of unusual colouring. The central mass of flowers is burgundy and tan, and the surrounding bracts are brick-red.

P. aristata CHRISTMAS PROTEA
Whereas most proteas flower in the cool months of the year this species bears its lovely flowers in early summer. It grows to 1,5 m and has pretty needle-like leaves, very different from those of most of the other species. It bears rose to pink flowers surrounded by velvety bracts of the same colour. This species will grow in soil that is slightly alkaline.

P. burchellii
(P. pulchra) GLEAMING PROTEA
An attractive species growing to 2 m rather bushy in habit. The bracts have a glistening texture and are shaded pink, rose or lime-green.

P. compacta BOT RIVER PROTEA
When in flower this is one of the prettiest of the proteas. The plant is rangy in habit of growth, reaching 2 m or more in height and becoming untidy if not trimmed to keep it compact in form. In winter it carries slender flowerheads of misty pink to rose. Their beautifully formed bracts have a rich satin or plush-like texture. The flowers are particularly decorative in arrangements.

P. cynaroides GIANT OR KING PROTEA
This species grows to 1 m and has somewhat leathery leaves sometimes grey rather than green in colour. It will grow in soil that is slightly alkaline. The large flowerheads are at their best from winter to summer. They are broad, measuring 25 cm across, and are subtly coloured, usually in shades of pink and rose. The outer bracts have a satiny sheen which adds to the impressive appearance of the flower.

P. eximia RAY-FLOWERED PROTEA
Reaches a height of 2 m and is erect in form. Has oval grey leaves with crimson margins. The flowerhead is made up of a central mass of flowers of lime-green to rose, tipped with chocolate-brown hairs. The surrounding spoon-shaped bracts are pale pink to rose with silvery hairs at the tips. It tolerates slightly alkaline soil. The flowering time is from autumn to spring.

P. grandiceps PEACH PROTEA
An exceptionally handsome protea with pretty foliage as well as beautiful flowers. The plant is 1 m in height and spread, and has large rounded grey leaves edged with rose. The flowers are enclosed within bracts of peach-pink to ruby-red. The upper bracts have a long silky, white or pink fringe which almost covers the inside of the flowerhead. It is outstanding in the garden and lovely in arrangements.

P. lacticolor
Grows to 3 m and has leathery leaves 4–8 cm long. The flowerheads have cream, pink or rose bracts which spread out wide around the central mass of flowers. It survives moderate frost and will grow in slightly alkaline soil. The flowering time is autumn to spring.

P. laurifolia
(P. marginata) FRINGED PROTEA
A tall plant suitable only for the large garden or park. It reaches 2 m or more in height, and has bracts of pink, rose or ice-green tipped with long silver or black hairs.

P. longiflora LONG-BUD PROTEA
This species is too large for the garden of average size. It may reach 3 m in height and has oval leathery leaves pointed at the tips. The flower buds are slender and the open flower is elegant with bracts of pink, cream or rosy-red. Its main flowering time is late spring and summer. It may grow in alkaline soil.

P. longifolia LONG-LEAFED PROTEA
Grows to 1,5 m and has slender pointed leaves, and long flowerheads. The black-tipped flowers form a sharp cone between waxy, pointed bracts of pale yellow or rose. The flowering time is autumn.

P. magnifica
(P. barbigera) BEARDED OR QUEEN PROTEA
A spectacular species 1,5 m in height and spread, with large grey-green leaves edged with rose. The huge flowerheads may measure as much as 25 cm across. The inner part of the head ends in a central cone of silky, silvery, black-tipped hairs. The bracts which are also fringed with silky hairs may be ivory-yellow, ice-green or pale pink to deep rose. It tolerates mildly alkaline soil.

P. nana MOUNTAIN ROSE
A small species growing to 1 m with slender pine-like leaves and drooping flowerheads with short cinnamon to mahogany bracts surrounding the mass of flowers in the centre. It is a dainty species for the small garden and for arrangements.

P. neriifolia OLEANDER-LEAFED PROTEA
The plant grows to 3 m but it can be cut back to keep it smaller in size. The large showy flowerheads are peach, salmon, rose or green, prettily tipped with a silky fringe of black or brown hairs. It shows a tolerance of alkaline soil. The flowering time is autumn and winter.

P. nitida
(P. arborea) WABOOM, TREE PROTEA
This species grows to tree size, reaching 3–4 m, and has a rounded tree-like crown. In winter and spring the new leaves coloured pink and rose glisten in the sunlight. The flowerheads consist of a large tuft of yellow flowers with small bracts at the base. The plant develops a rather gaunt but attractive form as it ages.

P. obtusifolia
Reaches a height of 2 m and has flowerheads somewhat like those of *P. repens*. In late winter and early spring it carries glossy heads of flowers of green flushed with rose at the top. They last for 2–3 weeks in arrangements. This species stands fairly alkaline soil.

P. pudens *(P. minor)* GROUND ROSE
This is a species with small flowers. It grows to 60 cm and has stems clothed with long and very slender leaves. The bracts, which enclose the

flowers, are of unusual shades of brown, tan and mahogany. The central mass of flowers is shaded from pink to maroon. The flowering time is late autumn and winter.

P. repens
(P. mellifera) SUGARBUSH PROTEA
Grows to 2–3 m and is upright in habit, with flowerheads varying in colour from pale green to lime and from blush-pink to rose. There is also a yellow form. The flowers are full of nectar that attracts birds. It makes a pretty show in arrangements.

P. scolymocephala
SMALL GREEN PROTEA
Produces dainty flowers of an unusual shade of pale green tipped with silver, surrounded by a bowl of bracts of the same subtle shades. Its flowers are unusual and look charming in corsages or small arrangements.

P. speciosa BROWN-BEARDED PROTEA
Reaches a height of 1,25 m and has broad and somewhat leathery leaves. The flowerheads are about 12 cm across, with pale to deep pink bracts tipped with a fringe of silky, cinnamon-coloured hairs. There is a creamy-yellow form of this one, too.

Prunus

FLOWERING ALMOND, CHERRY LAUREL
DESCRIPTION. Most of the flowering fruits which make such a glorious sight in spring are small trees, but there are some fine dwarf forms of prunus that never reach more than shrub size and which are bushy in habit. In full blossom, they can be numbered amongst the most decorative of all shrubs. They grow to 1–2 m or a little more, and are deciduous. The stems of flowers are highly ornamental in arrangements. To keep the plants neat, trim out some of the stems at flowering time. It is a good idea, also, to plant a specimen or two in a large container, kept in the backyard during the months when they are of little interest, and brought forward to the terrace or main garden when in full flower.
CULTURE. Plant them in fertile soil and water them well for the first two or three years. They enjoy cold and sur-

vive severe frost if not allowed to become too dry. They do well in slightly alkaline soil. Should it be necessary to limit their growth, prune them lightly immediately after flowering.

P. glandulosa BUSH CHERRY
A Chinese species with small, single, white flowers seldom planted now as the cultivars are much more attractive. 'Albo-plena', with double white flowers, and 'Roseo-plena' with rose-pink ones, are rewarding shrubs, beautiful in early spring when they bear their fountains of blossom.

P. laurocerasus CHERRY LAUREL
A shrub for the large garden. It can be trained to form a small tree by the removal of the bottom branches. The height and spread are about 6 m x 3 m. This is an evergreen with somewhat leathery, glossy oblong leaves about 12 cm long, that give it a handsome appearance throughout the year. Early in spring it bears tiny white flowers in racemes 10 to 15 cm long. Later small black berries appear. It will form a dense hedge or windbreak if close-planted. It likes cold growing conditions.

P. tenella RUSSIAN ALMOND
This species is native to south-eastern Europe. It is an arresting sight in late winter and early spring when it bears graceful stems of rose-pink flowers. Lovely in the garden and in large containers.

P. triloba DWARF FLOWERING ALMOND
Quick-growing to 2–3 m, with numerous stems forming a mound of colour in spring. The flowers of the species are single and white or blush-pink. The cultivar 'Flore-pleno' has double flowers of the same shades.

Pseudopanax LANCEWOOD

DESCRIPTION. This genus includes evergreens native to New Zealand, grown for their unusual foliage and form and not for flowers. They are effective standing alone in the garden or in a container on a patio or terrace. In their natural habitat they become trees but in the garden they are usually regarded as shrubs.

The leaves of Jade Plant or Spekboom (*Portulacaria afra*) may become colourful in late winter

Sugarbush Protea (*Protea repens*) has sculptured flowers on erect plants

The flowers of the Small Green Protea (*Protea scolymocephala*) are effective in small arrangements

CULTURE. They are tolerant of cold but not long periods of dry weather. Water well during dry periods of the year and plant in acid soil rich in humus. They will grow in coastal gardens.

P. discolor

Grows to about 2 m and has leaves which are bronze when young. This species makes a good container plant.

P. ferox

May reach a height of 6 m and assume tree form, but is generally a shrub of half this height. It is very slow-growing with deeply toothed grey-green leaves 30 cm in length and only 5 cm wide.

P. lessonii HOUPARA

Although this plant is usually grown as a container specimen it can be planted in the open ground and left to form a large shrub or small tree. The foliage is attractive in form and colour. The palmate leaves are divided into five sections and are dark green, leathery and slightly glossy. It grows in sun or shade and stands wind. Cultivars named 'Adiantifolius' and 'Lineari-folius' are decorative plants for the garden or for containers on a terrace.

Left
Bearded or Queen Protea (*Protea magnifica*) bears enormous heads of flowers

Opposite
Peach Protea (*Protea grandiceps*). One of the most ornamental of the proteas

Punica granatum POMEGRANATE

DESCRIPTION. This is a deciduous tree native to the Biblical lands and referred to in the Bible. It was no doubt a treasured tree in regions where the climate made it difficult to produce a variety of food. It is now seldom grown as a tree, being raised in containers, where it never grows to more than shrub size. It has oval, slightly glossy leaves 6–8 cm long and 2–3 cm wide. In spring, it bears terracotta funnel-shaped flowers with crinkled segments opening wide. In summer, it becomes festooned with large crimson fruits full of bright scarlet seeds, pleasant to eat. Where hot, dry conditions prevail, pomegranate makes a good dense hedge.

P. granatum 'Flora Plena' grows to 2–3 m and has attractive glossy oval leaves and double flowers of rich coral-red, somewhat like a carnation in form. It flowers in summer. *P. granatum* 'Alba Plena' has ivory-white to pale yellow flowers. *P. granatum* 'Legrelle' is 2 m tall and has creamy-yellow flowers striped with coral-red. A miniature form, known as *P. granatum* 'Nana', grows to only 60 cm and is a fine plant for the rock garden and for pot-culture. It has tiny rich green leaves and flowers of bright coral-red followed by miniature crimson fruits. Where autumn is dry and crisp the foliage turns pretty shades of yellow.

CULTURE. The species and cultivars grow well in poor soil and, when once established, they stand long periods of drought and fairly sharp frost. They are tolerant of slightly alkaline soil.

Pyracantha FIRETHORN

DESCRIPTION. These plants are usually grown for the beauty of their berries. They are evergreen shrubs with neat foliage and small but quite decorative flowers. Planted close, they form a good screen, large hedge or windbreak. They are attractive planted as specimen shrubs on a lawn or against a wall, and some of them can be trained to a single stem to form a small tree. Colourful berries appear from autumn to the end of winter. Pyracantha is related to cotoneaster but easily distinguished by its thorny branches and toothed leaves.

CULTURE. Pyracantha are useful plants for gardens where heat, drought and severe frost limit the range of plants which can be grown. They like an abundance of sunshine and grow well in alkaline or slightly acid soil. Prune by cutting some of the older stems low down on the plant, as shortening new growth all over is likely to inhibit the production of flowers and berries. Cutting stems of berries for arrangements will help to keep the plants from becoming too large.

P. angustifolia ORANGE PYRACANTHA
Grows to 2 m and spreads across as much. Has slender, neat leaves 5 cm long, dark green on the upper surface and grey-green underneath. Bears graceful stems of bright orange berries which persist through winter.

P. coccinea FIRETHORN
Reaches a height of 4 m and has scarlet berries on downy stalks. The narrow leaves are oval, finely-toothed and 2–5 cm long. Cultivars of this, which are smaller in size, are more suitable for gardens of moderate size. 'Lalandei' with flame-red berries and 'San Jose' with orange ones, are particularly showy in late autumn and early winter. 'Harlequin' has variegated leaves.

P. rogersiana CHINESE FIRETHORN
Is a spreading plant growing to 2 m if not trimmed. The narrow oval leaves taper to the base and are 1–4 cm long. It has clusters of white flowers in summer and reddish-orange or golden berries in autumn and winter. Makes a good, impenetrable hedge for a large property.

Reinwardtia indica

(Linum trigynum) YELLOW FLAX
DESCRIPTION. This delightful little shrub from India makes the garden glow at a season of the year when few plants are flowering. The flowers start opening in autumn and continue through most of winter. Each flower lasts a short time but the plant is crowded with gay yellow flowers week after week. It grows to 1 m in height and spread and has small, soft, oval leaves of a pleasant shade of mid-green. The flowers consist of a short

funnel opening to a wide saucer-like face of sparkling yellow. This is a rewarding plant anywhere in the garden and it looks effective also when grown in a container.

CULTURE. Although this shrub does best in tropical and subtropical gardens it will stand mild frost. Can be grown in fairly cold gardens provided it is sheltered by the overhang of a roof or tree. Does well in the open near the coast but, in gardens where the sunlight is intense, it is advisable to plant it in high shade. Trim plants back in spring as otherwise they tend to become straggly.

Rhamnus BUCKTHORN

DESCRIPTION. Evergreen and deciduous shrubs and small trees suitable for background or screen planting particularly where wind and drought make gardening difficult. The flowers are inconspicuous and the plants are grown for their foliage and resistance to hard conditions. They do well in coastal gardens.

CULTURE. Most species stand fairly severe frost, intense sun and wind, long periods with little water and slightly alkaline soil. They should, however, be watered during their first two years to get them established. Grow in sun or partial shade.

R. crocea REDBERRY
A small evergreen shrub growing to 1 m and spreading across more than this. It has stiff branches, small oval leaves that are spiny and slightly glossy, and bright red berries in summer.

R. crocea 'Ilicifolia'
HOLLY-LEAF REDBERRY
An evergreen, variable in growth. It may remain stunted or it may grow to 4 m. The small leaves have spiny margins – hence the common name. This is a plant for hot gardens where water is in short supply. It stands moderate frost.

R. purshiana CASCARA
Is a deciduous large shrub or small tree that reaches a height of 6 m or more. The pointed leaves are up to 20 cm in length and about 5 cm wide, dark green on the upper surface and pale

on the underside. In a cold climate they turn autumn tints before dropping. This species needs regular watering when young. It grows in shade or sun. The bark yields cascara sagrada.

Rhaphiolepis INDIAN HAWTHORN
DESCRIPTION. Shapely, slow-growing evergreen shrubs with leathery leaves, sometimes with slightly toothed edges. The plants grow to 1–2 m but can be trimmed to keep them small. Clusters of white to pink flowers appear in winter and early spring, and show up well against the jade-green of the leaves. They are followed by purple or blue-black berries. The flowers last well in arrangements. New leaves tend to be bronze or crimson, adding to the value of the shrub.
CULTURE. They grow well in full sun near the coast but prefer some shade in gardens inland where hot, dry winds blow and the sunlight is intense. Water well in winter to encourage flowering. They tolerate long dry periods in summer and moderate to severe frost.

R. delacourii PINK INDIAN HAWTHORN
Grows to 2 m and has neat, glossy foliage and small pink, five-petalled flowers about 2–3 cm across, in late winter.

R. indica INDIAN HAWTHORN
This species has white flowers tinged with pink. In late winter the new leaves flushed with bronze show up well against the olive-green colour of the old leaves. The cultivars 'Enchantress' and 'Springtime' are smaller in size and more suitable for suburban gardens.

R. umbellata YEDDO HAWTHORN
Is 2 m in height and has leathery leaves almost as broad as they are long, with lightly serrated or smooth margins. The fragrant white flowers are carried in small erect clusters and make a fine show in spring. They are followed by small blue-black berries.

Rhapis LADY PALM
DESCRIPTION. The genus includes two very attractive palms which are ornamental in the garden or when grown in containers indoors. They are slow-growing and evergreen, with unusual and graceful leaves.

CULTURE. Both species do best in warm, humid gardens but they can stand some frost. Plant in shade except near the coast where they do well in the open. Grow them in soil rich in humus and water regularly to encourage growth.

R. excelsa LADY PALM
A slow-growing plant from China which may reach 3 m but generally the height is not much more than half of this. It has a reed-like stem and deeply divided leaves that are very decorative. It grows in sun or partial shade and makes a good indoor plant.

R. humilis SLENDER LADY PALM
A Japanese species with a graceful habit of growth and larger leaves than *R. excelsa*. Prefers shade to full sunshine. Looks charming in a container indoors or on a shady patio or terrace.

Rhododendron RHODODENDRON
DESCRIPTION. These are among the most beautiful of all flowering shrubs and trees and it is unfortunate that their requirements are so specific that they can be grown successfully in only a limited number of regions. (Botanically, azaleas are included in the genus rhododendron, but, as gardeners continue to refer to them as azaleas they have been described under the name of azalea in this book.)

Rhododendrons have foliage which is usually handsome – often larger than that of azaleas, sometimes leathery in texture, dark green on the upper surface and pale on the underside, and carried in whorls. Many of the evergreen species are decorative throughout the year. The large round heads of flowers make a glorious show from late winter to late spring. Rhododendrons grow magnificently in many parts of England but they are not native to that country. Most plants in England and other parts of Europe are derived from the first plants imported at the beginning of the nineteenth century. Some of these were from America and Spain, but most of them were from the East – the Himalayas, China and Tibet. It is recorded that there are now something like 500 species in cultivation and thousands of named cultivars. Each year sees the introduction of more of

them, and keen growers are advised, therefore, to consult nurserymen who will know the names of those likely to thrive in their area, or to study the Rhododendron Year Book.

Rhododendrons vary a great deal in size. Some grow to tree size, spreading across 3 m whilst others are less than 1 m in height and spread. The form and colours of the flowers and leaves vary, too.
CULTURE. Plant rhododendrons in acid soil rich in leaf mould and in filtered shade, except in regions with mist, where they can be grown in the open. If hot dry winds prevail, shelter plants and water them abundantly to keep the air and soil moist. They enjoy moderate to severe frost. The plants have a fibrous root system and it is advisable to mulch the soil during dry periods of the year to retain moisture and to prevent the ground from heating up. Old oak leaves, decomposed pine needles and peat are excellent for this purpose as they are acid in nature. In regions where the water is likely to change the nature of the soil from acid to alkaline, apply a monthly sprinkling of aluminium sulphate, sulphur or iron sulphate. A tablespoon spread on the soil around the plant and watered in will usually correct a tendency to alkalinity. The smaller rhododendrons will flower well also when grown in large containers filled with peat and acid compost. Before planting, soak the peat thoroughly as otherwise it absorbs moisture from the plant. They need cool, moist conditions for their best development.

Ribes FLOWERING CURRANT
DESCRIPTION. The genus includes fruiting and ornamental plants of some decorative value. They are evergreen or deciduous shrubs that are fairly quick-growing and useful in providing a verdant effect in the new garden whilst the slow-growing shrubs are still small.
CULTURE. They like frost and generally do better when not subjected to intense sunshine and hot, dry winds. Plant them in semi-shade, except near the coast where they will grow well in full sun and water them well during dry periods of the year.

Flowering Pomegranate (*Punica granatum*) 'Flora Plena'). Its glossy leaves and pretty flowers are attractive in the garden

Yellow Flax (*Reinwardtia indica*) makes the garden glow in late autumn and winter

Rhododendrons like dappled shade and acid soil

R. aureum   GOLDEN CURRANT
Reaches a height of 2 m and has light-green leaves usually with three lobes, and coarsely toothed margins. In spring it has small loose clusters of yellow flowers with a spicy fragrance, and in summer, red or black berries appear. Deciduous.

R. sanguineum   PINK CURRANT
A deciduous shrub growing to 2 m in height and spread. It has three or five-lobed roundish leaves and small pink to rose flowers in ornamental clusters in spring, followed by blue-black berries in autumn.

R. speciosum   FUCHSIA GOOSEBERRY
Grows to 2 m and is evergreen or partly deciduous, with spines on the stems and thick three or five-lobed leaves. In spring it produces drooping, fuchsia-like flowers with protruding stamens. The flowers are red, and so are the fruits that follow. This species is tender to severe frost.

Grow plectranthus to brighten the garden with its purple flowers in autumn

Firethorn or Pyracantha (*Pyracantha coccinea*) stands frost and fairly long periods with little water

Ricinus communis
CASTOR OIL PLANT
DESCRIPTION. A striking plant from tropical Africa which grows quickly to 3 m. In warm regions it may reach 6 m in height. It has decorative glossy leaves which measure 20 to 30 cm across and are deeply cut and palmately lobed. They make a fine show for several months. The young leaves are particularly attractive as they are a rich bronze colour. The crimson seedheads are more decorative than the flowers. Although castor oil is extracted from these seeds, they are nevertheless extremely poisonous. As it seeds itself readily in any open place, children should be trained to recognise the plant and warned not to chew or swallow the seeds. This is a useful plant for quick cover whilst the slow-growing shrubs are taking time to mature.
CULTURE. It flourishes in warm districts and once established it will stand long periods with little water. Frost will kill plants to the ground.

Robinia hispida   ROSE ACACIA
DESCRIPTION. Is a delightful, deciduous shrub growing to 2 m or more, with stems covered with silky brown hairs. The graceful leaves are divided into slender small leaflets. The pea-shaped flowers, about 2–4 cm wide, are pretty shades of rose and carried in ornamental clusters in spring. The plant tends to sucker but is not difficult to keep

Castor Oil Plant (*Ricinus communis*). A quick-growing plant with decorative leaves and ornamental seedheads

California Tree Poppy (*Romneya coulteri*) endures drought and frost

151

under control. Standard plants grafted onto a different root-stock will not sucker and are exceptionally pretty. Plant them along a drive or to embellish any part of the garden.

CULTURE. When once established it stands frost, hot wind and long periods with little water. It is also fairly fast-growing, thriving in sand, gravel or clay.

Romneya coulteri
CALIFORNIAN TREE POPPY
DESCRIPTION. A herbaceous shrub that dies down in winter. It is a handsome plant which grows to 2 m sending up numerous stems from the base. The leaves are large, 10 cm across, of a pleasing shade of olive-green and deeply indented. In summer it carries lovely scented poppy-like flowers with crinkled petals surrounding a boss of golden stamens. The flowers may measure 20 cm across.

CULTURE. Grows in poor soil and stands long periods with little water. If cut back by frost it comes up again quickly. Is not suitable for sub-tropical gardens nor those with long periods which are cool and damp. Transplant it when very small or grow it from seed, as it resents disturbance of the roots.

Rondeletia amoena RONDELETIA
DESCRIPTION. An evergreen shrub from Mexico that reaches a height of 2 m and has handsome leaves measuring 6–12 cm in length. They are somewhat leathery, slender and pointed. The new growth is bronze and shines in the sunlight. In late winter and early spring it bears clusters of salmon-pink, tubular flowers with starry faces, marked with yellow in the throat. Two other species worth trying are *R. odorata* and *R. strigosa*. They have flowers similar to those of *R. amoena*, but their foliage is not as attractive.

CULTURE. Plant in acid soil rich in humus. They grow in the open near the coast but, where sunshine is intense, they need shade. They stand only moderate frost.

Rosmarinus officinalis
ROSEMARY
DESCRIPTION. An evergreen shrub growing to 1 m or more, with very small, almost heath-like leaves. They are dark green, aromatic, glossy on the upper surface and grey on the underside. From winter to autumn it bears small, salvia-shaped flowers of lavender blue. These are not showy but they attract bees. The leaves are used in sachets, for seasoning food and for making an essence of rosemary. If trimmed regularly rosemary makes a neat small hedge or specimen plant.

Rosemary was grown in gardens of ancient Rome and figures in literature and art. In *Hamlet*, Ophelia says: 'There's rosemary, that's for remembrance.' *R. lavandulaceus (R. officinalis prostratus)* is an aromatic, trailing form which looks effective as a ground cover or draped over a wall.

CULTURE. Once established it stands cold, heat, wind and dry air. It grows in alkaline or acid soil, clay, gravel or sand, but does not do well in cool, damp, shady places. To keep plants neat and compact and to prevent them from becoming woody at the base trim them back once or twice a year.

Russelia equisetiformis
(Russelia juncea) CORAL SHRUB
DESCRIPTION. A quick-growing shrub from Mexico which reaches a height of 1 m. It sends up masses of slender rush-like stems from the ground. The leaves are long and more slender than those of a willow. In summer the drooping stems are festooned with coral-red flowers marked with yellow at the tips. This is a good shrub to plant in the new garden to fill up space whilst slow-growing shrubs are developing.

CULTURE. It grows in acid or alkaline soil and stands long periods with little water. If frost cuts it back, it generally rises rapidly again to flower in summer.

Sambucus racemosa ELDER
DESCRIPTION. Occurs naturally in Europe and China. It is a large shrub reaching a height and spread of 2 to 3 m. The leaflets are oval or ovate about 10 cm long, slender, and sharply toothed.

The flowers appear in panicles in spring and are followed by berries in late summer. The most decorative forms are *S. racemosa laciniata aurea* and *S. racemosa plumosa aurea*, both of which have deeply cut golden leaves. These are among the best of the shrubs for foliage effect.

CULTURE. Grows in almost any soil and situation tolerating both frost and drought. Where the sun is intense, the foliage may be scorched during summer.

Santolina chamaecyparissus
LAVENDER COTTON
DESCRIPTION. This shrublet from the Mediterranean is grown for the colour and fineness of its foliage. It retains its tiny leaves throughout the year. It grows to 1 m in height and spread and has pearl-grey stems and very small, aromatic silver foliage. If it is not trimmed twice a year it tends to become woody and untidy. Plant it as a ground cover on a dry bank or wall, alternating it with rosemary for colour contrast in foliage, or use it as a low-growing hedge and trim frequently. *S. pinnata* is another decorative species. 'Nana' and 'Weston' are good dwarf forms suitable for a border or the rock garden. They bear little globular heads of yellow flowers in summer.

CULTURE. It does well in gravel, sand or clay. When frosted to the ground, it generally grows up again quickly. It likes an abundance of sunshine.

Sarcococca
SARCOCOCCA, SWEET BOX
DESCRIPTION. Small, slow-growing evergreen shrubs from China which do well in shade. They have pleasing foliage, fragrant flowers and decorative berries.

CULTURE. Plant under trees or on the south side of the house in soil rich in humus and water during dry periods of the year. These plants will not do well in regions where hot dry winds prevail. They stand severe frost provided they are shaded and not dried out. They grow in alkaline soil.

S. humilis
A low-growing species reaching 45 cm and spreading by means of underground stems. It has narrow glossy,

dark-green leaves and tiny, white scented flowers in winter, followed by purple-black berries.

S. ruscifolia SWEET BOX
Grows slowly to 1 m and has slender, glossy, waxy leaves of dark green. The white flowers that appear in winter have a faint scent. They are followed by crimson berries in summer and autumn.

Sasa BAMBOO
DESCRIPTION. This name includes small bamboos that can be used effectively in the garden. As they are rampant growers care should be taken to see that they do not become a pest. In the small garden plant them in strong containers sunk into the ground or in pots or tubs on a terrace. They are useful plants to stop erosion provided their spread is controlled.
CULTURE. The species described stand severe frost but not long periods of drought.

S. disticha DWARF FERNLEAF BAMBOO
A low-growing plant that reaches a height of 1 m and has small fern-like leaves. It grows from underground rhizomes which send out numerous runners. A good plant for a container.

S. palmata PALMATE BAMBOO
Grows to 3 m or more and has handsome leaves arranged like fingers on the hand. It makes a good container plant and is effective in the garden too. It is a rampant spreader.

Senecio DUSTY MILLER
DESCRIPTION. This is a large genus of plants comprising more than a thousand species. They grow easily and quickly. The species with silver, grey or white leaves are decorative plants creating a splendid foil to bright colours, and to the green leaves of surrounding shrubs and trees. Plant them in front of a shrub border, in the flower border, or as a foreground to a bed of roses. Their leaves add a feeling of light and coolness to the garden. The species described do not lose their leaves. The flowers of some are ornamental for a short period of the year.

CULTURE. They will grow in poor soil but do better if a little humus is added. They like sunshine and stand frost and fairly long periods with little water. They also grow well in coastal gardens. Trim them once a year to keep the plants neat and compact.

S. greyii
A vigorous and robust New Zealand species growing to 2 m with oblong leathery grey-green leaves felted white underneath, and showy clusters of yellow flowers in spring. The stems of leaves are pretty in arrangements. Prune hard once or twice a year to keep it from becoming straggly.

S. laxifolius
Another species from New Zealand which grows to 1 m in height and spread, and has grey-green, oval leaves 2–5 cm long and 2–3 cm broad. It produces yellow flowers in summer.

S. leucostachys
(S. candidissima) DUSTY MILLER
This species from Patagonia does very well in poor soil. It grows to 1 m or more and has delicately and deeply cut, pearl-white leaves. Pinch back the new growth occasionally to keep the plants compact. Grows best in full sun. This is one of the prettiest of the silver shrubs for a pot or the garden.

Serissa foetida SERISSA
DESCRIPTION. A fairly small evergreen shrub growing to about 1 m in height and spread. The small, ovate leaves, almost leathery, clothe the plant fairly densely and in spring it is decorated with tiny flowers. There is a form with double flowers and others with variegated leaves tinged with white or yellow. It is a useful shrub for the front of a large shrub border. Trim in summer when necessary.
CULTURE. It is not particular as to soil and once established, stands drought but not hard frost.

Serruria BLUSHING BRIDE
DESCRIPTION. These are decorative plants for gardens large and small. They grow to about 1 m in height and spread, and bear dainty flowers from winter to mid-spring. The leaves are graceful in form, divided into slender,

thread-like segments. They make a pretty show in the garden and provide fine flowers for arrangements.
CULTURE. Serruria belongs to the protea family and, like other members of this family, which occur naturally in Australia and South Africa, they do best in soil that is acid and that allows water to drain through readily. They do not grow well in a heavy clay that holds water for long periods. Where soil is impermeable they may grow if planted on a fairly steep slope or in a raised bed. They stand moderate frost provided they are watered in late autumn and winter. Where sharp frosts are likely to occur plant them where they will be shaded from the early morning sun in winter.

S. aemula CINDERELLA
Bears dainty, silky flowers with silvery hairs surrounded by bracts suffused with shades of palest pink to rose. They look charming in the garden and in arrangements.

S. barbigera SILKY SERRURIA
Has flowerheads similar to S. aemula, with clusters of pink to cyclamen flowers, fringed with silky, silvery hairs.

S. florida BLUSHING BRIDE
This species is becoming more and more popular as a cut-flower because the flowers last for a long time in arrangements. Months after they have been picked they still look attractive in dry arrangements. As young plants tend to become woody at the base it is advisable to plant new ones every three to five years to replace the older ones. The bracts look as though they have been made from spun glass or alabaster tinted from white to blush-pink.

S. pedunculata GREY SERRURIA
The flowerheads of this species are unusual rather than pretty, but the plant makes a fine show when in flower. The silvery flowerheads are ornamental in arrangements.

154

Skimmia japonica

JAPANESE SKIMMIA

DESCRIPTION. A slow-growing, ever-green shrub with pleasing foliage and ornamental berries. It grows to 1,25 m and has obovate dark green, somewhat leathery leaves. Clusters of white, star-shaped flowers appear in spring. If a male plant is grown as well as a female one, the latter will bear scarlet berries which remain colourful right through winter. *S. reevesiana* is a smaller species with slightly fragrant flowers and crimson berries on plants 60 cm tall. It is self-fertile.

CULTURE. Plant in holes to which compost has been added. They stand frost but no dryness and do better generally in partial shade than in full sun. Like acid soil.

Spartium junceum

SPANISH BROOM, YELLOW BROOM

DESCRIPTION. A quick-growing, decorative plant with rush-like almost leafless stems reaching 2–3 m in height. In spring the slender stems bear masses of pea-shaped flowers of a bright golden-yellow. They give off a faint vanilla scent, and are decorative in the garden and in arrangements. The plant is inclined to become leggy at the base if it is not trimmed back by one-third after flowering. Old, woody plants should be replaced by new young ones.

CULTURE. Spanish Broom grows in poor alkaline or acid soil and endures severe frost, wind and hot sunshine. It is also drought-resistant, and does well in coastal gardens and inland.

Opposite top
Rhododendrons are a lovely sight from early to late spring

Opposite bottom
A garden appears to be more spacious if shrubs are planted about the perimeter rather than within the lawn area

Top right
Where conditions suit it Skimmia produces flowers in spring and berries in autumn

Bottom right
Blushing Bride *(Serruria florida)* has pretty flowers in late winter

Spiraea

SPIRAEA, CAPE MAY, BRIDAL WREATH

DESCRIPTION. Several very attractive deciduous garden shrubs are included in this genus. The name is derived from a Greek word that indicates that the plants were used for garlands. With its showy flowers, often carried on long arching stems, one can imagine how delightful it must have looked when used for this purpose. The growth and flowering time varies from species to species. Some are fine plants for a formal or informal hedge.

CULTURE. Most species stand severe frost and, once established, many of them will also tolerate long periods with little water. Plant them in good soil to promote quick growth. Where the soil is sandy they will not die, but they will not make speedy growth. They grow in full sun or partial shade in soil that is slightly alkaline or acid, and they do fairly well also in coastal gardens. Prune the spring-flowering species when they have finished flowering, and the summer-flowering ones in late winter or early spring. When plants are large prune by cutting out some of the stems which have flowered, removing them near the base of the plant.

S. cantoniensis

(S. reevesiana) CAPE MAY

A robust and graceful plant with slender arching stems 2 m high and wide. It has soft, oval pointed leaves toothed at the ends and an abundance of round clusters of white flowers in early spring. When in full flower it makes a really splendid show. The flowers may be single or double like minute white roses, as in 'Flore Plena'. It makes a decorative informal hedge and is also very attractive as a trimmed hedge. If the trimming is done soon after flowering, the hedge will bear a mass of flowers the following year.

S. japonica

This species has given rise to several excellent cultivars suitable for gardens large and small. 'Alpina' makes a cushion of stems to almost a metre and produces small rose-coloured flowers in late spring. It does well in semi-shade. 'Anthony Waterer' has effective flat, plate-like heads of tiny carmine flowers in late spring and early summer. 'Bullata' is a decorative plant that reaches about 60 cm and has clusters of pink to rose flowers in summer. 'Bumalda' grows to a metre and has narrow leaves up to 8 cm in length and flat clusters of ivory to pink flowers in late spring. 'Goldflame' is worth growing for its foliage which is yellow with orange tints in spring. Rose-red flowers ornament this one in late spring. 'Little Princess' is a dwarf type of great merit, with crimson flowers.

S. nipponica

A bushy shrub to 2 m with arching stems of oval leaves, toothed at the apex. It becomes crowded with little snow-white flowers early in spring. 'Snowmound' is a good cultivar with white flowers in mid-spring.

S. prunifolia 'Plena'

BRIDAL WREATH SPIRAEA

A gracefully shaped plant growing to 2 m with a spread of as much. It has small soft, narrow leaves which turn pretty autumn colours when grown in a cold district. In late winter and early spring it bears flowers like miniature rosettes in great profusion. It trims easily into a pretty shape.

S. salicifolia

Grows quickly to 1–2 m. It tends to spread by suckers and is therefore not recommended for the small garden. Pale-rose flowers appear in late spring. The leaves are decorative for much of the year.

S. thunbergii

An old favourite which grows to 1 m or more, and has arching branches of narrow pale-green leaves that turn colour in autumn. In early spring tiny white single flowers are produced in clusters all along the branches. This species makes a charming informal hedge.

S. vanhouttei

A vigorous shrub with graceful arching branches. The leaves are obovate and coarsely toothed. The white flowers are carried in compact clusters in mid-spring.

Stephanandra tanakae

STEPHANANDRA

DESCRIPTION. Is a deciduous Japanese plant growing to 1 m with arching stems of triangular or almost heart-shaped leaves with toothed margins. They turn bright orange before falling in the autumn. In spring it carries tiny flowers in delicate sprays. If planted close together this species makes quite a good screen. *S. incisa* is another ornamental species with deeply lobed leaves. Both are worth growing for their foliage which is decorative in arrangements as well as in the garden.

CULTURE. They stand moderate frost but do not thrive in hot, dry places. Plant in soil rich in humus. Will grow in partial shade under trees.

Stranvaesia davidiana

DESCRIPTION. A large shrub or small evergreen tree native to China. It grows to 3 m or more and has dark-green oblong leaves up to 12 cm long. The new growth is tinged with bronze. The small white flowers which appear in summer are not showy. They are followed by colourful clusters of scarlet berries which are very ornamental in winter. In autumn the old leaves are orange to crimson. *S. undulata* is a smaller plant with orange berries.

CULTURE. Enjoys severe frost but not warm humid conditions. Grows in sun or partial shade.

Streptosolen jamesonii

MARMALADE BUSH

DESCRIPTION. A quick-growing evergreen shrub reaching 1 m or more in height and spread. It has oval leaves 3–5 cm long, dark green and slightly glossy on the upper surface and paler with prominent veins underneath. It is twiggy in habit and needs to be cut back once or twice a year to keep it neat and compact. In spring and summer, and on and off throughout the year, it carries showy clusters of funnel-shaped flowers, apricot in colour at the base with an orange face. A cultivar with flowers of golden-yellow is even more attractive than the species.

CULTURE. This pretty little shrub thrives in regions where the winters are not severe. It does well in coastal gardens and inland if watered during the dry seasons. Prune in summer to promote further flowering.

Sutherlandia frutescens
CAPE BALLOON PEA, GANSIES

DESCRIPTION. This quick-growing evergreen South African shrub is pleasing throughout the year because of its feathery, silver-grey leaves. In late winter it bears masses of pea-shaped coral-red flowers that show up beautifully against the grey of the leaves. These are followed by very large, balloon-like, inflated seedpods of ice-green tinged with crimson. It should be groomed to keep it from becoming straggly. The plant reaches a height of 2 m but looks better when pruned to keep it low. It is attractive when grown in a large container as well as in the garden.

CULTURE. This plant grows in sand, gravel or clay, thrives in hot dry situations and stands moderate frost. As plants tend to become woody after a few years it is advisable to raise new ones every two or three years. This is easily done from seed sown in spring or from cuttings.

Symphoricarpos SNOWBERRY
DESCRIPTION. A genus of deciduous shrubs, some of which are native to North America. They spread quickly by means of suckers and are useful for cold difficult gardens. The insignificant flowers are white or pink. They are followed by berries which remain on the plant in autumn, and are useful for arrangements.

CULTURE. They grow in any kind of soil and stand intense cold. These are not particularly attractive plants but useful ones for gardens where cold weather and poor soil make it difficult to grow a wide range of plants. They grow in light shade or sun.

S. albus COMMON SNOWBERRY
A shrub growing to 1 m, with arching stems and small rounded leaves. It has pink flowers followed by white berries in late summer and autumn.

S. orbiculatus
CORALBERRY, INDIAN CURRANT
Grows to 1 m. In regions that have frost the leaves colour in autumn.

'Foliis Variegatus' is a pleasing cultivar with pretty leaves margined with yellow. It needs sun for half the day to bring out the colour.

Syringa LILAC
DESCRIPTION. The genus includes some deciduous shrubs which have been popular for many years. Some of the species are attractive and there are many beautiful cultivars too. They vary in height and spread. The flowering time is spring, and the flowers may be scented as well as pretty.

CULTURE. Lilacs enjoy frosty growing conditions and will not do well in warm gardens. They need rich soil that is slightly alkaline. In areas where the soil is acid it is advisable to apply a sprinkling of lime to the ground around them once a year. They dislike hot dry situations and should be watered well during periods of dry weather. They flower best in regions with a crisp or cold autumn and winter.

S. x chinensis CHINESE LILAC
Grows slowly to 3 m and has graceful stems with pale green, oval, pointed leaves 3–5 cm long, and feathery clusters of fragrant cyclamen to lavender flowers. A variety with white flowers is also available but it is not as attractive. This is the only species which may do well in warm areas.

S. persica PERSIAN LILAC
Grows to 2 m or less and is elegant in form with arching stems of fairly long ovate leaves. In spring pretty clusters of fragrant, amethyst flowers are carried along the stems.

S. sweginzowii LATE LILAC
Reaches 3 m in height and has slender stems of ovate leaves 5–10 cm long. It carries conical clusters of lightly scented flowers after the other lilacs have finished flowering. Each tiny flower is tubular, with a starry face. They are of a delicate shell-pink colour.

S. villosa
This is a late-flowering species that produces large heads of lilac to pink flowers at the ends of the new shoots. It likes cool growing conditions. The leaves are broadly oval, pointed and 5–12 cm long.

S. vulgaris COMMON LILAC
A robust plant which grows to 3–6 m and flowers well only under cold growing conditions. It has large, almost heart-shaped, pointed leaves and spikes of scented lavender flowers. The following are the names of some beautiful cultivars: 'Charles X' (deep lilac); 'Clarke's Giant' (mauve-blue); 'Esther Staley' (carmine); 'Firmament' (mauve); 'Katharine Havemeyer' (royal blue); 'Massena' (maroon); 'Madame Lemoine' (white); 'Primrose' (lemon); 'Souvenir de Louis Spaeth' (burgundy).

Taxus YEW
DESCRIPTION. Although most species are trees, there are several forms and cultivars of shrub-size that are of ornamental value in the garden. These are excellent plants for the large rock or pebble garden, for a hedge or screen, to grow in a large container or to plant for landscape effect. Yews are evergreens with neat foliage. They belong to the group of plants known as conifers.

CULTURE. They are slow-growing plants which stand intense cold. They grow in full sun but, in regions where the sunlight is intense for much of the year, it is advisable to plant them in partial shade. They grow in slightly acid or slightly alkaline soil.

The following are the names of some ornamental forms of *Taxus baccata* (English Yew).

'Adpressa Variegata'
A sturdy cultivar which, after many years, will attain a height and spread of 2 m. It can however be trimmed lightly once a year to keep it from becoming too large. The young growth is deep golden-yellow, the older leaves are green with a yellow margin.

'Aurea' GOLDEN YEW
Too large a shrub for the garden of average size. It grows to 3 m in height and has rigid branches. The new growth is yellow, turning green as it matures.

'Elegantissima'
Dense in habit, with ascending branches. Its young leaves are deep yellow; the older leaves are green, edged with pale yellow. The final height is 3–5 m.

'Fastigiata' IRISH YEW
A columnar cultivar rising to 3 m or more, with dark-green foliage on erect, tightly packed branches. If it tends to look a little straggly, bind the branches in, and clip the side growth to retain a neat columnar form. It makes a fine small accent tree and looks effective planted on either side of an entrance. The Golden Irish Yew – 'Fastigiata Aurea' – is similar in form and has leaves tipped with gold.

'Repandens'
A low-growing plant seldom reaching more than 1 m. It spreads to form a mound of compact growth. The branches droop prettily at the tips. The foliage is a rich dark green. 'Repandens Aurea' is similar but has new growth tinged with gold.

'Repens Aurea'
This cultivar may eventually grow up to 60 cm. It is spreading in habit and looks effective in a rock or pebble garden. The leaves are edged with yellow. Plant where it has sun for half the day as, like all plants with golden foliage, it does not colour well in heavy or continual shade.

'Standishii'
Similar to the Golden Irish Yew. It is very slow-growing and suitable for the small garden where its dainty columnar form would not be out of scale.

Tecoma TECOMA

DESCRIPTION. The genus includes two decorative, fast-growing evergreen shrubs which bear pretty yellow flowers. They look effective when planted

Spiraea 'Anthony Waterer' bears its flowers in early summer

close together to form a screen or when grown with other shrubs in a shrubbery.

CULTURE. They survive moderate frost. Stems damaged by frost should be cut off. Such pruning does the plant more good than harm. They like an abundance of sunlight and do not thrive in shady, damp gardens. They do well near the coast, inland where the sunlight is intense, and in subtropical gardens.

T. alata   *(Stenolobium alatum)*
WINGED YELLOW TRUMPET
This one grows to 2 m or more and has attractively divided, fern-like leaves and large sprays of trumpet-shaped flowers about 5 cm in length. They are a glowing yellow tinged with orange. The flowering time is spring and early summer.

T. garrocha   ARGENTINE TECOMA
Grows to 3 m in height and spread, but can be trimmed to keep it smaller. The dainty leaflets are oval with toothed margins, creating a graceful effect. In spring and early summer it bears tubular flowers of orange-red and yellow.

Tecomaria capensis

CAPE HONEYSUCKLE, FIRE FLOWER
DESCRIPTION. This plant does not have the scent associated with honeysuckles but it grows quickly to 2–3 m and makes an ornamental low windbreak or tall hedge. It is a South African evergreen shrub with glossy dark green leaflets with serrated edges. In late summer and autumn it carries showy clusters of tubular orange flowers. *T. capensis* var. *aurea* is a pretty form with yellow flowers. When grown in the small garden, the plant should be cut back annually in late winter or early spring to keep it within bounds.

Top right
Spanish Broom *(Spartium junceum)* is colourful in spring

Bottom right
Cape May *(Spiraea cantoniensis)* heralds the approach of spring with a profusion of white flowers

CULTURE. Although this plant grows naturally in the warm, coastal regions of South Africa, it can tolerate moderate frost. Once established it will also endure long periods with little water; it is therefore a useful plant for gardens where water is in short supply. It does fairly well in seaside gardens too.

Telopea speciosissima
WARATAH

DESCRIPTION. This is one of the most striking of all shrubs. It is an evergreen, native to Australia, with decorative leaves and magnificent flowers. The leathery leaves are slender, up to 20 cm long and have toothed margins. They are a perfect foil to the rich ruby-red colour of the flowers which appear in late winter and early spring. The flowers are made up of a rounded head of tubular florets nestling in a halo of colourful bracts. They remain beautiful on the plant for a long time and keep fresh for two or more weeks when cut for arrangements. Where this plant is happy it will grow into a large bush, 3 m in height and more than this across. A mature plant may carry more than 200 flowers at a time. Unfortunately, however, it is not easy to grow, but nevertheless well worth trying where conditions are likely to suit it. Two other species worth planting are *T. oreades* (Victorian Waratah), which can become tree-size, and *T. truncata,* which is native to Tasmania, and which grows to 2 m or more.

CULTURE. The waratah is a member of the protea family and likes the same kind of growing conditions as the proteas: a loose, acid soil that drains readily. Heavy clay or soil that holds water does not suit them. Generally, they do better on sloping ground than on a level site where water may remain about the roots for long periods. Prepare holes with plenty of acid compost and a little peat. They need water in winter but do not mind being dry in summer. In hot dry periods of the year mulch the soil with acid material, such as well-rotted oak leaves or pine needles. They stand moderate frost but do not thrive in subtropical gardens. Transplant when very small.

Templetonia retusa
RED TEMPLETONIA

DESCRIPTION. An evergreen native to South and Western Australia. It is a somewhat straggly shrub growing to 2 m with small oval or obovate leaves. In late winter and spring it bears brick-red, pea-shaped flowers close to the stems. This is a good plant to make a low hedge in seaside gardens as it grows in alkaline soil and tolerates salty winds and spray.

CULTURE. Will stand moderate frost, poor soil and fairly long periods with little water. Prune the plant each year to keep it from becoming straggly.

Tetradenia riparia
(Iboza riparia) IBOZA

DESCRIPTION. A quick-growing, deciduous, South African plant, upright in habit, that reaches a height of 2 m. The leaves are soft in texture and heart-shaped, with serrated edges. It makes a charming show in autumn or winter when it bears its plumes of tiny misty mauve flowers at the ends of the bare stems. This is a good plant to grow between slow-growing shrubs. The flowers last fairly well in arrangements.

CULTURE. It likes warm growing conditions and is not suitable for gardens where frosts are severe. Plant it in partial shade or in full sun. Cut plants back lightly after their flowering period. It grows well in light sandy soils.

Tetrapanax papyriferus
RICE-PAPER PLANT

DESCRIPTION. This plant grows wild in south Japan and Taiwan and reaches a height of 3 m or more, and frequently sends up more than one stem from the base. The trunks often curve or lean, giving the plant a dramatic appearance. The leaves are huge – measuring 30 cm or more in length and width. They are deeply lobed, dark green on the upper surface and pale underneath. The new leaves are dove-grey. They stand erect until they unfurl, when the stems arch out away from the main stem. The foliage gives this plant an interesting silhouette throughout the year. It looks very effective planted next to a pool, alone near a wall, or as a patio tree. The creamy flowers that appear in winter are carried in large clusters above the leaves. The plant was used for the making of Chinese rice-paper.

CULTURE. A quick-growing plant that tends to send out suckers. It is not difficult, however, to dig these up. It stands moderate frost and grows in sun or partial shade. In gardens where the sunlight is intense it is advisable to plant it in partial shade and to water it during dry periods of the year.

Thevetia peruviana
YELLOW OLEANDER

DESCRIPTION. A quick-growing shrub from tropical America, reaching 3 m in two or three years. If not cut back it can grow to as much as 6 m and be trained as a small tree, by removing the lower branches. It has leaves which are very narrow, 7–15 cm long and only 10 mm wide, with deep veins on the upper surface. It produces gay clusters of flowers in summer. They are somewhat like a petunia in form and apricot or yellow in colour. Planted close together these plants will make a quick screen or shelter belt. *T. thevetioides* is a larger plant with leaves very like those of oleander and clusters of large, bright-yellow flowers in summer. The leaves are said to be poisonous.

CULTURE. They do well in subtropical and coastal gardens. Once established they will survive long periods with little water. They tolerate mild frost.

Thryptomene calycina
BUSHY THRYPTOMENE

DESCRIPTION. This is one of several species of this genus related to the myrtles. It is an evergreen Australian shrub growing to 1 m, with small dull green leaves only 1 cm long. It makes a delightful show in winter and early spring, when it bears masses of small white flowers with crimson centres. They last well on the bush and in arrangements. Other forms worth trying are *T. saxicola* 'Rosea' and *T. stenophylla,* both of which flower in winter and early spring.

CULTURE. They stand moderate frost and do well in sandy and gravelly soil which is acid in nature. The addition of compost will promote better growth. Transplant when very small.

Thuja THUYA, ARBORVITAE

DESCRIPTION. The genus includes shrubs as well as large trees. The small cultivars look attractive almost anywhere in the garden — beside a pool, on a bank, in a rock or pebble garden, or in a large tub. The evergreen scale-like foliage is arranged closely on flattened branchlets, producing a fern-like effect. It is green or variegated in colour. In foliage and manner of growth they resemble chamaecyparis.

CULTURE. These plants are hardy to severe frost but do not do well if left dry for long periods. It is therefore advisable to water them regularly during dry seasons of the year. In regions where the sunlight is intense and dry winds blow, plant them in semi-shade. They are slow-growing. Where the soil is poor make large holes and fill them with a mixture of humus and good soil. They grow in slightly alkaline or acid soil.

The following are the names of a few of the decorative cultivars of *Thuja occidentalis*:

'Aurea'
Grows to 1,5 m and is as broad. The foliage is flat at the tips and tinged with yellow.

'Ericoides'
Reaches 1,5 m and has blue-grey, needle-like leaves that turn bronze in autumn and winter.

'Globosa' TOM THUMB ARBORVITAE
Grows to 1 m and has flat sprays of tiny dark green leaves. Looks effective in a container, on a wall or bank, and in a pebble or rock garden. 'Globosa Little Gem' is similar but smaller. It makes a charming rockery subject.

'Hetz Midget'
A very small form. It is a dark green globular plant, ideal for the rock or pebble garden and for growing in a large container.

Marmalade Bush (*Streptosolen jamesonii*). Produces an abundance of flowers for many months of the year. Trim the plant lightly in early spring to keep it neat and shapely

The Common Lilac (*Syringa vulgaris*) bears charming flowers with a gentle fragrance

Overleaf
Shrubs and trees form a border which is easy to maintain

'Holmstrupensis'
Is conical in growth, reaching 1,5 m after several years. The foliage of deep, rich green is carried in dense, flat overlapping sprays.

'Lutea'
Has rich golden foliage in flat sprays. It grows to 2–3 m and is pyramidal in form. It is a fine accent plant. 'Lutea Nana' is a better one for the small garden.

'Pyramidalis'
An erect, columnar plant to 3 m, with pleasing dark green foliage. Good for formal planting.

'Rheingold'
A low-growing, spreading form reaching 1 m in height and spread, with foliage which is golden in summer and bronze in winter.

'Smaragd'
May reach a height of 3 m in time. It is narrow and pyramidal in form with bright emerald green foliage.

'Woodwardii'
A globe-shaped hybrid with flat sprays arranged in a vertical plane. The foliage is deep green and tinged with rust in winter. It reaches a height of a metre and spreads across more than this.

The following are the names of some cultivars of *Thuja orientalis*:

'Aurea Nana'
A low-growing plant 1,5 m in height with a rounded form. In spring the leaves are tinged with yellow at the ends.

'Beverleyensis'
An erect, columnar form reaching a height of 5 m or a little more. A good plant for formal planting. The fronds of foliage are tinged with gold.

'Elegantissima'
Grows to 3 m and has stiff green foliage tipped with gold. Is conical or columnar in form.

Waratah *(Telopea speciosissima)*. One of the most handsome of Australian shrubs

Lasiandra *(Tibouchina semidecandra)* produces its appealing flowers in summer and autumn

'Rosedalis'
Is a small form reaching 1,25 m. The foliage is lime-yellow in spring, changing to bronze in autumn. A charming one for the small garden.

Thuja plicata WESTERN RED CEDAR
Is a fast-growing North American tree which can be trimmed to make a hardy, dense hedge. The leaves have a pleasant aromatic scent when cut or crushed. The following are small forms of merit.

'Cuprea'
Is a very slow-growing, conical bush with dense foliage tipped with cream. It may grow to 1 m or a little more. A fine plant for a cool rock garden.

'Rogersii'
Grows very slowly to 1 m in height and spread. It has dense foliage forming a compact rounded or conical shrub. The foliage is tinged with gold.

'Stoneham Gold'
May reach a height of 2 m in a lifetime. Is very slow but decorative when very small. It is conical with dark green foliage tipped with gold.

'Zebrina'
Is pyramidal in growth to 3 m or more, and has attractive foliage of lime-green in gracefully arranged sprays.

Tibouchina semidecandra

LASIANDRA

DESCRIPTION. Is one species of a genus of very beautiful plants native to tropical areas of Brazil, some of which are small trees. This is an evergreen shrub growing rapidly to 2–3 m, with very pretty leaves. The plant may grow taller than the height given, but it is advisable to keep it trimmed back to this size as the stems are brittle and tend to break off in high wind. Silky hairs cover the new shoots and leaves, giving them a pleasant velvety appearance. The new growth is often col-

Enhance your garden steps by planting shrubs of low growth such as pelargoniums

oured a rich crimson, and so are the buds before they open. It carries most of its flowers in autumn and part of winter, but it has flowers at other seasons, too. They are of a rich luminous royal-purple, about 6 cm across, with five rounded petals making a shallow saucer. *T. semidecandra* 'Grandiflora' is not as tall and has larger flowers. Both are highly ornamental plants. Other species worth growing are *T. viminea,* with shining violet flowers, and *T. holosericea,* which has large panicles of purple flowers.

CULTURE. These plants thrive in subtropical gardens but they will endure mild frost. Plant them in soil with plenty of humus, and water them regularly during dry seasons of the year. Near the coast they do well in full sun but in hot interior regions they should be planted where they have some shade. Prune plants in summer to keep them compact.

Viburnum VIBURNUM, SNOWBALL

DESCRIPTION. The genus includes a diversity of ornamental deciduous and evergreen shrubs and small trees native to the cooler regions of the world – mostly China and Japan. Some of them have decorative foliage, others have pretty flowers and berries, and some have all three. A few have the additional merit of producing flowers with a sweet scent. These are rewarding shrubs which grow easily and flower in winter and spring. To encourage the production of berries several specimens should be planted as this will ensure cross-pollination.

CULTURE. Most viburnums tolerate a wide range of climatic conditions, but are not recommended for subtropical gardens. They do well in cold gardens. In areas in the interior which have extremely bright sunshine for much of the year it is advisable to plant them in partial shade. They need soil well enriched with humus, and water dur-

The colourful flowers of Cape Honeysuckle (*Tecomaria capensis*) appear in summer

166

ing dry periods of the year. Should plants become too large for their allotted space in the garden, cut out some stems at the base after their flowering period is over.

V. betulifolium
A deciduous shrub from China which reaches a height of 2–3 m and has coarsely toothed ovate leaves 5–10 cm long. The flat clusters of tiny white flowers are not as showy as the scarlet berries in autumn. To ensure the production of berries plant several specimens in a group.

V. bitchiuense   PINK VIBURNUM
A deciduous species growing to 2 m or more, with slightly downy ovate leaves 5–10 cm long. In spring it bears rounded clusters of fragrant, tubular pink flowers that fade to ivory. In autumn it has black berries.

V. bodnantense   BODNANT VIBURNUM
A fine shrub producing scented flowers in winter. It is a vigorous, deciduous plant reaching 3 m in height with oval leaves 5–10 cm long with serrated margins. They turn autumn colours before falling. In winter it bears small clusters of fragrant white flowers which are rose-pink in the bud.

V. burkwoodii   BURKWOOD VIBURNUM
This is one of the most decorative of the viburnums and one of the best for gardens of average size. It is generally evergreen with oval leaves, lustrous above and downy on the underside. The plant grows to 2 m but can be kept to smaller size by annual trimming. The buds are pink, opening to pure white flowers with a delightful gardenia-scent. They are carried in clusters in winter, and are followed by blue-black berries.

V. carlcephalum   FRAGRANT SNOWBALL
A deciduous shrub growing to 1,5 m in height and spread, with unevenly toothed, oval leaves 5–10 cm long. It

Guelder Rose *(Viburnum opulus)* enjoys cold growing conditions

Viburnum opulus – trained as a piece of bonsai, showing its lovely autumnal colouring

167

has broad, rounded flowerheads about 12 cm across. The little flowers making up the head are white and very sweetly scented. It is one of the most attractive species. The flowering time is late winter and early spring. Where autumn is frosty the leaves colour beautifully before falling.

V. carlesii KOREAN VIBURNUM

A viburnum which grows to 2 m, with irregularly toothed oval leaves, dull green on the upper surface and downy underneath. The flowers are pink in the bud and open pale pink flushed with white. They are sweetly scented and carried in small clusters in late winter and early spring. A charming deciduous species.

V. davidii

An evergreen species 1,25 m in height and spread. The oval or obovate dark-green leaves are deeply veined and 6–12 cm in length. The flowers are not showy; the plant is grown for its foliage. Plant in shade and water well. Likes acid soil.

V. dilatatum LINDEN VIBURNUM

This deciduous Japanese species has foliage that colours well in autumn, attractive heads of flowers in spring, and scarlet berries in autumn and winter. It grows to 2–3 m in height.

V. farreri (V. fragrans)

Is a vigorous deciduous Chinese shrub reaching 3 m. It has broadly oval, deeply veined, toothed leaves up to 8 cm long. They turn a pleasing shade of bronze in autumn. The small clusters of white flowers flushed with pink have a delicate fragrance. It flowers from late autumn to spring. The flowers are not spoiled by frost. After they fade the plant carries scarlet berries if satisfactory pollination has taken place.

Snowball (*Viburnum opulus*) 'Sterile' in spring when it carries its round clusters of flowers

Japanese Viburnum (*Viburnum plicatum* var. *tomentosum*) is picturesque in spring

Opposite
Trees in the background and shrubs cascading down over the sides of a pool create a charming intimate scene

V. japonicum JAPANESE VIBURNUM

A robust evergreen species growing to 2 m or more, with broadly oval leathery leaves up to 15 cm long. The new shoots are glossy and so are the leaves. In spring it bears clusters of small fragrant flowers. These are followed by red berries.

V. x 'Juddii'

Is a decorative species 2 m in height and spread. It is a deciduous plant with shoots clothed with tiny hairs and broadly oval, pointed, toothed leaves. In early spring it carries clusters of sweetly-scented, waxy, white flowers which are pretty in the garden and in arrangements.

V. macrocephalum 'Sterile'
CHINESE SNOWBALL

An evergreen shrub that may lose most of its leaves in areas with very severe winters. It grows to a height of 3 m, with numerous stems coming up from the ground. The individual flowers are 2–3 cm wide and carried close together to form large globular heads 12 cm in diameter rather like those of the common hydrangea. The leaves are oval. A plant in full bloom is a spectacular sight in spring.

V. odoratissimum SWEET VIBURNUM

Is an evergreen species for the large garden or park. It grows to 6 m and will spread across as much if not trimmed. It has large, glossy leathery leaves and fragrant white flowers in late spring.

V. opulus GUELDER ROSE

A deciduous shrub that will grow to 2–3 m if not trimmed back occasionally. It has deeply lobed leaves 10 cm long and broad, rather like those of a maple. In autumn they turn pretty shades of bronze and red before dropping. The flowers appear in spring in

Laurustinus (*Viburnum tinus*). An evergreen species with neat foliage and ornamental heads of flowers in winter

Chaste Bush (*Vitex agnus-castus*) is a robust shrub, tolerant of frost and dry conditions

Opposite
Weigela bears its elegant stems of flowers in spring. It is a handsome shrub for large or small gardens

A low maintenance garden in which pebbles cover the ground and dwarf conifers add interest and colour

large flat clusters and are followed by red berries in autumn. This is one of the most popular of the viburnums because of its colourful autumn foliage, its flowers and its berries. 'Aureum' is a cultivar with yellowish leaves. It needs some shade as the leaves tend to scorch in the sun.

V. opulus 'Sterile' SNOWBALL
A deciduous shrub with numerous stems rising from the ground, and deeply indented almost maple-like leaves with irregularly toothed margins. They turn glorious colours in autumn. In spring it bears huge round balls of ivory flowers which hang gracefully from the plant for a long time. It is highly ornamental in autumn and spring.

V. plicatum var. **tomentosum**
JAPANESE SNOWBALL
A deciduous species which reaches 3 m but it can be kept to smaller size. It has an interesting horizontal branch pattern

which adds to its ornamental value. The broadly oval leaves are neatly ser rated and so deeply veined as to give the effect of being pleated. They turn shades of bronze in autumn. In mid-spring it carries small ivory flowers in handsome plate-like heads about 10 cm across. 'Sterile' is another highly ornamental form. Its leaves are oval and pleated. The flowers are carried in globular heads very like those of the snowball. They appear a little earlier in spring and are prettily tinged with green before turning white. 'Lanarth', 'Mariesii' and 'Rowallane' are good cultivars. There seems to be some confusion as to the correct name of this species and it may be listed elsewhere as *V. plicatum*.

V. rhytidophyllum
LEATHERLEAF VIBURNUM
A large evergreen shrub or small tree reaching 3 m or more, with drooping slender leaves about 15 cm long, deep green in colour with a wrinkled surface. The white flowers are carried in loose clusters in early spring and are followed by oval crimson berries in

autumn and winter. To ensure berries, plant two or more, as single specimens do not fruit freely. It is recommended only for the large garden or park or for roadside planting. This species will grow in alkaline soil.

V. suspensum
An evergreen species for the large garden. It reaches 3 m in height and spread. The leaves are large, ovate or oval and glossy. The fragrant flowers that appear in spring are small but carried in fairly showy clusters and are followed by red berries in autumn.

V. tinus LAURUSTINUS
A vigorous evergreen for cold gardens, with dark-green leathery and somewhat glossy oval leaves which are decorative throughout the year. In winter, when little is in flower, it bears ivory-coloured flowers which show up beautifully against the dark green of its leaves. This plant which grows to 2–3 m makes a good tall screen or windbreak. Several cultivars are now available. One is dwarf in form, another 'Lucidum' has more lustrous leaves, and 'Variegatum' has leaves marked with

white and yellow. The flowers and leaves last well in arrangements.

V. trilobum CRANBERRY BUSH
A robust and hardy deciduous shrub with maple-like leaves and flat clusters of ivory flowers in spring. In autumn the leaves become crimson and it carries large clusters of ornamental crimson berries.

Vitex agnus-castus CHASTE BUSH
DESCRIPTION. This is a hardy deciduous large shrub or small tree 2–3 m tall and wide. It is an attractive and useful plant for gardens where the climate limits the number of plants which can be grown. The leaves are divided into five or seven leaflets, prettily arranged. They are of different sizes and radiate from a central point, each leaflet being pointed at both ends, green on the upper surface and grey-green on the underside. In summer it bears upright, pyramidal spikes of deep mauve to violet flowers with a faint scent. A form with variegated leaves is more suitable for suburban gardens.
CULTURE. Vitex grow in regions subject to sharp frost and long periods of drought. They do best in soil to which some humus has been added, but will do quite well in poor sandy or gravelly soil, too. To keep plants neat, trim them back hard after their flowering period is over. They grow in acid or alkaline soil.

Weigela florida
(Diervilla) WEIGELA
DESCRIPTION. A deciduous quick-growing shrub that is highly ornamental in spring when it flowers. The species has white and pale pink flowers but this is now seldom planted as there are so many lovely cultivars. The plants grow to 2–3 m but can be kept pruned to smaller size. They have several arching and spreading stems coming up from the base. The leaves are oval and pointed, dark green on the upper surface and paler on the underside. In spring, as the new leaves come out, the flowers appear in clusters all along the top 40 cm of the stems, making a really splendid show. Each flower is funnel-shaped in form with a starry face of five segments. The colours vary from palest pink to deep rose and bur-

gundy. This is a good shrub for background effect as its bare limbs can be hidden by low-growing shrubs during winter, and in spring the long stems of flowers will appear above the lower shrubs. Close-planted, it makes a good screen.

The following are the names of a few of the many pretty cultivars available: 'Abel Carrière' (large deep pink), 'Alba' (white), 'Bristol Ruby' (crimson), 'Candida' (white), 'Coquette' (shell pink), 'Eva Rathke' (crimson), 'Glory of Holland' (pink), 'Newport Red' (red) and 'Styriaca' (carmine). There is also a variegated form with apple-green leaves with broad yellow margins, and 'Foliis Purpureis', a small form, with purple-flushed foliage.
CULTURE. Weigela stands severe cold and, once established, it will also endure long periods with little water. To encourage an abundance of flowers the plants should be watered from winter to mid-spring when they flower. After flowering, prune branches that have carried flowers. Occasionally thin out some of the old growth from the base giving the newer stems more space to develop.

Westringia rosmariniformis
WESTRINGIA
DESCRIPTION. Native to the subtropical region of Australia, it grows to a height of 2 m with a spread of almost as much but it can be kept trimmed to smaller size. The slender leaves, 2–3 cm long, are carried in whorls of four. They are leathery, dark-green on the upper side and silvery white beneath. During spring it is covered with small white flowers tinged with lilac. Two other species worth growing are *W. fruticosa* and *W. glabra*.
CULTURE. Grows in any kind of soil but is not hardy to severe frost. It belongs to the mint family and does well in seaside gardens as it tolerates salt-laden wind. Trim mature plants to keep them shapely.

Wigandia caracasana
WIGANDIA
DESCRIPTION. A quick-growing evergreen shrub 4 m or more in height and spread. This plant is recommended for the large garden as it is difficult to keep

it within bounds in a small area. It is useful as a stop-gap shrub in a new garden to provide greenery whilst slow-growing plants are small. It has very large leaves with a coarse texture and almost triangular shape. Large clusters of mauve-blue flowers appear in spring, and on and off at other seasons too. Can be used as a screen or informal hedge or for roadside planting in a large area.
CULTURE. Tender to severe frost, but does well in subtropical regions. It will, however, stand fairly cold winters and dryness when established. It grows in any soil or situation.

Xylosma congestum
(X. senticosum)
DESCRIPTION. An evergreen shrub in regions where winters are not severe. In cold areas it may lose most of its leaves. Grows to 3 m with spreading stems that may need staking. Can be trimmed to keep it more compact. The leaves are oval and pointed, glossy and neat in form. The new growth has a coppery tinge. The flowers are insignificant but the plant is worth growing for its foliage and form, which is particularly good if the plant is trained against a wall. If the basal growth is cut out the shrub can be trained to tree form.
CULTURE. This is an adaptable plant which tolerates sharp frost and also long periods of brilliant sunshine and little water. It does best, however, if watered fairly regularly during dry periods of the year. Plant in acid soil for best results.

Yucca ADAM'S NEEDLE AND OTHERS
DESCRIPTION. Slow-growing evergreen perennials and shrubs of unusual and dramatic form suitable for the large rock or pebble garden, and for a special corner of a large terrace. They have sword-shaped leaves and ivory flowers. Some of them remain fairly small and some are almost tree-like.
CULTURE. These are fine plants for hot, dry gardens. They stand drought – almost desert-like conditions, and enjoy brilliant sunshine. They are hardy to frost.

Y. aloifolia SPANISH BAYONET

Reaches a height of 3 m and may be erect or sprawling in habit. It has tough dark-green, sharp-pointed leaves 1 m long and about 5 cm wide. In summer it carries large and handsome spikes of ivory flowers. 'Variegata' has leaves margined with cream.

Y. filamentosa ADAM'S NEEDLE

A splendid plant for a dry garden or to enhance a large rock or pebble garden. It has handsome dagger-like, grey-green leaves carried in rounded clusters. In summer the plant is a fine sight when it bears its elegant and impressive spikes of ivory flowers on stems 1–2 m high.

Y. recurvifolia

A native of the southwestern United States. It has pleasing, sharply-pointed blue-green leaves up to 1 m in length and only 5 cm wide. In summer the flower spike rises to 2 m and bears large, ivory-white flowers.

Y. whipplei

This species is native to dry areas of California. It has stout, dagger-like leaves of olive-green with sharp tips. The flower stem grows to 3 m and carries greenish-white flowers in summer.

Zenobia pulverulenta

(*Z. speciosa*) ZENOBIA
DESCRIPTION. A slow-growing, semi-deciduous or deciduous shrub which reaches a height and spread of 1 m or a little more. It has oval leaves 5 cm long. In spring it bears clusters of tiny white, scented, bell-like flowers, rather like those of lily-of-the-valley. This is a plant to grow for a woodland effect, or in a container.
CULTURE. It is related to the heaths and like them does well only in acid soil. Plant it in semi-shade and water during dry periods of the year. It enjoys frost and needs moist conditions.

Yucca is a dramatic plant to highlight the garden in summer

Opposite top: An informal grouping of shrubs will produce a garden which requires little maintenance

Opposite bottom: Small conifers are ideal plants for gardens large and small

Plan your garden

The plans which follow demonstrate how to set about planning your garden. In all cases shrubs play an important role in framing the house and garden and also in creating a vertical line.

The plans are suitable for gardens — large and small.

Shrubs of all sizes are planted to give a vertical line and to serve as a background to flowers. For those with little time to grow annuals this area could be planted with perennials such as agapanthus and shasta daisies or with small shrubs.

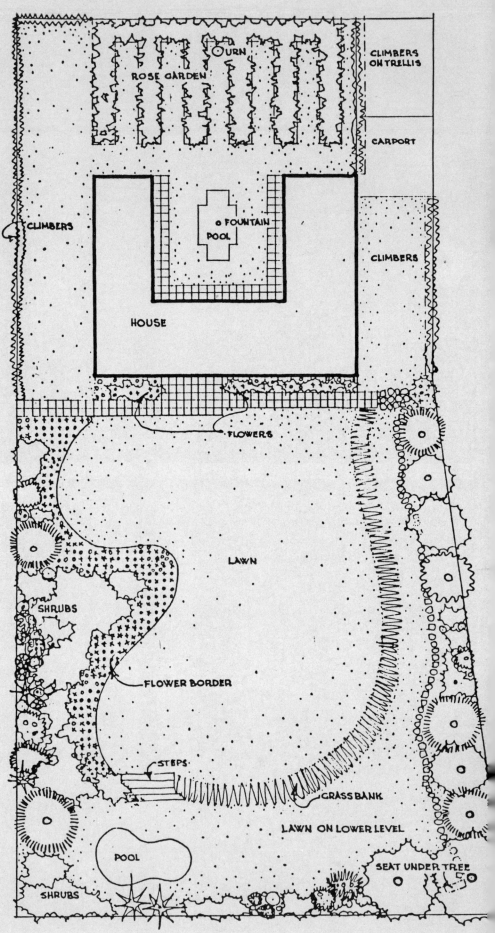

ROSE GARDEN
URN
CLIMBERS ON TRELLIS
CARPORT
CLIMBERS
FOUNTAIN
POOL
CLIMBERS
HOUSE
FLOWERS
LAWN
SHRUBS
FLOWER BORDER
STEPS
GRASS BANK
LAWN ON LOWER LEVEL
POOL
SEAT UNDER TREE
SHRUBS

An easy to keep garden, part of which is hidden from view by the shrubs which emphasize the curve of the lawn. Note how the shape of the lawn repeats the outline of the paving about the pool. Paving stones on the sides of the lawn suggest that there is something worth seeing behind the shrubs and lead to a birdbath on one side and a seat beneath trees on the other side.

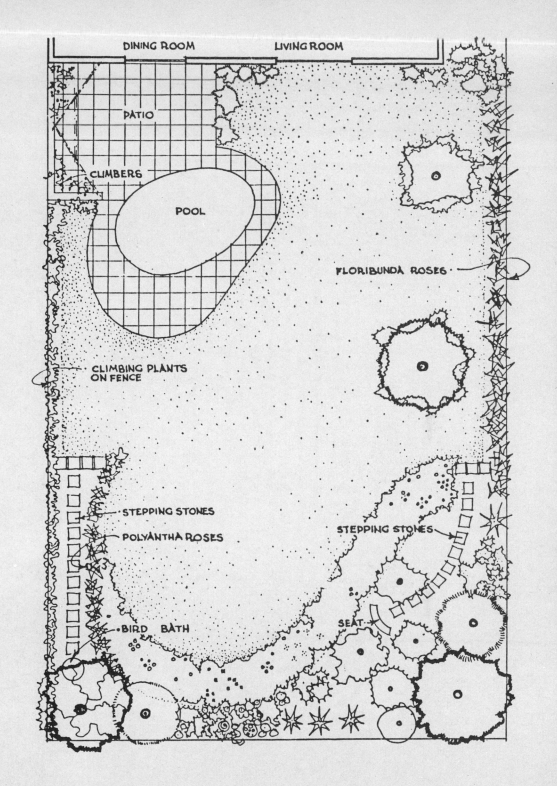

DINING ROOM   LIVING ROOM

PATIO

CLIMBERS

POOL

FLORIBUNDA ROSES

CLIMBING PLANTS
ON FENCE

STEPPING STONES

POLYANTHA ROSES

STEPPING STONES

SEAT

BIRD BATH

177

A garden on a steep slope is not easy to plan. Here the winding path leads down from a sloping terrace to another with steps between, the banks being grassed or planted with ground covers.

The bottom level has been planned as a small woodland area where shrubs and trees provide contrast in form and foliage. The flowers shown could be replaced by shrubs.

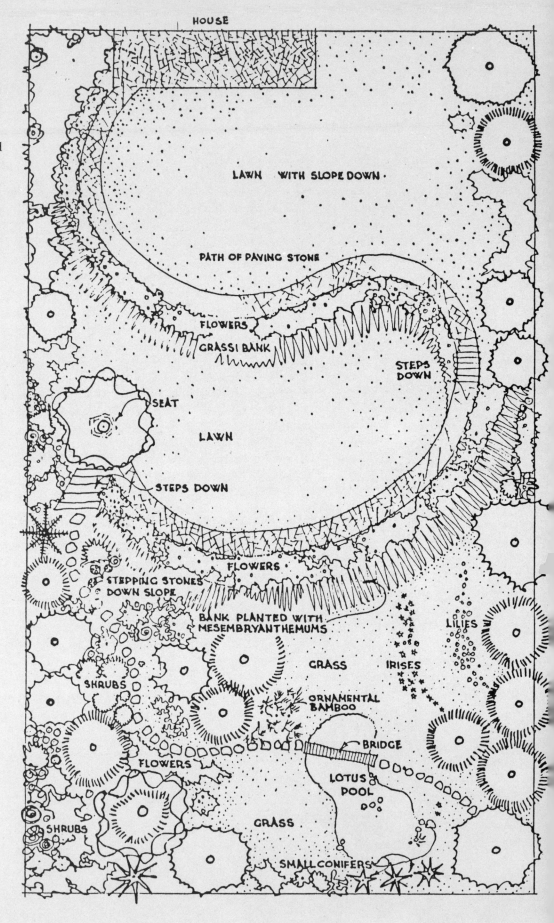

HOUSE

LAWN WITH SLOPE DOWN

PATH OF PAVING STONE

FLOWERS

GRASS BANK

STEPS DOWN

SEAT

LAWN

STEPS DOWN

FLOWERS

STEPPING STONES DOWN SLOPE

BANK PLANTED WITH MESEMBRYANTHEMUMS

LILIES

GRASS

IRISES

SHRUBS

ORNAMENTAL BAMBOO

BRIDGE

FLOWERS

LOTUS POOL

GRASS

SHRUBS

SMALL CONIFERS

A formal garden is easier to maintain than an informal one. In this garden the eye is drawn to the pool by the line of the beds of shrubs (or shrubs and roses) and by the hedge which should be not more than 30 cm high and wide.

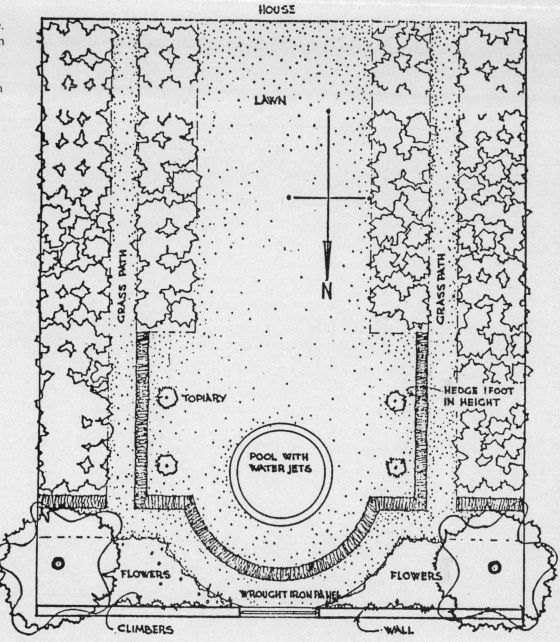

HOUSE

LAWN

N

GRASS PATH

GRASS PATH

TOPIARY

HEDGE 1 FOOT IN HEIGHT

POOL WITH WATER JETS

FLOWERS

FLOWERS

WROUGHT IRON PANEL

CLIMBERS

WALL

Index of common names